VETERANS ON TRIAL

Also by Barry R. Schaller

A Vision of American Law: Judging Law, Literature,
and the Stories We Tell (1997, 2001)

Understanding Bioethics and the Law: The Promises and Perils
of the Brave New World of Biotechnology (2008)

Related Titles from Potomac Books

The Veteran's PTSD Handbook: How to File and Collect on Claims
for Post-Traumatic Stress Disorder
—John D. Roche

Claim Denied! How to Appeal a VA Denial of Benefits
—John D. Roche

A Warrior's Guide to Psychology and Performance: What You
Should Know about Yourself and Others
—George Mastroianni, Barbara Palmer, David Penetar,
and Victoria Tepe

Through Veterans' Eyes: The Iraq and Afghanistan Experience
—Larry Minear

Minefields of the Heart: A Mother's Stories of a Son at War
—Sue Diaz

"War Stories": False Atrocity Tales, Swift Boaters, and Winter
Soldiers—What Really Happened in Vietnam
—Gary Kulik

VETERANS
ON TRIAL
THE COMING COURT BATTLES OVER PTSD

BARRY R. SCHALLER

Foreword by Todd Brewster

Potomac Books
Washington, D.C.

Library of Congress Cataloging-in-Publication Data
Schaller, Barry R., 1938–
    Veterans on trial : the coming court battles over PTSD / Barry R. Schaller ; foreword by Todd Brewster. — 1st ed.
        p. ; cm.
    Includes bibliographical references and index.
    ISBN 978-1-59797-696-1 (hardcover : alk. paper)
    ISBN 978-1-59797-860-6 (electronic)
    I. Title.
    [DNLM: 1. Combat Disorders. 2. Stress Disorders, Post-Traumatic. 3. Veterans—legislation & jurisprudence. 4. Veterans—psychology. 5. War. WM 184]
    LC Classification not assigned
    616.85'21—dc23
                                                                                  2012012981

Printed in the United States of America on acid-free paper that meets the American National Standards Institute Z39-48 Standard.

Potomac Books
22841 Quicksilver Drive
Dulles, Virginia 20166

First Edition

10 9 8 7 6 5 4 3 2 1

To Carol V. C. Schaller
and
the men and women of the U.S. military who sacrifice
so much in times of war, those who care for them,
and those who follow in their footsteps

CONTENTS

PART IV: BATTLES ON THE HOME FRONT

FOREWORD

More than twenty years ago, at the outset of the first Persian Gulf War, there was considerable enthusiasm over the possibility that new combat technologies such as "smart bombs" would make modern battle relatively bloodless. It was one of those dreams, as irresistible as they are impossible, about escaping the human condition: achievement without journey, pleasure without pain, war without suffering. There were attendant worries about whether this might also make war too easy, more like a video game than a life-and-death matter. But the thought persisted: How much better would the world be if we could find a way of completing the mission of war without having to sacrifice our own blood or, for that matter, the innocent blood of our enemy? How much easier would it be to endure the consequences of a warrior life if we could adjust its proximity to the cool distance provided by a computer screen?

Two decades later, in the midst of a long (and ongoing) battle against terrorist insurgencies, that seems like so much foolishness. Yes, technology has made war more efficient. But, sadly, war is war, and the price we pay for engaging in it remains as steep as ever. Even as we have removed some of its horror, we have revealed new horrors. Think, for instance, of this combination of the primitive and the modern as experienced by a hypothetical soldier in the first decade of the twenty-first century: an infantryman on his third or fourth deployment working to quell the insurgency in Iraq conducts a search-and-destroy mission, going door to door, confronting deadly threats from the shadows of every street corner, alert for the hidden "improvised explosive device"

(IED)—a new name for an old weapon we used to call the booby trap—that might be tripped by his next step. His heart races, his mind leaps. Is the man on the balcony over there, holding a cell phone, gossiping with a friend or coding a device to explode in the soldier's path? Is that child running toward him looking to play or has he been strapped with explosives? The rules of engagement tell the infantryman he can do "this," but not "that," and yet he must decide "this" from "that" in a split second. The enemy combatants are not in uniform and are not directed from a central command. They are haphazard and anonymous, and the acts of violence they commit are spontaneous and unreasonable. The battlefield is the village itself, and the enemy may nod and smile at you one moment and try to kill you the next. After skirting brief encounters, some real, most imagined, the infantryman returns to the desert FOB (forward operating base) and wearily goes on Skype to visit with his wife back in Arkansas. The kids are doing poorly in school, she tells him. The grass needs to be cut, the car needs repair, and, oh, when are you coming home?

This scenario is a good day at work. A bad day would include taking and returning fire; killing or wounding the enemy; watching others, including friends and colleagues, die; receiving debilitating injuries; watching a mission fail; fighting back doubts that the mission is worthy or doable. The soldier's life has always been one of crushing boredom punctuated by short, intense episodes of sheer terror, episodes when many veterans claim to have felt more alive than they have ever felt before, if only because in those moments they are so very close to death. It is a special kind of tedium, one interrupted by fits of black chaos that will hang in the memory for as long as one lives, if allowed to, and not just any old black chaos either, but one that grips the soldier with the anguish of guilt. If only I had acted differently in that moment, would lives have been saved? Would the mission have been more successful? Would I have lived up to my standard, my superior's standard, as a warrior worthy of respect? Would I have been able to go home proud?

As the director of the Center for Oral History at West Point, I have listened to many veterans recount war experiences. None was more riveting than a company commander from Pensacola, Florida, who found himself in Afghanistan, laughing at the absurdity of a war in which he found himself mingling with sheepherders who didn't know what the Taliban was, much less why the Americans were there, on their land, looking for it. To the soldier, this was the tedium part, though at least it had the element of the ridiculous to keep him entertained. Then he was redeployed to Iraq and in less than two weeks had lost three men under his command to a gruesome IED attack.

Commanders don't like to have subordinates do what they themselves won't do, and so, in an act of leadership, this soldier took up the task of returning to the site of the explosion and, holding a cardboard box, retrieving the body parts of the dead, one of them a close friend who had children the same age as the commander's. The friend had been reduced to a spray of stray body tissue and severed digits, scattered around a central mass of blood and indistinguishable organs lying inert in the hot dust.

Can the mind adapt to such absurd juxtapositions of the sacred and the profane? Thirty years ago, when veterans of the Vietnam War complained of what we now call post-traumatic stress disorder (PTSD), they were received with little sympathy. The war was unpopular, and veterans of it were looked upon with resentment and shame. In fact, these men were expressing what soldiers have long expressed: that the experience of making war leaves a person changed, and changed for the worse. In World War II, the problem went by the comparatively benign term "combat fatigue"; in World War I, "shell shock"; before that, less specific terms such as "mental exhaustion" described the warrior's psychological state.

With the first professional studies of PTSD came some perplexing questions, and even today they remain unsettled. Is PTSD a normal reaction that dissipates over time and treatment, or is it a state of permanence? Is PTSD a mental illness that can be explained as a contributor to later criminal behavior and used as a defense or at the very least as a mitigating factor in sentencing? Finally, are the scarring experiences of war derived only from memories in the most vivid sense of that term, or can they be experiences that are powerfully suppressed only to spring back with a vengeance years or even decades later when the will to resist them has been relaxed? These are the sorts of questions that are at the heart of this much-needed study by Justice Barry Schaller, whose sensitivity to the subject is matched by the depth of his analysis.

The overarching message of this work is a sobering one: war is not over with the last hostile shot. It lingers and the price grows, often quietly, over time, presenting daunting and very modern challenges for the time-honored practice of the law. Justice Schaller shows that from being freer from the horrors of war, the kind of conflicts that grip us in the twenty-first century are likely to leave even deeper and more mysterious psychological scars. This last point is worth dwelling on, because there are those who believe that the mental wounds of war are an invention of modern psychology, perhaps equally with modern politics, and that they serve as a convenient excuse for antisocial or even criminal behavior, as a way of blaming the state for the moral failures of the individual. People have been making war since the beginning of time, they reason, so why should today's warrior be diagnosed with a "condition" that others for so long have simply accepted as their lot?

Yes, war is as ancient as man himself, but the experience of war, horrible in all incarnations, has been radically different from one generation to the next. Thanks to the advances of modern medicine, injuries that would have killed a soldier a century ago—even half a century ago—can now be successfully treated to the point where we have a whole new population of veterans whose dark tales of injury have never been told before.

Of course, soldiers in all the wars of history have had to explain to themselves why killing, a criminal and immoral act, is somehow legal and moral when it is done by them as soldiers. In the context of war killing is seen as serving some cause greater than the moral wrong. Believing that is never easy, but it is harder now, particularly when, in fighting crudely conceived insurgencies, the objectives of battle are not easily or clearly defined, and when fighting a war as ambiguous as a Global War on Terror, there is no foreseeable path to the comfort of closure. The human mind thrives on ordering experiences according to narrative, and when there is no clear beginning, middle, and end—no first shot, battle royal, and armistice rendering the holy grail of "purpose"—the result is psychological torment. Gen. Martin Dempsey, chairman of the Joint Chiefs of Staff, has told me that he looks upon the Global War on Terror as a thirty years' war. But, sadly, among prognosticators one would have to label him an optimist. As Justice Schaller says in his epilogue, a war on terror may well be an endless war, a permanent war, war more as a state of being than a temporary interruption to the peace.

Everyone with a stake in this subject attempts to make sense of it from a different perspective: the soldier, the psychologist, the legislator, the general, the lawyer. Justice Schaller provides a first-rate description of the problem and advice for each profession. But he also warns against the temptation to look too much to the courts for a solution. In America, law is a reactive discipline. Judges do not formulate policy (at least they are not supposed to); instead, they must work purely from cases and controversies, seeking to find answers in the sorting out of real-world problems. Misunderstanding the role of the judiciary, some states have sought to distinguish the experience of veterans on trial from *others* on trial by actually creating separate veterans courts, at least for nonviolent crimes, a peculiar development in a country where "equal protection before the law" is a sacred Fourteenth Amendment principle. Once we begin to create a special class of courts looking to provide a special brand of justice, Justice Schaller asks, don't we risk the "me too" argument from others who feel as though their situation—poverty, abuse, discrimination—forced them to go wrong? More emphatically, he argues that the business of healing the psychological wounds of war belongs not with the courts, but with those—the political branches, the military—who sent these men and women out to do the dangerous work that brought them such scars in the first place. Courts, after all, don't see the evidence of such trauma until a crime is committed, when it may already be too late.

Shortly after returning from losing his three colleagues in Iraq, the company commander in the preceding story was at his home at an army base in Virginia. His sleep had been restless, so he left his bed and retired to the living room couch. In the morning, his wife came downstairs to wake him. As she shook his body, the soldier leaped from a dream, pinning his wife against the wall and threatening her with an imaginary weapon. He recovered himself and withdrew, horrified at what had overcome him. Still, like so many, he did not see his situation as remarkable, did not look upon his own evident PTSD as a reason to stop being a soldier. Indeed, six months later, with the surge of forces returning to Afghanistan, he was on a plane headed for Bagram Air Force Base and the start of his third deployment.

Justice Schaller rightly says that we have only begun to see the effects of these multiple tours. In essence, we, as a society, will be suffering from them for decades to come. But this book does not portray a utopian vision, simply decrying war. It is a realistic, even courageous, one that asks this question: If we must engage in war, should we not also directly face its long-term psychological consequences? Don't we owe this to our veterans who have undergone such trauma not out of choice but as the furthering of national aims? We may never be able to sanitize war—and maybe we should not even seek to—but we can adjust our compassion toward those we ask to engage in it. That—even more than smart bombs—would appear to be the emblem of an enlightened society.

Todd Brewster, director of the Center for Oral History
at the U.S. Military Academy, West Point,
and coauthor, with Peter Jennings, of *The Century*
and *In Search of America*

PREFACE

Since the beginning of the Iraq and Afghanistan Wars, the American public has borne witness to the personal experiences—the boredom and tedium as well as the anxiety and agony—of soldiers in both theaters. Although traditional media sources provided much of the coverage in the early years, more and more the soldiers have told their own stories by means of their personal mobile devices. Armed with digital technology, such as mobile phones and video cameras, and a new spirit of openness, American service members communicate directly with the public through blogs, videos posted on the Internet, and social networks.

Hundreds—perhaps thousands—of homemade videos have appeared on websites like YouTube, filmed and narrated by the soldiers themselves. The public—if it cares to pay attention—has available for the first time in history daily reports of the action. Soldiers speak openly, not only about combat and their views on the wars, but also about their psychological stress, anxieties, and concerns. Some speak directly about their post-traumatic stress disorder (PTSD), a psychiatric disorder that has become widely known within popular as well as military culture. For those of us who have long been deeply interested in trying to understand today's military culture and the history of wars from the point of view of the men and women who are fighting them, the Internet has become a rich resource.

INCEPTION OF THE BOOK

An opportunity that arose in 2007 led directly to writing this book. After many years of research and writing at the Yale Interdisciplinary Bioethics Center, where

I pursued interests in bioethics and public health ethics, I was invited to join a group whose purpose was to discuss and write about PTSD from multidisciplinary perspectives. My assignment was to write about PTSD and the law. Although my paper focused mainly on civilian uses of PTSD, I became intrigued by the disorder as it arises in the military context. Researching the book has led me to study not only PTSD and the way it has been used in court,* but also military history; war psychiatry; women's health issues, including military sexual trauma (MST); and the hundreds of court cases involving PTSD as a defense. To ground my work in the everyday lives of veterans, I spoke with a great many veterans of American wars who have suffered from PTSD and have been involved in the criminal justice system, including veterans from the Korean War, the Vietnam War, the first Gulf War, and the wars in Iraq and Afghanistan. The book incorporates the personal reflections and observations made by some of these veterans. Their timely and insightful comments reflect the wide range of their war experiences, their PTSD, and their lives before and after the war. Their compelling stories, reflecting courage and determination as well as suffering and loss, have left me with an indelible impression of the human cost of war.

POINT OF VIEW

My observations and conclusions about combat PTSD, by which I mean PTSD arising in the course of war or other military service, may not follow the popular wisdom about PTSD or military combat or support the self-proclaimed expert opinion about these subjects. No individual or group has a corner on the market on these subjects, which have been marked by profound misunderstanding and confusion, misstatement, and fallacies for so long. These subjects are still marked by uncertainty, and discussion of PTSD may change depending on the interests that are being served.

THE JARGON PROBLEM

Jargon—the technical *encoded* language that develops idiosyncratically within institutions, bureaucracies, and professional disciplines—is a problem when addressing

---

* This book addresses legal issues arising in state and federal civilian courts and not in the separate United States military justice system, which operates according to specialized rules. See Timothy P. Hayes Jr., "Post-Traumatic Stress Disorder on Trial," *Military Law Review* 190/191 (Winter 2006–Spring 2007): 67.

a topic that involves the government, the military, the courts, and the psychiatric profession, four institutions that lead the way in spawning volumes of specialized language. Most institutions and professional disciplines develop over time a language of their own, which practitioners use to communicate with each other in ways that shortcut complicated explanations, terms, definitions, and names. This shorthand language can be very difficult for outsiders to understand. It often involves complicated terms, for which codes and acronyms are used. Although a rationale for these special languages exists, they can be far more confusing and cumbersome for outsiders to navigate than the original terms would have been. Discussing combat PTSD and the courts creates a jargon problem of huge proportions.

Each of the institutions—the law, psychiatry, government, and the military—has its own set of concepts, language, and acronyms. Avoiding the use of any jargon would necessitate repeating cumbersome terms and names. To help navigate this treacherous course, I substitute nontechnical language whenever possible, and with respect to terms that cannot easily be avoided, I add explanations. I do not use acronyms without explanation. It is necessary to use some technical terms in order to familiarize readers with vocabulary they are certain to confront in the media and other sources. Consistent with maintaining a smooth flow of the narrative, I state new terms in full and explain how they will be referred to thereafter. In addition, when I use my own shorthand method of avoiding the repetition of cumbersome terms and phrases (such as referring to "soldiers" to mean military personnel of all services, "veterans" as referring not only to those who have retired from military service but those who continue in the ranks, and "war" as meaning armed conflict, regardless of specific designation), I so indicate.

PERSONAL STORIES

To illustrate how PTSD impacts some soldiers and veterans, I provide pertinent excerpts from the personal stories of selected veterans who have suffered from PTSD and its consequences as a result of their military service. The stories appear throughout the book where relevant to the subject matter. They are, in some respects, the stories behind the story of PTSD—accounts that bring the legal, psychiatric, and military concepts to life. Although telling veterans' personal stories is not the main purpose of this book, these narratives put a face on the problems of combat PTSD.

With one exception, Dax Carpenter, who had already been the subject of a pub-licly posted interview,* the privacy of these veterans is protected, first, by avoiding use of their names and, second, by modifying, where absolutely necessary, certain factual details about them. The men and women whose stories appear are veterans of the Vietnam War, the Persian Gulf War, and the Iraq and Afghanistan Wars. The stories are striking for their differences as well as their similarities. They are all classic stories of combat and PTSD, but each has unique features. None of them experienced involvement in major crimes or significant incarceration. All of them eventually recovered from their illness, some more than others. All of them completed, to an extent, the cycle of enlistment, combat, trauma, PTSD, reentry to civilian life, recov-ery, and reintegration into civilian life. In that sense, their experience differs from other veterans, many of whom are still struggling or whose lives took tragic turns.

Despite the differences among the individuals in this group of interviewees, certain patterns are visible concerning the factors that led to PTSD and the way the conse-quences developed. Since it is impossible to tell the stories in their entirety, I focus on stages of military service that are critical to PTSD: signing up (life before and enlisting); training and initiation (conditioning and preparing); deployment to combat (adjust-ing to violence and trauma); transitioning back (return and readjustment to civilian life); PTSD strikes (symptoms and consequences); and the road to recovery (combat-ing PTSD and looking ahead). The lives of individuals are far more complicated of course, but common patterns emerge from examination of the wartime experiences.

> **JAY:** The first story belongs to Jay, a veteran of the Vietnam War. Jay was drafted into the army at the age of nineteen in 1969 and served for the better part of a year with an airborne division in Vietnam.
>
> **RON:** Ron enlisted in the navy at age seventeen. He ended up in what was called the Brown Water Navy in Vietnam. He spent two years patrolling the Mekong Delta.
>
> **ART:** Art enlisted in the Marines in the late 1980s. He spent his first four years in the service in a variety of bases at home and abroad. He was deployed to the Persian Gulf during the first Gulf War, Desert Storm.

---

* Dax Ashlee Carpenter Collection (AFC/2001/001/57035), Veterans History Project, American Folklife Center, Library of Congress.

ALAN: Alan spent nearly four years in the Marines, including his seven-month deployment to the Al Asad region of Iraq starting in late 2006. His platoon spent most of its time on patrols.

RAY: After enlisting in the army at the age of nineteen, Ray qualified as a Ranger. During his two deployments to Afghanistan, he served as a sniper.

LINDA: Linda enlisted in the Marines in 2001 after attending one year of college. She was deployed to Iraq not long after the beginning of the war in 2003. She spent part of her time driving a supply truck and the rest of the time behind the gun mounted on top.

JULIA: Julia was in the Army Reserve and was deployed with her unit to Iraq for a year. Although she was not exposed to combat, she was a victim of sexual harassment and assault.

DAX: Dax enlisted in the Marines in 1999 when he was seventeen years old and still an Arkansas high school student. He was deployed for three tours, one in Afghanistan and two in Iraq.

THE STORY LINE: PTSD FROM BATTLEFIELD TO COURTROOM

Chapter 1 provides an introduction to issues and themes, including a historical account of the predecessors of PTSD identified in wars before Vietnam.

Chapter 2 opens with a description of the evolution of PTSD in the *Diagnostic and Statistical Manual of Mental Disorders* (*DSM*), the guide to psychiatric disorders maintained by the American Psychiatric Association (APA). The current version of the manual, which is revised periodically, is the *DSM-IV-TR*. Although chapter 2 provides the current definition of PTSD in general terms and a short introduction to the precursors of PTSD, chapters 3 and 4 give a more detailed account of its origins in wartime. Combat PTSD is not a separate disorder but rather is included in the general category of stress disorders.

Chapter 3 traces the history of the combat stress reaction now called PTSD from the American Civil War through World Wars I and II and the Korean War. Although the condition was not identified or explained medically in current terms, it has existed as a human reaction to the stress of wartime for centuries. It was frequently unrecognized and undiagnosed as a psychiatric disorder, dismissed, misunderstood, or attributed to a variety of social and medical causes that no longer seem relevant. Although combat PTSD has a lineage extending back to the origins of societal warfare, accurate understanding of it from one war to the next appears to be obscured by the fog of war.* The next stage of the story takes place in chapter 4, which consists of a narrative about the Vietnam War and the role of psychiatric casualties during the war. Chapter 5 recounts the campaign for the acceptance of PTSD in the *DSM*. Although the Vietnam War ended in 1975, and thousands of American troops returned home suffering from symptoms of mental illness as well as physical injuries, five years elapsed before PTSD was formally introduced into the *DSM* and thereby gained recognition as an authentic psychiatric disorder in its own right.

PTSD, by one name or another, has been used as a defense in criminal cases since at least 1978. Its use rose significantly when the APA officially designated it as a disorder in the *DSM-III* in 1980. Although the recognition was a long time coming, once officially recognized within the mental health community, its use in court increased. The revitalized use of combat stress as a defense in criminal cases is the subject of chapter 6. The social impact of its surge in the courts is not easy to measure because, prior to the psychiatric community's official recognition, the condition had been identified by many different names and descriptions. Only after PTSD achieved official psychiatric recognition as a disorder that could be diagnosed and treated was it capable of being accurately identified in court cases.

The wars in Iraq and Afghanistan represent the first time that all relevant institutions—and the soldiers themselves—are familiar with the disorder. As the discussion in chapter 7 reveals, the present wars are likely to produce an increased number of PTSD responses. Statistics drawn from studies of returning troops already provide evidence to support that prediction. The impact of PTSD is well under way.

Chapter 8 develops the criminal court experience of soldiers and veterans to date as well as future predictions concerning veterans of these wars. Because the existence of PTSD usually depends on proving a single traumatic event rather than a complex set of causative factors, PTSD is better suited than other mental disorders for use in

---

* The term "fog of war" originally described the phenomenon that existed when the chaos of combat obscured the details of battlefield action so that commanders found it difficult to discern what was happening. In today's warfare, although combat action is not only readily accessible but even simultaneously filmed, the inception, progress, and goals of war are often obscured. I use the term in the latter sense.

the legal system. It may be the only disease that is defined as having a single trigger-ing causal event as part of the basic diagnostic criteria. It might even be said that PTSD was, in a sense, perfectly designed for courtroom use. The single event cause is the kind of straightforward and unambiguous factor that the legal system demands.

Chapters 9 and 10 address the new and expanded role of women in the U.S. military and the corresponding increase in PTSD in women as spouses, veterans, and victims of sexual assault. Chapter 9 discusses women's roles as military spouses or partners and as soldiers. Chapter 10 focuses on MST (harassment and assault), which women regularly suffer at the hands of their fellow soldiers, not the enemy, while serving in today's military. With increasing numbers of women in the mili-tary and virtually all soldiers in Iraq and Afghanistan facing direct exposure to vio-lence as a result of combat and sexual assault, women are more likely to acquire PTSD, even if they are still technically not assigned to combat positions. The inclu-sion of more women in the volunteer military under these circumstances will mean that women veterans will be returning home to their families with PTSD, a novel situation. Although women serving in military roles prior to the present conflicts may well have suffered from PTSD, that possibility received little attention. The effects of war on women remain to be seen.

Chapter 11 draws together many of the ideas and themes of the book as they are revealed in the personal stories of the veterans whom I interviewed. This serves as a prelude to addressing what military and civilian leadership, psychiatric pro-fessionals, and courts can do to solve the problems resulting from the anticipated impact of PTSD on society. Chapter 12 addresses measures that courts, in partic-ular, as well as the psychiatric profession and military and civilian leadership, can take before the next surge of mental health casualties in order to avoid (or at least alleviate) many of the types of problems that arose in the post-Vietnam years. Although no easy remedies exist, both short- and long-term measures can help deal with this problem. I detail the steps that can be taken in the immediate future to ease the burden on veterans, who desperately need help before they find them-selves entangled in the criminal justice system.

In addressing the challenges that courts face, I note that some states have already created special veterans treatment courts to handle criminal problems of returning troops. Although special problem-solving courts are commonplace and accepted within the judicial field, they generally are structured by type of offense rather than on the identity of the defendants. Veterans courts operate on a different basis. I present viable steps that court systems and lawyers can take to assist veterans while not compromising the guarantee of equal protection of the laws.

The epilogue attempts to predict how combat PTSD may arise out of future conflicts. The future may well hold a generation-long war marked by periodic combat with terrorist groups as well as with militant nations. I discuss the likelihood that PTSD may be even more prevalent in the future, unless psychiatric casualties of war are taken into account before wars are undertaken.

ACKNOWLEDGMENTS

I extend special thanks to Laurie Harkness, PhD, founder and director of the Errera Community Care Center in West Haven, Connecticut, for assisting me in so many ways. I also thank Helen Hart-Gai, BSN, MS, for helping me understand the consequences of PTSD in female combat veterans. I am grateful to Peter Karsten, professor of history at the University of Pittsburgh, for reading and commenting thoughtfully on an earlier draft and for guiding me to important military history sources. Tony Booth provided invaluable research guidance and support.

I am greatly indebted to several people who helped in research and editing. Jennifer Amdur provided outstanding contributions to the crucial final editing process and took on the task of checking my research sources. Elise Minter edited an earlier draft with proficiency and made valuable suggestions. Alexander Kuehling assisted me with research and footnoting. Tracey Dunbrook provided research, and Skye MacDonald assisted me with several interviews. Tracey Rogers patiently worked to make sense of my notes and records of interviews with veterans.

I am grateful to my colleagues who participated in the PTSD project at the Yale Interdisciplinary Bioethics Center. Their work and comments on my paper informed me about many aspects of PTSD. I am particularly grateful to Deane Aikens, PhD, for reading and commenting so carefully on earlier drafts of several chapters.

I deeply appreciate the willingness of many veterans of American wars—in Korea, Vietnam, the Persian Gulf, Iraq, and Afghanistan—to speak candidly with me about their combat and PTSD experiences. Their determination and courage are inspiring. Although the promise of confidentiality prevents acknowledging most of them by name, their voices speak in these pages.

My wife, Carol V. C. Schaller, above all, deserves my heartfelt thanks for her love and support as I wrote this book and for offering me the benefit of her illuminating observations, insights into human behavior, and wisdom.

PART I

SETTING THE STAGE

The Battle That Never Ends

One-fifth to one-quarter of the estimated 2 million American troops that have served in Operation Iraqi Freedom (the Iraq War) and Operation Enduring Freedom (the Afghanistan War) are likely to return to U.S. civilian life plagued by serious psychological symptoms of post-traumatic stress disorder (PTSD), according to recent government and medical reports.[1] Statistics from U.S. military engagements in Korea and Vietnam indicate this percentage is likely to increase dramatically over time. The number of Vietnam veterans who suffer from PTSD has increased substantially since that war ended, with estimates ranging from 30 percent to as high as 70 percent of veterans experiencing PTSD symptoms. Likewise, 30 percent of Korean War veterans may have suffered from the symptoms of PTSD.[2] The estimates, viewed in light of the historical experience of past wars, suggest that, in the long run, 30 to 40 percent of Iraq and Afghanistan veterans will suffer from PTSD.

The occurrence of PTSD in combat veterans will have a substantial impact on American society for decades to come. Aside from personal medical and mental health problems, social and relationship problems, and economic problems, some studies suggest that increased exposure to combat may increase the likelihood of criminal arrest and conviction.[3] A U.S. Department of Veterans Affairs (VA) study indicated that many veterans of the current wars will experience fates similar to those of Vietnam War veterans.[4] Another report suggested that some 25 percent of Vietnam veterans who had heavy combat experience have been charged with criminal offenses since the end of the war.[5] No comparable statistics for nonveterans were given, however, and the subject remains highly controversial. Although the connection between combat exposure and criminal behavior, both violent and nonviolent, is supported by PTSD statistics from the post-Vietnam period, other studies show that veterans are less likely to be incarcerated than nonveterans. The most frequently cited study on the comparative rates of imprisonment of veterans and nonveterans was published by the Bureau of Justice Statistics in 2007. The report, which related to a 2004 research study, indicated that male veterans were less than half as likely as nonveterans to be in prison. The rate was 630 prisoners per 100,000 veterans, compared with 1,390 prisoners per 100,000 nonveteran U.S. residents.[6] Other studies have produced different findings. One indicated that the frequency of certain types of crimes, such as sexual assaults, may increase with combat exposure.[7] Another study found that risk of incarceration increased based on other variables such as the time period studied and the racial and ethnic group considered.[8]

It is difficult to interpret the conflicting findings of these studies since the populations studied, the subject of the studies, and the time periods vary among them. Some studies focus on violent behavior; others center on risk of arrest or risk of incarceration. Comparative statistics concerning groups of nonveterans are missing. Predictions based on the various studies seem purely speculative. There is no doubt, however, that PTSD is related to combat experience; that veterans with PTSD have demonstrable personal, mental health, substance abuse, social, relationship, and economic problems; and that PTSD causes serious disruption of lives and relationships. This combination of factors frequently leads veterans suffering PTSD to antisocial behavior, which ultimately produces criminal conduct.

Moreover, even comparative statistics, regardless of what they show, fail to recognize that the population of veterans should be an exceptionally disciplined, law-abiding population. After all, veterans have undergone enlistment screening for antisocial behavior of many types, rigorous training, and specialized education. They are trained to follow, not only the law, but strict conduct rules. They are taught to protect—and respect—civilians, and perhaps more than any other group in society, they are instructed in patriotic values. They learn to place the well-being of colleagues and others ahead of their personal comfort and safety. If their rates of criminal activity, arrest, conviction, and imprisonment are not dramatically *lower* than comparable populations of nonveterans, the system has failed. Veterans should be at least as well prepared to reenter society as they were to enter the military in the first place. Their training actually should make them better prepared to lead law-abiding, productive civilian lives. If a significant proportion of veterans is, instead, beset with disabling mental health problems, dysfunctional relationships, suicidal propensities, and criminal behavior, it is clear that the system is not managing the root causes of this destructive and self-destructive behavior.

If the trend of problems resulting from veterans' PTSD continues, a surge of cases in which PTSD is asserted as a defense could deluge criminal courts for decades to come. The impact of PTSD and related criminal court cases will be felt, not only by the veterans, but also by their families, friends, employers, potential crime victims, health-care and social service agencies, and society as a whole.

Many articles and books about PTSD in the context of the ongoing wars have already been written. Some of these sources approach the subject from the perspective of military psychiatry. One book, *Odysseus in America*, takes a literary approach, referring to Homer's Greek classics, *The Iliad* and *The Odyssey*. This book recounts how Odysseus, a warrior chief making his long and fateful journey home from the wars, may be the earliest literary example of a hero who suffers from post-combat stress. Worn and anguished by war, a series of postwar battles, and other encounters, Odysseus is a forerunner of all veterans who suffer from combat stress. When he finally arrives home, his struggles continue as he faces a new series of challenges in his never-ending battle.[9]

IDENTIFYING PTSD

The rationale that leads from the prevalence of PTSD to the disorder's powerful impact on American society and the court system, in particular, is clear and logical. Experience with prior wars and the subsequent incidence of mental injury among veterans indicates that PTSD has consistently followed in the wake of combat stress. Because of the specific nature of the present wars, which share common features with several prior U.S. wars of the twentieth century, notably the Vietnam War and the Korean War, researchers can predict—and already have seen—that PTSD resulting from the current conflicts will be more prevalent than ever and will profoundly impact society.

My focus is on *combat* PTSD, which has never been a distinct psychiatric disorder with its own set of diagnostic criteria. PTSD, whether arising in civilian life or military life, is represented by a single, uniform set of criteria. Trauma that occurs outside a combat setting is typically based on an unusual event experienced by a civilian in the course of ordinary life, such as a criminal assault, an accident, or a natural disaster. Combat PTSD arises from trauma that occurs in combat, in combat support, or during combat training.*

PTSD is a disease, or, perhaps more accurately, an injury, affecting human identity in the aftermath of a traumatic event or series of events that cannot be fully comprehended or absorbed by the human mind or soul. It arises when the limits of human endurance are extended beyond capacity. The current *DSM* definition of PTSD requires that symptoms persist for more than a month before a PTSD diagnosis can be made; this is referred to as the one-month recovery period. This requirement recognizes that the experience of mental stress is common and cannot immediately be assumed to be symptomatic of a psychiatric disorder.

The concept of PTSD is not the exclusive province of the mental health professionals who diagnose and treat the disorder. Nor is it the province of courts or lawyers who apply it in the course of litigation. PTSD belongs to those whose lives have been disrupted or destroyed by the disorder and its consequences. Many such individuals are presently serving or have served in the military, and many have had their lives directly or indirectly affected by problems of veterans with PTSD. Although an examination of the societal cost of combat PTSD, especially in terms of social, economic, legal, and medical consequences, is important, it is equally essential to pay close attention to the compelling personal stories of veterans.

COMBAT PTSD

In combat, a soldier, with a freshly minted identity as warrior, is in an extraordinarily challenging situation. The soldier is far removed from the security of ordinary life with its familiar support system. The alien environment is inescapable. The soldier may be conflicted about the mission and its goals. He

---

* Another term in use is "combat operational stress," referring to the symptoms of combat stress that have not fully ripened into PTSD by virtue of the duration of symptoms. I use the terms "PTSD" or "combat PTSD" regardless of symptom duration since PTSD diagnoses are not usually given during deployment. See Robert D. Haycock, *Arming Commanders to Combat PTSD: A Time for Change— Attacking the Stressors vice the Symptoms* (Fort Leavenworth, KS: School of Advanced Military Studies, U.S. Army Command and General Staff College, 2009), 4.

or she is typically motivated by the duty to carry out whatever missions have been ordered against enemy forces, by personal loyalty to a unit, and of course, by the need to survive. The dual goals of killing and surviving may be in conflict. Soldiers in support roles are subject to substantial stress, although they may be operating in environments that are less directly exposed to the risks and demands of combat.[10] Combat trauma is unique, however. Trauma resulting from a catastrophic event, such as an accident, a crime, or a natural disaster, may shatter a person's complacency, confidence, and security, but it rarely calls into question the essence of a person's identity. Combat trauma challenges personal identity because of the alien context in which it occurs and because the measures that must be taken to survive as well as to carry out orders may be contrary to or even the antithesis of the moral and ethical standards that govern life outside military service for the soldier.

Certain factors that cause or contribute to PTSD in the combat setting differ from factors that arise in the civilian setting. Combat PTSD arises, not in ordinary life situations, but in situations where individuals have been stripped of their own identities and given new warrior identities. They even undergo special training in order to shed or, at least, modify their civilian identities in favor of military ones. The Battlemind Program is designed to train individuals for combat situations and for the new roles they must perform that would be incompatible with conduct in a civilian environment.[11] Individuals are uprooted from family, community, and civilian life and, after training, deposited in a foreign, hostile environment, in the midst of unimaginable chaos. They are at constant risk of life and limb. Their mental and emotional endurance is pushed to the limit—and they are trained and ordered to perform actions that would otherwise be criminal.

They must routinely wound and kill other humans based, not on deliberation or civilian legal standards, but on suspicion—sometimes a slender reed of suspicion. At the same time, they are ordered to use restraint and caution to avoid killing or injuring civilians. They face risk, guilt, fear, anxiety, and repulsion as they witness their friends being killed or injured. Through it all, they are expected to display resilience, a term that is gaining strength among psychologists and psychiatrists, meaning the positive capacity to cope with stress and catastrophe. It is apparent that the capacity for resilience varies from person to person and does not prevent PTSD under conditions of extreme stress. In the military, however, a reaction that reveals lack of resilience in the face of extraordinary stress may be characterized as cowardly. Another concept that is gaining research attention within the mental health community is "post-traumatic growth." Current research suggests that encounters with severe trauma can lead to positive changes in some individuals.[12] Despite the normal one-month recovery period, studies show that, when a stress reaction is suppressed or unresolved, which is common in combat situations, it may emerge as a delayed reaction weeks, months, years, or even decades after the traumatic events.

Before the impact of combat PTSD on society in general—and on courts, in particular—can be demonstrated, it is necessary to understand what it is and how its features differ from those of other forms of PTSD as well as to explore its place in the *DSM*, the standard classification of mental disorders used by mental health professionals in the United States. PTSD in general remains the subject of sharp controversy within the field of psychiatry. Neither courts nor other societal institutions can deal with PTSD of any type unless they begin with a clear understanding and appreciation of the disorder and its debilitating effects. Chapter 2 presents a short explanation of PTSD, with emphasis on combat origins.

The inclusion of PTSD in the third edition of the *DSM* (known as *DSM-III*) in 1980 was a giant step forward in the long overdue official acknowledgment that emotional distress is a legitimate, disabling psychiatric combat injury. The disorder is, in one sense, a well-known condition that has existed virtually as long as war has been a part of the human enterprise. In another sense, the phenomenon has also been shaped by twentieth and twenty-first century American culture and by the nature of later U.S. conflicts, engagements, and wars (all of which I refer to as "wars" regardless of technical distinctions or changing status).* Americans today display far greater awareness of psychiatric symptoms and disorders than in earlier times, in part because of increased understanding of the medicalizing (that is, defining human problems as psychiatric or medical conditions) of ordinary life conditions and symptoms. The expanding practice of advertising prescription and over-the-counter drugs for many of these disorders directly to patients also contributes to heightened cultural awareness. The official designation and criteria of PTSD were not recog-

---

* Despite the changing terminology used to describe the continuing role of the United States in Iraq and Afghanistan, I continue to designate these military engagements as "wars."

nized in the *DSM* until five years after the Vietnam War. The Persian Gulf War was the first war in which PTSD, as such, was acknowledged. The Iraq War and the Afghanistan War are the first wars in which the troops themselves have had widespread knowledge of PTSD before they entered combat.

The *DSM* provides a standardized model of the criteria that indicate when a victim's response to trauma constitutes a psychiatric disorder. PTSD is unusual among *DSM* disorders in that it relies on trauma as a specific causational factor.[13] During the 1980s, traumatology, the study of injuries caused by accidents and violence, exploded on the national scene in psychiatry and law. Some critics of PTSD diagnosis criticize the expansion of traumatology and argue that "as a diagnosis, PTSD has become so flabby and overstretched, so much a part of the culture, that we are almost certainly mistaking other problems as PTSD and thus mistreating them."[14] In any event, trauma is more widely understood today by the public as well as by professionals than at any other time in history.

CAMPAIGN FOR PTSD AND ONGOING CONTROVERSY

The initial battle to establish the legitimacy of PTSD originating from wartime trauma was won after a campaign that took more than five years. The controversy about the legitimacy of the disorder and the changing criteria has continued. The complexity of PTSD and, in particular, combat PTSD has yet to be fully recognized. PTSD is a psychiatric construct (with strong social and legal implications) consisting of precursor conditions that are not always clearly identified, including events, memories, symptoms, personal responses, beliefs, injuries, and diseases, such as major depressive disorder (MDD) and traumatic brain injury (TBI). The *DSM* definition of PTSD remains a moving target, with the disorder undergoing changes in each revision of the manual. The changes in diagnostic criteria require close attention when interpreting the use of PTSD in criminal cases.

The centuries-old history of psychiatric casualties of combat, virtually as old as war itself, is still not fully appreciated, as shown by the variations in language and concepts over the years. PTSD, as now framed, is a concept designed for identifying actual human problems that emerge in the wake of traumatic events. It is not a theoretical concept but, rather, a functional diagnosis geared to real-world problems, most immediately those that were observed in Vietnam veterans before and after the war ended.

PTSD is, in one sense, an expected human response to trauma that is beyond the immediate capacity of a particular individual to manage. Some people experience, in the course of their lifetimes, a single traumatic human-made event, such as the terrorist attacks of September 11, 2001, or natural event, such as a tsunami or earthquake. Others, such as refugees in ongoing civil wars, suffer those types of traumatic events frequently. Still others, including soldiers, are literally caught up in a constant barrage of traumatic events, that is, not only significant single events such as improvised explosive device (IED) explosions, but repetitive events that occur in the combat environment over long periods of time. Soldiers constantly face the threat of what is now called "moral injury," injury to the psyche from performing actions that run counter to moral or ethical beliefs. The need to take lives is as much a part of the PTSD risk for combat troops as the danger of losing their own lives.

Reentry into marriage, family, job, and the community presents challenges for veterans—especially those who anticipate future deployment after dwell time, the time spent at home between trips to war zones. In the past, psychiatrists in charge of revising the *DSM* have periodically modified the criteria without clearly explaining the basis for the changes or relating them to study results. It is useful to recognize that there is no magic to any particular set of criteria. Each diagnostic category governs mental health practice until it is modified in a subsequent edition of the *DSM*. Although the *DSM* is authoritative for purposes of diagnosis, treatment, and health insurance, the psychiatric profession does not control the definition for all purposes. Courts and lawyers, for example, change the criteria in a sense as they adapt and apply it to various factual scenarios that arise in the course of legal proceedings.

PARADOXES OF PTSD

PTSD has been dealt with over the years in ways that are rife with misconceptions and misunderstandings, fallacies, and paradoxes. PTSD represents, depending on the point of view, either normal behavior in abnormal times or abnormal behavior in normal times. An extraordinary reaction to extreme stress is, in one sense, perfectly normal human behavior in response to an inhuman demand, that is, a demand that exceeds human capacity. A reaction to combat stress, which is expected and, therefore, normal, would be considered a disorder and, therefore, abnormal, only if it persists for more than a month. One expert in the field, Col. Charles W. Hoge, U.S. Army (Ret.), an army psychiatrist, takes the position that PTSD is both a normal stress response and an abnormal response. The *DSM* definition, however, does not seem to recognize the complexity of the matter but, instead, sees the disorder as turning on the length of time symptoms have been experienced. As Colonel Hoge put it, "By considering PTSD within the framework of normal reactions, it doesn't mean that we don't also consider it a disorder. PTSD is both, and the more we become aware of this contradiction, the further our understanding will evolve in how best to help each other get through difficult experiences."[15]

Actions that would be criminal in civilian life become acceptable—even required—in military life. Upon return to civilian life, those actions become criminal again. The civilized prohibition of extreme behavior, such as killing other humans, is a normal restraint on antisocial behavior, but in war, killing is necessary and required, and can even be highly desirable behavior. Guilt and remorse can have positive effects on human behavior in civilian life, but in war, they can be crippling and undesirable.

Another paradox is that PTSD was incorporated into the *DSM* in part to acknowledge the postwar distress of Vietnam veterans, to facilitate their disability claims, and to make available a mental health defense (using the term "defense" liberally) in criminal cases. The diagnosis, however, was not drafted to limit it to veterans of the Vietnam War or any other war but was broadly drafted to include people who experienced traumas in civilian life. The expanding use of the term by civilian claimants over the years has, in some respects, undermined its use by war veterans by creating controversy about the diagnosis and, therefore, casting doubt on its credibility and its legitimacy.

PTSD is a phenomenon of the present, the past, and the future. It is measured by present stress symptoms, but in view of its potentially delayed onset, the initial trauma might be years in the past. Even when the reaction is immediate, it is not considered PTSD unless it persists for a month. Delayed onset, however, appears to conflict with the one-month durational criterion. This criterion is one of the key elements of the construct of PTSD; it is, in a sense, the demarcation between normal and abnormal response. One would think that variations in individual lifestyles that occur within the month-long recovery period would be critical factors to consider in making a diagnosis, but they do not appear to be. Moreover, since PTSD can be delayed in onset for months and even years, it would seem logical that the multitude of life events that occur during the months and years between the original trauma and the appearance of symptoms would be a major consideration in making a diagnosis. How delayed onset affects the one-month criterion is uncertain.

The return to traditional civilian life may be difficult or easy for a veteran depending on a wide range of circumstances. Recruits for the volunteer military, some studies have shown, are drawn from social and economic groups that have less stability, certainty, security, and support than others.[16] Aside from urgent demands created by wartime troop shortages, as occurred during World War II, recruiting is likely to be more successful among those who need employment, the promise of education and training, or general social support. It would seem sensible to assume that, generally speaking (and not considering factors such as a family military tradition or sense of patriotic duty), individuals who need economic and social support would be more likely candidates for a volunteer army than people who are secure, prosperous, and well-situated. Studies have suggested that the former group is apt to be less successful in avoiding a draft than those with social and economic resources. That proved to be the case during the Vietnam War.[17]

The extent to which factors such as economic and social stability contribute to post-service PTSD is uncertain, given existing information. It seems logical that people who are having trouble sustaining themselves before entering military service are likely to have more trouble after military service without special help from the government. If returning veterans are suffering from mental injury in addition to dealing with predictable readjustment problems, it is unlikely that they will recover easily within the one-month period. They are at risk for chronic PTSD.

The military's goal is to return soldiers to combat, whereas the goal of mental health professionals is to provide care to serve their patients' best interests. Although military psychiatrists doubtless strive to accomplish both goals, treatment is generally designed to assist patients in recovering in order to return them to the scene of the stressor trauma itself—combat.

EARLY HISTORICAL NARRATIVES

Richard Gabriel, a prominent political scientist, has written, "If fear has been a constant companion in war, so has madness. Even a cursory reading of the

accounts of battles over the ages provides numerous examples of men manifesting various forms of psychiatric and emotional symptoms brought on by the
fear and stress of war. Today we recognize such symptoms for what they are
and call them 'combat reactions.'"[18]

PTSD has antecedents that can be found throughout the history of warfare.[19] It is common knowledge that trauma in the form of overwhelming terror produces troubling memories, arousal, and avoidance responses.[20] Long
before the nature of traumatic experiences was identified and defined in terms
that one would recognize today, the toxic effects of trauma were reported in
mythological, literary, and historical sources. According to Old Testament literature, in ancient Hebrew civilization, soldiers suffered from the stress that
followed combat. For example, in Psalms 25:3–5 (King James), King David, a
renowned warrior who lived in the eleventh century BC related, "because of the
voice of the enemy, because of the oppression of the wicked . . . my heart is sore
pained within me: and the terrors of death are fallen upon me. Fearfulness and
trembling are come upon me, and horror hath overwhelmed me."[21] Medical literature dating back to Egyptian civilization reveals discussion of clinical symptoms similar to PTSD: in 1900 BC, an Egyptian physician described the
hysterical reactions of a patient after a traumatic experience.[22] In a letter written almost three thousand years ago, an Egyptian combat veteran wrote, "You
determine to go forward. . . . Shuddering seizes you, the hair of your head
stands on end, your soul lies in your hand."[23]

Ancient Greek literature contains many references to battle stress. Homer,
the Greek poet, whose vision provided penetrating insights into human nature,
wrote two epic poems on the subject of war and its human wreckage. In *The
Iliad*, composed in 730 BC, he recounted the horrors of war and human reactions experienced by ancient Hellenic combatants, notably Achilles. In another
epic poem, *The Odyssey*, he followed with a narrative of the postwar experiences of Odysseus in his journey home. The ten-year journey, marked with
one battle after another, is a metaphor for the long journey home that many
war veterans experience.[24]

Jonathan Shay, a psychiatrist who is interested in the effects of modern-day
PTSD, has written about parallels in Achilles and Odysseus to veterans of more
recent wars suffering from the disorder. Achilles is shown to suffer the effects of
traumatic stress in battle. When he learns of the death of a friend in combat, he

expresses his anguish. Odysseus appears to suffer what is now called PTSD as he journeys home after the wars. At one point, Homer asks, "Must you have battle in your heart forever? The bloody toil of combat?"[25]

Homer also described the impact of war on widows and others in a timely parallel to the suffering of spouses, partners, and families of returning veterans. His insights concerning combat and reintegration were prescient. The current prevalence of PTSD cases has brought about a revival of interest in ancient Greek plays that portray the experience of warriors in wartime. Sponsored by the Department of Defense, the Theatre of War performs readings of plays by Sophocles and others for active-duty service members and their families in locations around the country as part of an effort to inspire discussion and help to heal the emotional wounds of current soldiers and veterans.[26]

Roman military medicine first appeared during the Punic Wars in the period 264–146 BC. The guiding principle for this service was the same as for today's military medicine, that is, to return as many people as possible to combat. One result of the Romans' institutionalization of military medicine was the creation of a record-keeping system. The records contain many accounts of combat stress, especially stress that leads to self-inflicted wounds. The problem was serious enough to cause regulations to be adopted specifying the punishment for self-inflicted wounds—death. The phenomenon of self-inflicted wounds and "accidents" appears repeatedly throughout the history of warfare up to and including the Vietnam War. The American military, for example, has considered a high incidence of trench-foot and frostbite in a unit as "clear indication of emotional stress approaching breakdown."[27] Reactions to battle stress can have various lethal consequences, including the assassination of officers believed to be incompetent, and, of course, a high incidence of suicide—a problem that continues to plague the military in ever-increasing ways.[28]

Although early narratives in literature and cultural mythology described the effects of combat stress, it was not until the late seventeenth century that the effects began to be described in medical terms. The first medical diagnosis of combat stress used the term "nostalgia." The condition was first called the Swiss disease because it was prevalent in young Swiss men who left their home villages to fight for mercenary armies, such as the Swiss Guard, and who often were assigned to fight for the kings of France, from the late Middle Ages on. A Swiss physician, Johannes Hofer, coined the term "nostalgia" to refer to cases of homesickness, a condition that afflicted the Swiss troops stationed far from home. German and French physicians also diagnosed the condition as homesickness. It became recognized as a universal condition by the middle of the eighteenth century and became established as nostalgia in medical literature. One of the early descriptions of this condition emphasized separation from homeland and hopelessness about a safe return.[29] Nostalgia continued to be discussed within the psychiatric community for two centuries until it faded from usage early in the twentieth century.[30]

During the Napoleonic era, French physicians identified a number of factors that they considered important in producing or preventing nostalgia, many of which psychiatrists today would still recognize as relevant. They noted, for example, cultural conditions, such as whether the conscripts were from rural or urban areas, and social conditions, such as whether camp conditions were disorganized or boring. They also noted the significance of weather conditions and the success of battle in contributing to the development of the condition. They prescribed a regimen that would give soldiers a sense of good health, the mastery of weapons, and a sense of group cohesion. They sought to bring an end to the policy of evacuating soldiers from the battlefield to their homes that had been in use in order to minimize any secondary gain from being ill.[31]

ILLUSIONS OF WAR: REMEMBERING AND FORGETTING

The standard most often used to evaluate the Vietnam War experience is World War II, the war that enjoys a uniquely positive and appealing image in the public perception. The military historian, Roger Spiller, points out that the United States has fought "revolutionary wars, guerrilla wars, punitive wars, imperial wars, limited wars for the finer points of policy, wars marked by low and grudging social support, wars that consumed disproportionately younger men, wars whose supposed nobility was spoiled by atrocity, wars in which the rhythms of life at home were hardly interrupted, and wars in which the soldiers had only the most meager idea of why they were fighting. Indeed, the Vietnam War has been described in all these ways." Spiller adds that, although Vietnam has been conceived of as a unique war, World War II has a "much more compelling claim to uniqueness than Vietnam ever could."[32]

Spiller emphasizes that the traditional standards of judging wars do not provide the information necessary to understand combat trauma. In his words, "PTSD belongs to the soldier's history of war, a history that until recently has been hidden from view, seldom celebrated, poorly documented, hardly remembered, almost never studied." The soldier's history is the secret history of war—"the darkest corner of all that has to do with war's essential, defining feature: combat—what it is like to have lived through it and to have lived with one's own combat history for the rest of one's life."[33]

Because soldiers' starkly realistic views about the painful experiences of war are often repressed once the war has ended, and the public is eager to forget and move on, a simplistic and often romanticized view of war persists. World War II provides a good illustration of this phenomenon. Although the devastation of the Civil War should have ended for all time any romantic notion of war in America, a combination of repression and moving on produced a kind of amnesia that precluded learning from the experience. After the Civil War, the public avoided awkward questions about mental illness and injury because of the lack of psychiatric awareness in the mid-nineteenth century and out of deference to the more palatable illusions about warfare that took over once the fighting ended. With so many devastating physical injuries to treat, "invisible wounds," including traumatic stress injuries, were not welcomed, and this led to repression. Claims of mental injury were considered first as a form of insanity and later, as nostalgia, a vague diagnosis at best.[34] This practice continued into the twentieth-century American wars—that is, until Vietnam.

PTSD IN THE LATER WARS

Because thorough analysis of American wars of the last half of the twentieth century and the twenty-first century (Vietnam, Persian Gulf, Iraq, and Afghanistan—the later wars) is complicated, I confine my remarks to observations concerning PTSD. The later wars have had distinctly different features from earlier wars (World War I and World War II—the "world wars"—and the Korean War).* Although all the wars share common elements, they have affected the individuals who fought them differently and have had a different impact on American society. Whether the incidence of traumatic stress has been quantitatively different in reality for the soldiers who fought the wars is an open question.

---

* The Korean War could be placed in either the earlier or later war category because it represents a bridge between the two. Although it was a forerunner of the Vietnam War in Southeast Asia, it took place only a few years after the close of World War II. With respect to military attitudes, including those of the soldiers themselves, very little change from World War II was evident. I do not discuss several other U.S. military engagements in the nineteenth and twentieth centuries.

PREVALENCE OF PTSD

I noted previously that, since October 2001, an estimated 2 million U.S. service personnel in the all-volunteer military have been deployed as part of the Afghanistan and Iraq Wars. The pace and rhythm of deployments has exceeded that of prior conflicts in several respects. A greater proportion of the armed forces has been deployed, deployments have been longer, multiple redeployments have been routine, and intervals between deployments have been shorter. Many other features of the present conflicts set them apart from past wars. Notwithstanding the intensity of combat at times, the current military operations have used lower troop levels than in the past, and they have produced casualty rates—both deaths and injuries—that are lower than those in the Korean and Vietnam Wars. Advances in body armor and in medical technology probably account for the relatively low death rates. More soldiers now survive incidents that would likely have resulted in death in prior wars. The result, according to U.S. Army sources, has been a higher rate of reported TBI, especially a type called mild traumatic brain injury (MTBI); PTSD; and depressive disorders (MDD and others).[35]

The three conditions, TBI, PTSD, and MDD, exist in a comorbid relationship, that is, they are diseases or disorders that regularly appear together in various combinations. One report estimated the prevalence of PTSD among Iraq War veterans at one in five. Many veterans have already returned and many more will return with significant mental health problems. A Rand study found that 14 percent of returning veterans from the wars reported current symptoms of PTSD and 14 percent reported MDD, while 9 percent reported symptoms of both disorders.[36] Other studies have found symptoms of PTSD alone in as many as approximately 22 percent of the veterans. Based on its own statistics, Rand estimated that, as of April 2008, approximately 300,000 Iraq and Afghanistan veterans were suffering from PTSD or MDD but that some underrepresented groups may be at higher risk of the conditions.[37] Accepting that conservative estimate, which was based on a deployment number of 1.64 million, one can predict that the number could easily grow to 360,000. Using the 22 percent statistic, the figures would rise to well over 400,000 soldiers with PTSD or major depressive disorder. This probably is the best-case scenario.

Other studies, taking into account that PTSD can take years to develop, have projected that 35 percent of the soldiers deployed to Iraq and Afghanistan may suffer from PTSD at some point in their lives.[38] By this reckoning, the number of veterans suffering from PTSD could approach 700,000. The worst-case scenario may exceed even this catastrophic total. Considering that PTSD's consequences will be multiplied many times as family members and others are directly affected by returning veterans with mental health problems, one can see that a problem of huge proportions faces American society. The secondary impact on mental health providers, courts, and social service agencies outside the military sphere will dramatically increase the impact on society.

IMPLICATIONS FOR SOCIETY

That is not the only bad news. Estimates are that 20 percent of soldiers in the regular army and 42 percent of those coming from reserve units returning from these wars have some kind of psychiatric problem.[39] Worse, longitudinal (that is, long-range) studies of Vietnam veterans have shown that, as of 1988, 70 percent had been diagnosed with PTSD at some point in their lives.[40]

In addition, army suicides, which some view as often related to PTSD, have more than doubled since 2001 and reached a high point in 2008. Research indicates that the number of army suicides in some periods of time during the wars have exceeded the number of soldiers who have died in combat during the same periods. The army suicide rate has reportedly exceeded the civilian suicide rate for the first time since the Vietnam War.[41]

Another research study found that 25 percent of the soldiers who fought in and survived heavy combat in Vietnam have been charged with a criminal offense.[42] This statistic, projected into the future on the basis of the present wars, could have dire implications for the criminal justice system. It would mean that some 400,000 to 500,000 veterans with new criminal cases are headed for the court system, many with serious mental health issues and, doubtless, substance abuse problems. That estimate is conservative because it is based on current deployment figures. If outbreaks of conflict against terrorist groups occur regularly or even sporadically during the next few decades the impact will be far greater. On this score, some commentators predict that the Global War on Terror (GWOT), typically involving asymmetrical warfare and counterinsurgency operations, will lead the country to engage in an era of persistent and complex conflict. Since resources needed to wage war for extended periods are limited, the application of force must be limited as well in order to protect the nation's treasure, which includes—first and foremost—preserving those who are sent to fight the wars.[43]

Regardless of outcome, the tragedy is that those veterans, specifically those who are likely to be involved with the criminal courts, have been and perhaps still are law-abiding men and women who have volunteered to devote portions of their lives to serve in the military. Many of them may be people who—by virtue of their economic and social situations before entering military service—are vulnerable under the best of circumstances, even without health problems, to readjustment difficulties upon their return to civilian life. In other words, the postwar PTSD problems are predictable on two fronts: (1) their prior history and circumstances and (2) the combat trauma of war. A compelling question is whether these problems were properly anticipated and taken into account in the political and military decision making that led to U.S. involvement and continues to lead to U.S. involvement in overseas conflicts.

INSTITUTIONAL FACTORS AT WORK

Many institutional forces are at work behind the scenes in military operations. War is an institutional enterprise that subjects ordinary individuals to disruptions in their lives beyond their control. The institutions—mainly political and military, but also medical and psychiatric, and occasionally judicial—often disagree over the goals and methods of military operations. The government makes the political decision to wage war, and the military is ordered to carry out the task, often amid changing public opinion and ambiguous, shifting, and uncertain political goals. The mental health community created the PTSD construct to enable the provision of care for returning soldiers, but within the military, a conflict of interest exists for those whose responsibility it is to provide psychiatric care for soldiers. Legal institutions are reactive; they are charged with deciding controversies that have not been resolved in other areas of society. These institutional forces can be seen as part of the backdrop of the problems of PTSD for returning veterans that will be discussed in the course of this book.

FOCUS ON THE COURTROOM

My focus is on the potential impact of the influx of veterans with PTSD following deployment in Iraq and Afghanistan on the court system. My approach will be to examine PTSD itself, within the historical context of war, with particular emphasis on the Vietnam War and its aftermath, including the involvement of Vietnam veterans in criminal court in the years following the war. Vietnam was a watershed with respect to the official recognition of PTSD and the subsequent litigation of PTSD issues in the courts. With that background, and the background provided by the mental health and court experience of Iraq and Afghanistan veterans, one can make a sound prediction of what lies ahead for the court system.

Since courts in America stand uniquely on the front lines of dealing with the unsolved problems of society, courts will bear the brunt of postwar mental health problems.[44] In the legal community, criminal arraignment courts are even colloquially called the "trenches," a reference to their function as the front line. Unlike social service and health-care institutions, which also are on the front line with respect to this problem in some respects, courts are empowered with authority, not only to screen and refer cases to other agencies, but also to make final decisions. How courts handle these cases in the first instance is crucial. Judges, lawyers, and court personnel need to understand the origin, long history, and nature of PTSD in order to deal effectively and fairly with those affected by it. This is no small order since PTSD as a disorder has been, more often than not, unrecognized, undiagnosed, underestimated, misunderstood, and even disingenuously disregarded at times by the government, including the military and the courts, the general public, and the field of psychiatry itself.

PTSD, however labeled and understood, can be very complex. Its cause and manifestations can reflect an individual's experience prior to military service, after completing service, and during military service. The dynamics of the syndrome in any individual can be intricate and their identification and diagnosis the subject of conflicting interpretations. These conditions can make it difficult to identify, interpret, and explain PTSD, especially in circumstances such as a veteran seeking understanding from family, seeking assistance from the VA, and in judicial proceedings. Nevertheless, the syndrome is real and must be dealt with accordingly. Although interpretation and explanation must be as clear as possible, the difficulties should be recognized and taken into account.

With regard to the use of PTSD as a defense in court, American culture is highly adversarial in terms of litigating disputed claims. With that characteristic comes an increasing willingness to pursue claims of PTSD in criminal and civil cases through the legal system. The legal systems of most states have evolved from purely adjudicative (that is, decision-making) tribunals to problem-solving institutions that are geared to doing intake and referral work. Increasingly, they are structured to differentiate cases that must be formally decided from cases that are suitable for referral to social agencies and other institutions for handling. This is important for those who suffer from combat PTSD. Problem-solving courts, such as community courts and drug courts, are common today. Since the Iraq and Afghanistan Wars have been under way, many states have created veterans courts, a subject for later discussion.

When the PTSD concept is applied for a specific purpose, whether it is for treatment or for court use, there is a natural inclination to reshape the facts to fit the category. Courts have been the principal places where the construct has been used (aside from disability panels), and judges have sometimes altered the way the construct is applied. The legal profession relies on skillful interpretation and integration of facts and law and that skill carries over to integrating facts and medical and scientific concepts. How the concept has actually been used by judges and juries cannot always be ascertained with certainty because of the institutional features of the judicial system. Juries, for example, do not have to offer explanations of their verdicts, and courts often decide cases, especially criminal matters, in conclusory language that does not explain reasons in detail. Court decisions do not necessarily preserve and maintain the integrity of medical and psychiatric concepts for future application in the legal context. At best, psychiatry and law engage in an interactive and dynamic relationship in an effort to achieve practical and fair results.

Not only has the definition of PTSD changed in revisions of the *DSM*, but no consensus exists concerning treatment. In addition, new long-range studies have revealed that veterans of older wars have suffered for a lifetime and that rates of PTSD are likely to increase with time. It is remarkable that these discoveries are being made with respect to a disorder that has been an obvious by-product of war for hundreds, if not thousands, of years. It was largely ignored until it could no longer be contained, as the country reeled in confusion and contention over the long and costly Vietnam War. When pressured to confront the situation, the psychiatric community defined it and the military acknowledged it. PTSD still faces controversy within the mental health community and skepticism within the military.

Through all the changes in the terminology identifying PTSD and its predecessors, American society has undergone change as well. Tracing the history of
PTSD in combat and in the aftermath of war, therefore, requires a study of
the patterns of the changes in both the criteria and American society.
Developments in American culture have played a prominent role in the emergence of PTSD as an authentic disorder. Whether readjustment by veterans to
present-day society is easier or more difficult than in the past is debatable.

COURTS: THE FRONT LINE OF SOCIETY

I will explain basic features of the operation of courts when I discuss, in chapter 6, several post-Vietnam criminal cases in which PTSD played an important
role. A few words are in order, however, about why the court system serves as
the front line of society in today's culture. The court system has traditionally
been an institution that is central to the functioning of America's constitutional
democracy. It is elemental that the judicial branch operates in a way that is
equal to—but separate from—the other two branches. From their earliest days,
courts have played a unique and powerful role in American society.[45]

Courts traditionally have maintained a certain detachment from the tumult
of society and the political activities of the other branches by performing a
purely decision-making role. In the last few decades of the twentieth century,
however, the role of courts diversified and expanded. Criminal arraignment
courts—trial courts in which defendants who have been arrested are first presented for bail setting and initial pleas—began to engage in more of a social
service role. In this capacity, they began to screen cases for referral to specialized services (such as alcohol or drug rehabilitation, mental health screening,
or domestic violence counseling) within or outside the judicial branch. In many
states, the judicial branch grew institutionally and encompassed support services that reached far beyond the traditional structure of the judiciary.

In the past ten years, this practice has led to the creation and expansion of
specialized problem-solving courts to deal with situations involving alcohol and
drug abuse, mental health problems, school truancy, conflicts within local populations ("community courts"), complex business litigation, complex juvenile
and family cases, domestic relations violations (which had become criminalized), and other specialty matters. Judges became managers, social service screen-
ers, problem solvers, and mediators, as well as maintaining their traditional roles

as decision makers. State court administrative staffs grew into huge bureaucracies. Continuing with this trend, veterans courts are the latest brand of problem-solving courts to come along, a subject that I will explore in chapter 12.

Now that the role of courts has been expanded to include problem-solving functions, they serve, more than ever, as intake agencies for virtually all of society's unsolved problems. Not only do they decide traditional criminal, civil, and family cases, but they process an ever-expanding list of controversies and issues. It is difficult to think of any type of conflict or controversy that does not first appear publicly in court.

PERSONAL STORIES: ENLISTMENT AND INITIATION

The personal stories that led to enlisting, a step along the path to PTSD, are diverse. For some, like Art, enlisting straight out of high school fulfilled the ambition to be a marine. Art had wanted to be a marine since the sixth grade. "Everyone else in my family is either army or navy and I wanted something different," he said. He understood that his commitment was four years. That period passed uneventfully. "My first four years were not in combat," he said. "There was stress from the training . . . just being on the base. . . . When we were in the field, I was more comfortable. When we were not in the field, life could be pretty stressful. Someone was always in your face. . . . You had to . . . watch everything you did. There was a lot of showing off but I expected that being a marine would be rugged. I had three disciplinary incidents and almost got thrown in the brig for a fight with a noncommissioned officer."

Dax was motivated by his family tradition of military service. In his words, "My grandfather was a World War II veteran, my uncle was a Vietnam veteran. . . . I always wanted to be in the military." He started boot camp in San Diego in July 2000 after finishing high school. He became a "squad leader right off the bat" and finished with the rank of private first class because of his dedicated performance despite pain from a meniscus tear. He said about the Marine Corps, "Their whole goal and mentality is to break you down from civilian status all the way to the point of nothing, and then build you back up in the image . . . which they perceive, which is a United States marine, and that's not an easy task for the drill instructors." When he went home for his first ten-day leave, he felt as though he had matured "so much faster in those three months than most people do in a lifetime."

For others, like Alan, who enlisted in the Marines at twenty-five, a lack of direction and inability to find satisfying work was a motivating factor. He had always loved the military as he was growing up and thought about signing up immediately after high school but kept putting it off year by year—even after September 11, 2001. In the meantime, he went from job to job—video store manager, landscaper, missionary, and even garbage collector. "I could never find anything that really interested me," he said. He suspected that he probably had attention deficit disorder (ADD). He had a few minor scrapes with the law: "Youthful offender things. . . . I was just going nowhere fast so that's why I joined the Marines." As to his concentration problem, he said, "there's a waiver for everything in the military."

As to basic training, he said, "The whole point is to break you down and then build you back up as a marine. They strip you of . . . your dignity . . . everything. They build you back up to be basically a war machine." He was singled out in basic training because of his age. He knew he was "the twenty-five-year-old screw-up because I had nothing going on in my life when I joined up." At twenty-five, he was the "old man"; another recruit, twenty-nine, was "grandpa."

Most of the veterans interviewed had practical goals. They were looking for ways to improve their lives with training, increased security, financial help for education, or the promise of a career and a better life. Few of them felt they were better off after serving. In retrospect, their lives were on hold in the service, and they had little to show for it. Several felt even more desperate about their circumstances after getting out. Although they acknowledged that their benefits were important, few felt they had gained helpful knowledge or skills. Julia alone had enlisted from a position of strength. She was in her third year of college when she signed up, and she went on to graduate before deploying to Iraq. She had a promising career ahead of her and enlisted mainly to secure help with student loans and graduate school expenses.

Ray felt that he enlisted "almost by accident" in late 1998. His father had been in the military, but he felt no pressure to follow in his footsteps. He had turned down recruiters while he was in high school. He recalled, "About a year after high school, I was in community college. I was completely wasting my time. I was a typical eighteen-year-old male. I had no direction. I didn't know anything. I was frustrated with everything, and when a recruiter talked to me, instead of blowing him off, I said, 'Sure, what the heck.' Within a few days, I was down at the MEPS [military entrance processing station]." After he learned about an opportunity to be in special operations, he waived the mandatory waiting period, and "in a whirlwind," he was on his way to Fort Benning, Georgia. "It was a chance to run away . . . a chance to do something I thought was going to be fun because it wasn't what I considered to be like a regular job." He envisioned "Hollywood type stuff, jumping out of planes and other special operations stuff." He was interested in the educational benefits of the GI bill. After basic training, Ray went on to the sniper training program. He had no reason to expect a full-out war at that point.

After Linda graduated from high school, she went to college for a year. She had been sheltered by her parents while she was growing up. College was her first chance to be on her own. She wasn't doing well as the first semester drew to a close. She recalled, "About that time, I was a rape victim and so my grades went downhill. I was partying a lot and my parents didn't want to send me back because they were paying. So, in 2001 I decided to go into the Marine Corps. . . . I wanted to do the hardest thing . . . so I could prove myself, especially to my parents. . . . I was kind of emotional . . . and my parents didn't understand. . . . I grew up in a family where we don't talk about feelings. My friend and I went to see the recruiters many times. I became friends with them and just decided to join up." In basic training, Linda broke her wrists and had several surgeries. When she went off to Iraq, she had pins and plates in her wrists.

Ron knew that, by enlisting at seventeen, he would have to commit to only three years, rather than the four that would be required if he waited until he turned eighteen. His life was not going particularly well. He had been asked to leave his high school during his freshman year. After spending a couple of years drifting aimlessly, he decided to enlist in the navy; he thought he would probably be drafted into the army unless he acted first.

Jay is the only one of the interview group who was drafted. He recalled, "When I was drafted at the age of nineteen, I was upset because I was the only one of all my friends who was drafted. I knew, though, that it was just the result of the lottery system. I was on vacation when I got the draft letter. I didn't expect that to happen." Jay had completed high school, had a full-time job, and had started taking community college courses. Although he could not afford it at the time, he intended to become a full-time student. "I chose airborne duty in hopes

I would not be sent to Vietnam. But the day after basic training ended, my name was on the list with a postal address of San Francisco, which I knew meant that I'd be sent to Vietnam." Within days, his journey to the jungles of Vietnam was under way. His life, which had been in order, was now in turmoil.

With these introductions to themes and stories, I turn to PTSD—the battle that never ends.

Combat PTSD
A Moving Target

Leaders of U.S. military and civilian institutions, including the VA,* are paying close attention to the psychiatric injuries suffered by the veterans of the Iraq and Afghanistan Wars. Beyond that, the extensive media coverage of the current mental health issues arising from these wars has led the general public to be far more aware of the effects of combat trauma on military personnel than in past wars. Major newspapers and television programs carry frequent reports and studies of the effects of combat trauma on American troops. The Internet is awash with talk of PTSD in blogs, social networks, and videos, many posted directly by soldiers in the field.

This chapter will provide an explanation of PTSD and a brief look at the history of the conditions that predated the adoption of PTSD in the *DSM-III* in 1980. The predecessor conditions all had their genesis in war. Psychiatric stress, by various names, has been seen in soldiers and veterans of virtually all wars. Until 1980, however, no consensus existed as to its definition or diagnostic criteria. The condition now identified as PTSD was subject to many different medical and social interpretations over the course of history. Since its official recognition in the *DSM*, it has been modified in every revision of the *DSM* and is likely to be modified again in the *DSM-5*.

The Rand Center for Military Health Policy Research published a report in 2008 of an extensive study of PTSD and its projected consequences.[1] The

---

* This reference is to the Department of Veterans Affairs. When I refer to the VA hereafter, unless otherwise specified, I refer to the medical assistance component, the Veterans Health Administration.

military and the VA have put programs in place to deal with the mental health problems of veterans when they return from deployments, and as part of the Battlemind Program, soldiers are supposed to receive "peacetime mind" training before returning to civilian society.[2] At no time in the history of war has so much study and media attention been devoted to mental health injuries from combat. Although this awareness is a positive development, the test of its value will lie in the extent to which the knowledge gained is used now and in the future. Soldiers and veterans are more aware than in past wars of the realities and risks of mental health disorders, but studies suggest that only a small percentage of those with symptoms have received help from mental health professionals.[3] When they do seek professional help, it is usually only after considerable time has elapsed.[4]

Although the term "PTSD" is now commonly used among soldiers themselves, it is often misapplied to explain any postwar behavioral problems, such as anger, fighting, alcohol or substance abuse, and the inability to hold a job or maintain a successful marriage and family relationship. The term is sometimes used interchangeably with combat stress, post-traumatic stress, combat stress reaction, and acute stress reaction. All those terms refer to specific conditions that share common features with PTSD but that do not meet the current criteria for a diagnosis of PTSD.[5] The condition, which is deeply rooted in the human experience of combat trauma, has historically been misunderstood.

Although PTSD is, by definition, a psychiatric disorder, it is accompanied by physical symptoms and changes that affect the entire body, including brain tissue, cardiovascular function, hormonal balance, and the immune system. The emerging science of stress physiology studies the normal and abnormal responses to stress. It is clear that PTSD is not merely an emotional or psychological problem, but also a physiological condition that includes physical, emotional, psychological, and behavioral reactions.[6] Medical experts now suspect that PTSD may also have long-term effects on memory and the development of dementia, including Alzheimer's disease. Although this is the subject of ongoing study, present indications are that PTSD may double the incidence of dementia in older veterans.[7] PTSD affects the spectrum of human activity, including thinking, feeling, remembering, working, playing, and even sleeping.

The disorder remains controversial within the field of psychiatry even though thirty years have passed since its adoption. Its criteria are challenged each time the *DSM* is revised. The latest *DSM* edition is scheduled for publication in 2013. Present criticisms directed at the PTSD criteria are as strident as ever. The controversy includes both debate over the nature and order of symptoms and debate over PTSD claims at the VA, which provides medical care, and the Veterans Benefits Administration (VB), which provides financial, educational, vocational, and other kinds of assistance to veterans.

The controversy within the psychiatric profession is important to the legal community because the starting point for legal consideration of mental diseases and disorders is the *DSM*. The psychiatric guidelines specified in the *DSM* generally come before courts through testimony of psychiatric expert witnesses. One caveat about courts is that expert testimony about medical and psychiatric standards is not binding or conclusive because lawyers and judges are bound, first and foremost, by legal precedent and legal principles even when they are applying medical or scientific concepts.

Courts cannot deal fairly and effectively with the mental health problems of veterans and others whose lives are affected by PTSD unless judges and lawyers, as well as social and health-care agencies, understand what PTSD is and how it affects human behavior. In the years following the initial recognition of PTSD in the *DSM-III*, many courts and lawyers had to decide how the disorder should apply in civil, family, and criminal courts. Since that time, legal use of PTSD has become far more common.

As noted, soldiers on active duty and veterans are speaking out about the impact of war trauma on their lives. It is evident from media reports, however, that the public in general, including many political leaders, lacks accurate understanding about what this epidemic of mental injuries means. Outdated stereotypes and assumptions continue to play a role in the discussion, and the full impact of PTSD in veterans returning from the current wars has yet to be fully appreciated.

ORIGINS OF PTSD

PTSD, as a formally recognized mental disorder, had its origins in war—specifically the Vietnam War and postwar period. PTSD symptoms of soldiers and veterans that arise from actual combat experience satisfy the criteria most convincingly. The definition of PTSD is broad enough, however, to include symptoms arising from noncombat experiences, such as carrying out support roles or training for combat. The first official recognition of PTSD occurred in response to a concerted effort by Vietnam War veterans' groups and others lobbying on their behalf, a story that I will tell in chapter 5. After the initial acceptance into the *DSM*, PTSD migrated into the American legal system, where it was widely adapted to legal uses by survivors of a range of trauma and advanced as an explanation for and defense of behavior, especially criminal behavior.

The psychiatric community has consistently defined PTSD in general terms that would be adaptable to use in civilian as well as military situations, although the disorder has gained the most visibility in combat soldiers and veterans. Ironically, the changes in diagnostic criteria with each revision of the *DSM* seem to stem from applications that refer to noncombat situations, mainly crimes, accidents, abuse trauma, and traumas occurring in civilian social settings rather than from combat situations. As a result, combat veterans who suffer from PTSD and seek to make use of the diagnosis are directly affected by the way the psychiatric community accounts for trauma in civilian life. Soldiers and veterans who suffer mental health problems stemming from war experiences must display causes and symptoms that conform to the prevailing criteria, even when the criteria seem to be geared more toward civilian than military applications. This is so even though combat PTSD is produced, in large part, by some key factors that are not found in civilian trauma. Those factors include the reprogramming of the mind that occurs during combat training of recruits; training to kill the enemy under circumstances that would cause those actions to be immoral or, at least, illegal in civilian life; and exposure to circumstances of continuous danger of being killed and seeing close friends killed.

The American Psychiatric Association (APA) has, in the past, failed to explain thoroughly its reasons for making changes in the *DSM*. The deliberations of the committee drafting the latest revision of the *DSM*, however, have taken place with greater transparency. Veterans who suffer PTSD injuries or illnesses deserve to be evaluated, diagnosed, treated, and compensated where appropriate, based on a consistent and predictable set of criteria that are relevant to combat. Specifically, when it comes to benefits, they should not be evaluated according to standards defined and changed for reasons that have little to do with combat experience, or that are based on inconsistent methodology. Without transparency in the process and convincing explanations for changes, it is impossible for practitioners and the public to know whether the new criteria were fairly and sensibly developed based on proper evidence and experience. In a promising step in the direction of candor, the APA has posted proposed revisions to the *DSM-5* on the Internet.

SOCIAL AND POLITICAL INFLUENCES

It is important to keep in mind that the *DSM* is designed to provide a way for mental health professionals to communicate with each other and with healthcare providers and insurers concerning the problems that they see in patients. Colonel Hoge wrote, "Most people . . . don't realize that the diagnoses contained in the *DSM* were essentially created by committees of doctors sitting around conference tables. They are best guesses regarding which groups of symptoms should be considered discrete disorders, based on the doctors' clinical experience treating patients with mental health problems, and their interpretation of published studies."[8] The point of diagnostic specificity was to provide a basis for treatment specificity. The disorder was framed principally as a social and political response to a specific problem—the suffering and needs of Vietnam War veterans. It was designed for that purpose, although not the way the proponents originally proposed, which was to give it a specific name, such as "Vietnam stress reaction." Its criteria did not arise originally from research into the psychiatric symptoms themselves.

In another sense, the *DSM* is a social and political document as well as a medical and psychiatric one because the formulations are made with the social and political culture of the time in mind. Indeed, PTSD is a social and cultural concept just as its predecessor concepts were, but the underlying stress reaction and its symptoms are real. The shifting criteria reflect not so much the changes perceived in the underlying psychiatric problems as the prevailing social and political needs.

It may be that a greater shortcoming than diagnosis clarity has been the inability to provide a full range of effective treatments for this multifaceted disorder. The issue of combat stress has arisen each time the country has engaged in a war. Identifying PTSD involves the coalescence of several factors, including gradual recognition and acknowledgment of symptoms observed in soldiers, slowly evolving medical knowledge, and military expediency. Treatment of the disorder in a traditional medical sense was somewhere toward the bottom of the priority list. The prevailing goal each time was to promote enough recovery to enable the affected soldiers to return to the combat area—the scene of the stressors. The pattern was relatively consistent during the course of each war. Following the end of each war, the same mistakes were made. As Colonel Hoge succinctly wrote,

> Rather than recognize that going to war can change the body's physiology in a number of ways and identify the best treatments for the full range of health problems that warriors experience, postwar symptoms are attributed to causes that are highly influenced by prevailing politics. After every war, veterans are told that their war-related symptoms are "stress-related" or "psychological" . . . and the medical community becomes embroiled in divisive debates as to whether the causes of war-related symptoms are predominantly "psychological" or "physical" (or environmental) in origin.[9]

EVOLUTION OF PTSD CRITERIA

In the latter part of the nineteenth century, the term "fright neurosis" was used to describe anxiety symptoms following accidents. After World War II and the Korean War, the first edition of the *DSM*, *DSM-I*, used the term "gross stress reaction" to identify such symptoms. Although that edition did not list detailed criteria for the disorder, it basically provided a diagnosis for normal people who suffered symptoms as a result of extreme stress.[10] During the Vietnam War, when the *DSM-II* was issued, this diagnostic category was eliminated, but a condition described as "transient situational disturbance" was added. The disorders were often wrongly thought to be caused by or associated with personal weakness or medical deficiencies, such as so-called soldier's heart and railway spine, rather than the result of external situational trauma.*

In 1980 the *DSM-III* included PTSD as an official diagnosis. The disorder, classified under anxiety disorders, had four criteria: (1) the existence of a recognizable stressor that would evoke symptoms in nearly anyone (hence the elimination of personal fault); (2) at least one of three ways of reexperiencing symptoms, including intrusive recollections, recurrent dreams, or acting as

---

* The term "soldier's heart" was used to refer to combat stress in the Civil War, implying that the heart had been "changed" by war. "Railway spine" was a nineteenth-century diagnosis for passengers involved in railroad accidents that complained of nerve problems such as chronic pain and fatigue.

though the event were recurring; (3) at least one indicator of numbing of response to the world around, such as diminished interest, detachment, or reduced affect; and (4) at least two other symptoms, such as startle reaction, disturbed sleep, survivor guilt, avoidance, lack of concentration, or impaired memory.[11] The disorder could be of two types: acute, if limited to the first six months after the trauma, or delayed or chronic, meaning onset or duration beyond six months. Those distinctions often prove worthless to clinicians when taking into account the length of wars. The inclusion of PTSD in the *DSM* gratified supporters of veterans' groups that had lobbied for that result. It also satisfied members of various social movements that, in the 1970s, had focused attention on the consequences of various other types of trauma, such as domestic violence episodes. All types of traumatic events were pooled into this single diagnostic category, in large part because the campaign for the original "Vietnam War adjustment disorder" was faltering until the veterans' lobbyist groups joined up with abuse victims' lobbyist groups.

The next revision, *DSM-III-TR* (*DSM-III Text Revision*), published in 1987, provided the criteria that exist today with only minor changes. This edition identified five criteria: (1) the stressor (trauma); (2) reexperiencing symptoms (minimum of one); (3) avoidance symptoms (minimum of three); (4) arousal symptoms (at least two); and (5) duration more than one month. The stressor criterion continued to define stressors to be events "outside the range of usual human experience." In other words, they could not include common events such as grief, illness, marital strife, or business setbacks. This became an important issue for people concerned about communities in which highly traumatic events such as abuse or criminal violence were frequent occurrences. The stressor that caused PTSD usually would be accompanied by intense fear, terror, and helplessness.[12]

DSM-IV AND *DSM-IV-TR*

Additional changes were made in the *DSM-IV* and *DSM-IV-TR*. According to the most recent formulation of criteria in *DSM-IV-TR*, PTSD includes exposure to a life-threatening or other traumatic event (criterion A) together with symptoms from each of the following criteria groups: intrusive recollections (B), avoidant/numbing symptoms (C), and hyperarousal symptoms (D). Two other criteria must be met—duration and a new criterion of "significance," which involves impact of the symptoms on the individual's daily functioning.[13]

To sum up, in the present *DSM-IV-TR*, a person may be diagnosed with PTSD if "the person experienced, witnessed, or was confronted with an event or events that involved actual or threatened death or serious injury, or a threat to the physical integrity of self or others," and "the person's response involved intense fear, helplessness, or horror." The person also must consistently reexperience the event psychologically with (1) "recurrent and intrusive distressing recollections of the event"; (2) "recurrent distressing dreams of the event," such as by reliving the experience, illusions, hallucinations, and flashbacks; (3) "acting or feeling as if the traumatic event were recurring"; (4) "intense psychological distress" when exposed to "cues that symbolize or resemble an aspect of the traumatic event"; or (5) "physiological reactivity" after exposure to cues that symbolize or resemble an aspect of the event.

The current version also requires the presence of two persistent symptoms of increased arousal that were not present before the traumatic event. These can include such symptoms as irritability, difficulty sleeping, difficulty concentrating, hypervigilance, exaggerated startle response, or avoidance of stimuli associated with the trauma. Finally, the symptoms must persist for more than one month and must cause "clinically significant distress or impairment in social, occupational, or other important areas of functioning."

Although traumatic experiences at this level do not occur frequently in ordinary civilian life, they do occur frequently—even routinely—in wartime. Every item listed as a symptom in the definition can also be a routine or normal response to life-threatening events or the normal way the body responds to extreme stressors. In terms of combat experience, reactions that psychiatrists diagnose as PTSD may be reactions expected of soldiers in combat situations. In this sense, PTSD represents a paradox with regard to the normal/abnormal characterization.

Normal, however, is an elusive concept since no one can point to a perfect definition or illustration of what is normal human behavior.[14] Reactions to traumatic experiences vary from person to person. Not all individuals react negatively to trauma, and when they do, not all have persisting symptoms. When people do have persisting symptoms, generally speaking, three factors seem to influence the outcome—the nature of the trauma, the personality and life experience of the person exposed to the trauma, and the support that the person receives, before, during, and after the traumatic event.[15] Victims of

PTSD suffer a wide variety of behavioral, emotional, and social disturbances. Some people have a sensation of reliving the experience during nightmares or in waking flashbacks. In some cases, individuals may act as though they are actually reexperiencing the event.

CRITERIA CHANGES

The cause of PTSD as originally described in the *DSM-III* consisted of a trauma beyond the range of normal that would be distressing for anyone who experienced it. In the *DSM-IV*, however, trauma came to be seen as an event that could cause death, serious injury, or harm but that was not necessarily beyond the range of normal. Starting with the *DSM-III*, the disorder was defined as a pathological anxiety that occurred after an individual experienced or witnessed severe trauma that threatened the physical integrity or life of the individual or another person.[16] In the *DSM-IV-TR*, however, the definition of what qualified as a trauma was changed, and in this formulation, the event qualified if it inspired intense fear, helplessness, or horror in the victim. The *DSM-IV-TR* expanded the definition to include events that were within the normal range, that is, events that previously had not qualified as causing PTSD. The reaction of the individual now played a more prominent role than the event itself. Further, the *DSM-IV-TR* added the provision that the individual need not experience the event directly; merely witnessing an event or being exposed in some other way, such as hearing about it, could also cause PTSD under this definition. This expansion has come under criticism.

Many of the changes that have been made since the original inclusion of PTSD in the manual have little to do with trauma experienced during combat. Most combat PTSD claims would be valid under any of the *DSM* versions. Although the changes appear to be directed at clarifying, limiting, or expanding PTSD in civilian and military noncombat situations, combat soldiers and veterans must exhibit a stressor and symptoms that comply with the changing standards to secure diagnosis and treatment. Victims of traumatic experiences in the civilian world benefit from many of the liberalizing changes, as do military victims who have not seen any combat exposure. Direct exposure to combat trauma is not a threshold for PTSD.

Individual variability clearly is an important consideration since it is well known that not everyone exposed to war or other highly unusual trauma ends up developing PTSD. Most people, in fact, do not develop PTSD as a reaction to trauma.[17] Some people, however, have been known to develop PTSD from experiences not generally associated with trauma, which confounds the prediction process. For example, PTSD has occurred in soldiers whose only military experience has been training in stateside bases.[18] It also appears that symptoms of PTSD can begin long after the trauma is over. The concept of delayed onset can cover a multitude of variations in manifestation of the disorder. While research continues to contribute to the changing conceptions of PTSD, changing social, economic, and political needs also contribute.

The most significant area of change from *DSM* edition to *DSM* edition has been with criterion A, which serves a gatekeeping role. With this criterion, the *DSM* requires designating the probable cause of the disorder, namely, the presence of an explicit traumatic stressor. In specifying the cause as one of the criteria, PTSD's entry differs from those of most other disorders in the *DSM* (although brain injury and intoxication disorders also require an explicit external etiology). To receive a diagnosis of PTSD, the individual must experience an extreme life-threatening stressor. This factor is very important in terms of proving PTSD in the legal context. It is this specific, straightforward traumatic cause that makes PTSD useful as a defense for criminal charges as well as for civil cases.

NEW PHENOMENON OR NEW EXPRESSION OF AN AGE-OLD CONCEPT?

According to one source, some experts have argued that PTSD is a "relatively common human problem [that] has been known for many hundreds of years, although under different names." Others contend that PTSD is a "culture-derived diagnosis and can only have existed in the late twentieth century." Still others argue that PTSD should be seen as "the product not of trauma in itself but of trauma and culture acting together." They argue that PTSD is not a timeless phenomenon and that earlier responses to extreme stress, such as shell shock, are not the same thing.[19]

It is not clear how PTSD, as it is now defined, is related to the wide variety of psychiatric symptoms that manifested themselves during every war recorded in history. Until the wars of the late twentieth century, Vietnam in particular, the psychiatric problems that received attention were those that arose during wartime, especially in combat conditions, not after. They got attention because they seriously hampered the war effort—in every major war in which the United States was engaged. Very little attention was paid to manifestations of symptoms that occurred after the wars. They were a matter of common observation about some veterans but received almost no attention from military or psychiatric personnel.[20] Once the wars were over, whatever residual problems veterans had were their personal problems, not the government's—except, of course, to the extent that the VA had to deal with problems later in the veterans' lives.

The ongoing debates within the psychiatric profession, however, will not be quickly or easily resolved. Regardless, the evidence points unmistakably to the fact that PTSD, by whatever name, is a condition deeply rooted in human experience, especially wartime experience. The perception of stress or trauma is bound to change with the culture of the times. Traumatic stress is not only a medical or psychiatric condition; it has social, economic, political, ethical, and legal aspects. The way PTSD appears to people will differ over time, and the way it will be interpreted and characterized will change as well. It was inevitable, then, that the manifestation of PTSD would be perceived differently from war to war. Trauma—and even the experience of warfare—may have been a frequent or constant occurrence at times. At other times, it may have been episodic and infrequent.

People have to cope with traumas of all kinds within society. Historically, the American experience with war has been sporadic, but some commentators predict that warfare, characterized by occasional violent outbreaks, some on domestic soil, may become a constant presence for the next few generations.[21] Apart from the origin of combat stress far back in the history of war, it is evident that the current version of PTSD displays pervasive elements of contemporary culture. It is a twenty-first-century version of a phenomenon that is deeply rooted in human history. If the present criteria were to be applied in a future situation, the results would be quite different depending on the nature of trauma, the perception of the trauma, and the different circumstances of the other criteria. Despite the long history and the vast amount of literature describing the nature of warfare and the immediate and long-term consequences it holds, Americans have learned little from the war experience. Since the late twentieth century, Americans have approached the subject as neophytes, arguing and making choices as though for the first time and ever surprised by mistakes as they forge ahead to make new ones.

The applications of PTSD in the civilian context—that is, in connection with civil claims for damages from accidents, crimes, and disasters alike—are, beyond question, a contemporary phenomenon without precedent in earlier times. There is great value in studying the past and in examining PTSD's manifestation in other cultural contexts. That process not only authenticates the condition, but also helps one understand it and how it should be interpreted and applied in forensic situations. In addition, it serves as a guide in treating PTSD in medical, psychiatric, and social terms. The wisdom of having a single, one-size-fits-all set of criteria that applies to combat trauma as well as natural disasters, accidents, and crimes remains an open question.

Both views of PTSD—as a new phenomenon and as an age-old problem—have some merit. PTSD is a current manifestation of a condition that is well documented throughout human history, as an examination of American wars will reveal. The political scientist Richard Gabriel has written persuasively about the psychiatric illness that will beset nearly every person if the conditions are stressful enough.[22] Rachel Yehuda, PhD, has written eloquently about the validity of the PTSD formulation.[23] Others, such as Edgar Jones, have discussed the implications of the impact of recent history and culture on the PTSD condition.[24] Still others, such as Hans Pols and Stephanie Oak, have viewed the phenomenon from a combined historical and public health perspective, reaching back into U.S. military history for insights into the disorder.[25] Because PTSD is a serious public health problem, given the number of veterans of the present wars who have been and will be returning home during the decade ahead, treating the disorder within the public health framework is a vital, if presently neglected, enterprise. Moreover, psychiatrists, including Steven Southwick, continue to study what has been called the million-dollar question: "Why do some warriors develop serious symptoms of PTSD after combat, while others from the same units do not?"[26] Are some individuals susceptible and others resilient when it comes to PTSD? When conclusive evidence about why some people develop PTSD and others do not becomes available, this information can be used in recruiting men and women for warfare.

What does this mean for those who suffer from combat PTSD? The long-term effects continue to be discovered. Ongoing studies that focus on veterans of previous wars, especially the Korean and Vietnam Wars, however, reveal long-term, even lifetime, effects of PTSD, some appearing for the first time in the later part of life. Among many new findings are those referred to earlier that suggest that PTSD contributes to dementia in older veterans.

PROBLEMATIC FEATURES OF PTSD

Recognizing PTSD—Trauma

The diagnostic criteria of the *DSM-IV-TR* depend on an external cause (the trauma) rather than on internal factors. This element of the disorder's definition was designed, at least in part, to make the diagnosis workable for victims filing disability claims and involved in lawsuits. In addition to the external causative criterion, the diagnosis has other controversial features, including the shifting focus on present or future, the absence of a predisposition or prior illness criterion, overlap with other disorders, the changing standards for the trauma, and the confusing normal/abnormal dichotomy. Many factors present in the military experience, such as separation from home; severe, continuous, or variable trauma; adjustment problems upon return stateside; and training to use violence, are all missing from the criteria.

The basic premise that underlies the inclusion of PTSD—by whatever name—in the *DSM* as an officially recognized disorder is that it existed in the world prior to being recognized. In other words, identifying the disorder did not create it but merely acknowledged its existence. The story of PTSD, therefore, is the story of how certain people, organizations, and forces in society "brought [the disorder] to light as an always-already-there object in the world, relevant to medical work." When a condition is recognized in one edition of the *DSM* but removed from the next, the fiction falters. The fiction that a disorder can exist before it is recognized but ceases to exist upon withdrawal of recognition is a more difficult concept to accept.[27]

Delayed Onset

Delayed onset ordinarily refers to a delay in the appearance of symptoms. In reality, however, symptoms may be present long before they are identified as such and reported to a mental health professional. Who is to say when the symptoms of PTSD actually began? Does PTSD begin with the appearance of one symptom, or must there be enough for a full diagnosis? How does this determination relate to the one-month criterion? The symptoms must be present for a month before a diagnosis is appropriate. That depends on when the symptoms appear, and are recognized, which may depend on when they are reported to a mental health professional. The significance of the one-month duration in light of identifying the first appearance of symptoms and delayed onset may be unclear in any given situation.

The study of delayed onset PTSD is ongoing. Information about the delayed onset of the disorder uncovered in long-range research will have a major impact on future long-term assessment of PTSD. Further study of the lifelong impact of PTSD on veterans exposed to combat is necessary. The lack of sufficient information complicates the assessment of delayed-onset PTSD.[28] Delayed onset of the disorder can obviously complicate the matter of connecting PTSD with a specific trauma or a specific crime. For example, if a Korean War veteran has a record of many years of criminal behavior but no recognized PTSD symptoms, or at least none recognized and reported until many years after the war and after the criminal behavior, are his PTSD and criminal behavior causally connected to military combat?

Long-Term Effects

Long-range research has shown that PTSD can become a chronic psychiatric disorder that lasts for decades, sometimes for an entire lifetime. An example of such research is an ongoing study into the long-term effects of combat trauma on veterans of the world wars and the Korean War. The veterans may exhibit intermittent remissions and relapses over the course of the study. A delayed variant also exists in which individuals exposed to a traumatic event do not exhibit the syndrome for many months or even years. The factor that precipitates the PTSD response is often a situation that resembles the original trauma in a significant way.[29]

If a person meets diagnostic criteria for PTSD, it is likely that the person will also meet *DSM-IV-TR* criteria for other psychiatric diagnoses as well. Most often, the other diagnoses—classified as comorbid diagnoses—include major affective disorders, chronic depression, substance abuse disorders, anxiety disorders, or personality disorders. In fact, PTSD may be more common in people with a history of these disorders.[30] The high rate of comorbidity among PTSD patients is the subject of ongoing controversy within the mental health field and, in particular, with regard to what the *DSM-5* should contain. High rates of comorbidity obviously complicate diagnosis and treatment because providers must treat multiple disorders.

The relationship (comorbidity) of PTSD with MTBI is a concern within the psychiatric community today. Both MTBI and PTSD are commonly called signature injuries of the current wars. Although they are very different injuries, they may be difficult to distinguish because they have overlapping symptoms. To complicate matters more, within the category of MTBI, as opposed to more severe TBI, physicians have recognized injuries caused by the force of an explosion that does not directly impact the head as well as injuries resulting from a direct blow to the head. Some advocates for MTBI victims have suggested that blast-related TBI is a new form of brain injury and that PTSD may be caused by MTBI alone.[31]

How this debate among psychiatrists and neurologists will play out remains to be seen. Blast-related TBI resembles the concept of shell shock during and after World War II, which I discuss in chapter 3.

A diagnosis of PTSD may be acute or chronic, depending on whether the symptoms last for more or less than three months, and may be labeled delayed onset if symptoms do not appear until six months after the initial trauma. Although the precise cause is unknown—beyond the occurrence of the requisite traumatic event—several factors are thought to contribute to the onset of PTSD in an individual. Those include genetic, psychological, physical, and social factors as well as prior mental illness and prior exposure to trauma.[32]

Diagnosis Obstacles for Veterans

Specificity and sensitivity are important to the scientific and medical value of the diagnosis. Clinicians achieve specificity by asking for behavioral anchors. It is important, for example, to ask for specifics beyond claims of "I feel bad" or "I don't sleep well" or "I drink a bit." The clinician, therefore, seeks to elicit responses that give more behavioral detail, such as "I feel so bad I haven't been able to hold a job for the last two years," or "I only sleep three hours a night on average." Other responses include, "I only drink two cases of beer a week, and people don't like drinking with me anymore." This specificity is important for a military community sample because unanchored emotions themselves have limited relevance and value. The specific manifestations of PTSD pose a serious problem because a portion of the symptoms listed in the *DSM* are shared by other disorders, in particular major depressive disorder (MDD) and alcohol/drug abuse/dependence. A person who scores high with regard to one of these disorders is more likely to meet full criteria for a related disorder.

Another problem is that some of the PTSD criteria can also falsely conflate with diagnoses of other disorders, especially psychotic ones, such as bipolar disorder, that involve concerns of harm to self. The important difference is that people with psychotic disorders generally cannot point to specific causes of their disorders, whereas PTSD patients can attempt to make connections between their current apprehension and their past exposure to trauma. This is an important differential diagnostic issue that only a discrete and competent diagnostician will recognize.

To further add to the problem, diagnosis for veterans has an additional consequence when compensation and pension benefits are involved. Unlike the VA, the VB tends to view veterans' claims with skepticism. All PTSD victims who are seeking redress for an injury must provide supporting evidence. Depending on the legal proceeding involved, rape or abuse victims, for example, may have to present corroborating evidence of trauma and an explanation of the psychic injury by a care provider, or they may have to explain in court how PTSD has negatively affected their life activities. For veterans, however, this means thoroughly documenting the trauma, the absence of mental illness prior to the trauma, and the presence of illness claims post-trauma and, in many cases, during active duty. Career goals and other reasons preclude soldiers from documenting PTSD during active duty. This complicates the matter of making claims once they become veterans within the civilian world. Unlike in many civilian professions (but not dissimilar to law enforcement), in the military there are strong secondary motivations for underreporting mental illness.

A Predictable Response

PTSD is a predictable reaction to the stress of military service, combat in particular. The word "predictable" is preferable to "normal" because, as Colonel Hoge, a military psychiatrist, has pointed out, mental health professionals "aren't in the business of 'normal' because we don't know how to define what normal looks like."[33]

Experience from ancient times to the present supports the prevalence of PTSD. Although it is likely that virtually all people could develop PTSD at some stress level, there is great variation in the way individuals respond to trauma. The point at which a diagnosis can be made or when partial symptoms arise differs from person to person.

The current *DSM* diagnostic criteria for PTSD are not perfect, but they are, with a few notable exceptions, adequate to cover combat stress. Again, as Colonel Hoge emphasized, diagnostic categories in the *DSM* are "best guesses regarding which groups of symptoms should be considered discrete disorders, based on the doctors' clinical experience treating patients with mental health problems and their interpretation of published studies." He added, "The various disorders outlined in *DSM* overlap extensively with each other. They are not distinct conditions, like bacterial infections. They blur together, and it has been proven . . . that different mental health professionals will frequently diagnose different disorders when they interview the same patient."[34]

As previously discussed, confusion surrounds the relationship between delayed-onset PTSD and the durational factor in PTSD symptoms. Still more confusion surrounds what I call "personal identity characteristics in the causative chain" leading to symptoms and behavior that flow from the traumatic stressor—that is, the sum total of experiences, concerns, and conflicting emotions that a particular individual displays. This has been described in terms of predisposition or vulnerability. Finally, there is further uncertainty concerning the invisible impact of partial PTSD.

Soldiers in combat face traumatic experiences while they are in alien surroundings, separated from families and familiar environments. In those situations, they are often anxious, not only about the dangers they encounter, but also about the difficulties that their families are confronting at home. Despite the problematic nature of the current *DSM* criteria, however, the inescapable fact is that a straightforward set of criteria will serve veterans who are charged with crimes better than a complex, detailed set of criteria. The more complex the criteria are, the more difficult it will become for veterans to use them. For example, establishing that a veteran was predisposed to PTSD because of individual characteristics and experience is more difficult than establishing a traumatic stressor. The concept of trauma may be overly simplistic, but still victims can point to it as a single cause of symptoms and antisocial behavior. One might say that PTSD may not be the true diagnosis (in terms of ultimate truth), but it is the right diagnosis (most effective) for veterans' problems—as long as patients and psychiatrists are not troubled by having to reshape events and reactions to fit within the PTSD framework. A similar process is followed in legal matters as factual narratives are reshaped to fit existing substantive and procedural rules and criteria for legal claims.

The psychosomatic aspects of PTSD have long been recognized. As noted earlier, although PTSD is a mental disorder, it has physical effects on the body. It is a physical condition that affects the whole body and is studied through an emerging field of medicine called stress physiology. Colonel Hoge writes, "PTSD can result in physical, cognitive, psychological, emotional, and behavioral reactions that all have a physiological basis."[35] Early definitions of combat stress centered on the combined mental and physical manifestations of stress. Remarkably, for all the early mistakes in diagnosis of psychiatric injuries, the diagnosticians were often closer to the mark than one might expect.

The diverse causes of PTSD are rarely fully recognized. It is obvious from the personal stories included in this book that each veteran's PTSD resulted from different traumas and different combinations of factors. Some of these stories may test the limits of the diagnostic criteria. And yet all involved some common elements, such as displacement, training to overcome the resistance to killing, moral conflict, risk of injury or death to self or others, and constant exposure to traumatic events. None of the veterans were fully prepared for what they experienced, and all felt some degree of fear, anxiety, guilt, and remorse. None were fully prepared for their return to civilian society.

The causal connection between military combat and PTSD is well established and well documented throughout American history. Recent experiences in Iraq and Afghanistan reaffirm the strong connection despite misrepresentations and misunderstandings. But then, misattribution of the symptoms to combat events has been common over the course of many wars.

Recent Research

Recent research has demonstrated that evidence of PTSD can be observed through the use of new medical technology. For example, the effects of PTSD on the brain's chemical process have been studied. In addition, neuroscientists have undertaken studies of PTSD using neuroimaging tools, such as magnetic resonance imaging (MRI). An MRI study has shown that people suffering from PTSD may have a smaller or damaged hippocampus (part of the brain that involves memory and emotional experience). Damage to the hippocampus impairs the ability to store and recall information and to manage fear responses. This affects an individual's ability to react appropriately to stimuli from the outside world. Individuals may, for example, respond violently to what they perceive as a threat and, in the process, harm other people, resulting in criminal charges.[36] These novel developments, which doubtless will have increasing impact on diagnosis and treatment of PTSD, have been challenged by some critics, who contend that they represent inappropriate attempts to medicalize the condition further.

SOCIETAL AND CULTURAL ISSUES

Legal Applications

The human response to combat stress in war is well known, and PTSD has existed in one form or another throughout history. Whether an adverse response to extreme trauma (based on vulnerability) is so common as to be considered the default response or whether resistance to trauma (resilience) is the default response is in dispute, although statistics certainly do not show by any means that acute or chronic PTSD is the majority response. Medical professionals who believe PTSD is probably underreported and underestimated are not surprised by the long-term effects that have been revealed by recent studies. These professionals might concede that PTSD has been overused in the civilian arena, but they would argue that combat stress is age old and that people have not evolved to the point at which they can undergo the stresses of war without ill effects.

Another group of psychiatrists points out that most people are sufficiently resilient to recover within a short period of time, namely, a month. This group considers PTSD overestimated and does not anticipate long-term effects from past and present conflicts. They view American society as enamored or even obsessed with trauma and as having exaggerated the PTSD response so that it applies to all kinds of trauma, small and large. They see the excessive diagnosis of PTSD as harmful because it has trivialized the disorder and caused the development of a system at the VA in which veterans benefit from chronic illness. They complain that veterans come to see themselves as ill and disabled as a by-product of their dependence on continued support from the government.

This dispute, which has erupted again now that drafting of the *DSM-5* is in process, conflates several different controversies. One is the nature and prevalence of war and the combat stress reaction. Another is the question of whether PTSD is a normal reaction to abnormal stress or an abnormal reaction to normal stress. In other words, is psychic injury the normal response or is resilience the normal response? Still another question is whether the focus should be on the patient's success or failure in recovering in timely fashion or whether it should be on the severity and duration of the reaction itself. An additional issue concerns the use or overuse of PTSD in forensic psychiatry for civil and criminal court actions.

There is no escaping the fact that the VB traditionally has been the most forceful proponent of the argument that PTSD is merely a social construct. If that view of PTSD were to prevail, it would discourage many claims and result in huge savings in compensation and disability benefits. Critics of PTSD argue that the present system of benefits discourages recovery because victims become financially dependent on their benefits.[37] Changes in the benefits system have recently been made, however, to make it easier for veterans with PTSD to receive benefits.[38]

Military Expediency

The name and description of the disorder have changed over time through a complicated process of development—a combination of knowledge and expediency. This process has repeated itself in nearly every war. It typically begins with preconceptions and assumptions and progresses based on knowledge that is acquired gradually through experience—often through measures that do not work—but this evolution is always subject to overriding military goals. For the military, illness or injury, whether physical or mental, can limit manpower resources. Consideration of sufficient troop levels, while perfectly understandable, does raise the specter of conflicting goals and purposes. When a major component of an army is beset by physical and mental disorders, real or imagined, the result can be crippling to the war effort and, therefore, inspires finding immediate solutions, generally of a short-term nature.

PTSD may be the only disorder that has been recognized and acted upon in concert with—and sometimes at the convenience of—political, social, and military goals. Although mental health treatment surely meant in part to equip patients to return to normal life activities, few treatment plans aim to prepare patients for return to the source of exposure to the cause of their illness—even when the patients could potentially suffer from the reexposure to trauma. Preparing soldiers to return to the battlefield is one of the controversial purposes of military psychiatry in the case of traumatic stress disorders. The greater goal of military victory typically has too often subsumed the less urgent goal of bringing about and securing the mental health of the individual soldier.

The conflicting roles of military psychiatrists influence the recognition and treatment of PTSD in wartime. The story of combat stress, in fact, is as much the story of war psychiatry and military psychiatrists as it is the story of the trauma of war. Whether psychiatrists are in private practice or employed by the military, they are bound by the same set of ethical responsibilities. The Belmont Report, a document published in 1979, established standards for research with human subjects. Among the report's widely accepted principles was that psychiatrists must respect the patient as a person (respect for persons, autonomy), do no harm, do good, and act with justice in the allocation of the benefit and burden of resources and services.[39] A major question in the case of PTSD is whether psychiatrists are acting ethically when they provide treatment to soldiers for the purpose of returning them to combat, with the risk of relapse. Should the focus be on long-term recovery and adjustment to civilian life? Does sending a soldier back to the battlefield, to be exposed to more trauma that could cause a relapse when the physician knows that the patient has not had enough time or treatment to recover fully, respect the soldier's personhood and autonomy? What autonomy should a physician recognize in the case of an enlisted soldier? Does reexposing the patient to more trauma constitute doing harm? What does a fair distribution of benefit and burden (justice) mean in the context of war? Should military leaders or physicians treat people who volunteer for military duty, thus self-selecting for trauma exposure, differently from those who were conscripted in prior wars? Although these are all difficult questions, physicians and researchers have an ethical duty to protect the individual, not the military and its goals, in all situations.

Moral Injury: A Missing Element?

In the *DSM-III* definition of PTSD, one of the symptoms was "guilt about surviving while others have not, *or about behavior required for survival* [emphasis added]." One commentator attributed the inclusion of survival behavior to the "predominance of thinking about the phenomenology of Vietnam veterans and clinical care experience with veterans of war."[40] This symptom generated some consideration of moral conflict in the framework of PTSD until it was removed. In 1981 a psychiatric expert stated, "Guilt figures strongly in post-Vietnam syndrome and includes not only survivor guilt because close friends were killed in combat, but also guilt about Vietnamese (especially women and children) who were killed in the line of duty."[41] Little formal attention was paid to moral conflict, however, until the publication in 2009 of an article by a group of mental health experts from the National Center for PTSD in Boston and other medical centers headed by Brett Litz, PhD.[42]

According to the article, moral injury can happen when a person acts in ways "that transgress deeply held moral beliefs, witness that in others or witness intense human suffering and cruelty."[43] The group claimed not to be arguing for a new diagnostic category, nor did they wish to make the moral and ethical distress of soldiers or veterans seem pathological. They did claim, however, that they wanted to stimulate research and explore treatment options. Essentially, they asserted that the current wars might be creating additional risk of exposure to morally or ethically questionable situations and other threats. For example, soldiers in Iraq and Afghanistan are likely to mistakenly kill civilians whom they believe to be insurgents, kill enemy combatants, witness dead bodies or human remains, or see suffering women or children whom they cannot help. Most of the attention on the part of clinicians is devoted to the impact of life-threatening trauma, which is understandable given the clear focus of the present criteria of PTSD.

The concept of suffering moral injury because of one's own action is controversial because it can be asserted on behalf of people who have participated in committing or failing to prevent atrocities or other immoral actions. It is possible, however, that even in the absence of morally injurious behavior, the inner conflict caused by the requirements of military service and survival may cause distress and intensify the effect of other traumatic experiences. In addition to the anxiety of displacement, another layer of anxiety exists—that is, doing one's duty and abiding by one's moral standards. Moral injury may also be considered an ethical problem rather than a psychiatric one, and in that context, it raises questions about ethical and moral standards and conduct that transcend military psychiatry. The implications of moral injury extend far beyond the realm of events that may qualify as traumas for purposes of PTSD. Whose morality or ethical code is at issue? What is the source of the moral or ethical standards? Should all moral or ethical standards receive the same recognition? Another question is: How should the concept of moral injury be taken into account in PTSD assessment? Should it be identified as a trauma criterion or as a situational criterion? Or should it be merely a symptom? Should it be part of PTSD at all?

If tendencies or predispositions were introduced into the *DSM* criteria, the result might be a more realistic assessment of PTSD, but it would complicate the use of PTSD in court because it would open up inquiry into the individual's history and life activities.

Simplicity of Definition for Veterans

For the sake of veterans with PTSD, the most useful definition of the causational factor is a simple one of a traumatic experience without regard to predispositional factors. Effective forensic use of a mental disorder relies on simple, straightforward, uncomplicated testimony about matters that juries and judges can readily grasp and apply. When medical and psychiatric criteria become too complicated, fact finders can easily get bogged down in detail and in doubt. PTSD was formulated primarily for forensic use with Vietnam veterans in mind. The basic definition of trauma as the gatekeeping factor was designed to be workable for them, despite being framed in general language. Certain changes may be appropriate and useful. Some changes in *DSM* criteria, however, even if they genuinely reflect the complexity of PTSD, may hinder, rather than help, veterans (and other claimants).

In particular, if the *DSM-5* further expands the causative criterion (trauma) to accommodate more civilian claimants who seek treatment, this may lead to more questions about the legitimacy of the disorder and may undermine the legal use of the disorder by veterans. In addition, the more complicated the PTSD defense becomes and the more factors imported into the criteria, the more difficult it will be for veterans claiming PTSD—and others in civilian situations—to prove they have the disorder. The door may be open for probing inquiry into preexisting factors—genetic, psychological, experiential, physical, and social.

The criteria for PTSD do not include some of the crucial distinguishing factors of combat PTSD, which I have previously noted, including, in brief, separation from home, psychological preparation and training as warriors, and

developing a new warrior personality that allows one to kill without compunction or remorse. In combat circumstances, development of group loyalty
temporarily replaces devotion to family and friends. Risk and the need for
hypervigilance are constant companions in wartime. Both are always dangerous, chaotic, and unpredictable. The death and destruction of human beings,
which is felt deeply when happening among one's own group but observed
with detachment if happening among the enemy, becomes commonplace, even
if not accepted at the core of being. All these factors contribute to developing
PTSD.

The Criminal Connection

The connection between combat PTSD and crime depends on the particular
behavior in question, for example, physical violence or driving while intoxicated. It is important to note that in the criminal justice system, a general relationship between a mental condition and a crime is not legally significant. Only
the relationship between a specific mental health condition and a specific crime
has legal relevance. Even when a relationship is established, it may be complicated by facts and circumstances that relate to the alleged criminal conduct.

Studies have shown that people who suffer PTSD from combat are more
prone to aggression, either directed at themselves or others. Male veterans with
PTSD show higher rates of violent outbursts and aggressive behavior than those
without the disorder. They express more hostility and have poorer anger control. Although all the reasons for this relationship are not understood yet, combat exposure is naturally associated with aggression, in part because violence is
reinforced as a part of military service. One theory explored at the National
Center for PTSD is that PTSD combined with depression may account for
aggression in men with the disorder. Another is that various negative emotions,
such as being irritable, ashamed, guilty, hostile, or upset, may contribute to
the phenomenon. The findings of the National Center study, however, support the idea that PTSD symptoms are a significant contributor to aggressive
behavior and violence.[44]

Research on combat PTSD's role in producing criminal behavior is in the
early stages, although anecdotal evidence of the relationship is well known. It
would seem, however, that studies are not necessary to predict that some types
of criminal problems will result from the disorder. One police official in a city

near a military base said, for example, "It doesn't take a study to know the potential for problems is going to be there."[45] It is clear that veterans will have difficulty turning off their warrior persona and mentality, which are necessary for protection in combat settings, in civilian life. Moreover, social factors that accompany reentry of veterans, such as alcoholism, divorce, unemployment, and homelessness, contribute to poor decision making. A series of bad decisions can propel a veteran toward lawless behavior, such as use of illegal drugs or domestic violence, and can result in criminal prosecutions. Other criminal activity, however, can result from psychological problems that need treatment. Whether PTSD causes or merely correlates with criminal conduct remains an open question.

Although studies on the relationship between crime and PTSD are in their infancy, news reporters have begun using anecdotal evidence and court cases involving PTSD as proof of the correlation. Most attempts to use PTSD as a defense in court rely on the reasoning that, when veterans are confronted by situations that in wartime would trigger a violent response, they will react in ways in which they have been conditioned to react. In these situations, crucial factors are the event that triggered the veteran's reactions and the PTSD symptoms involved in the response. Was the event an ordinary, nonthreatening action? Was it a threatening remark or physical assault? Perceived threats or violations of a veteran's sense of justice, anger and irritability, hypervigilance, startle response or depression, and emotional numbing can all lead to criminal behavior and appear to be fairly logically connected to PTSD. Many instances of criminal behavior cannot be explained by simple causal relationships. The effect of flashbacks, troublesome memories, or violence that bears no simple explanation may need deeper psychological probing to determine whether the PTSD is causally related. As I continue the story of PTSD past and present, it will become clearer that the mental injuries suffered by veterans during the present wars will be immense and will challenge courts as they grapple with society's unsolved problems.

PART II

AMERICAN WARS PRIOR TO SEPTEMBER 11, 2001

3

Across the Ages

PTSD from the Civil War to Korea

As I review the role of combat stress in the early American wars, my focus is on the value of the information in predicting the impact of PTSD on veterans of the wars in Iraq and Afghanistan. The view that the Vietnam War was unique and that Vietnam veterans were exceptional among all American veterans does not hold up under close scrutiny. Traumatic stress symptoms occurred during all the earlier wars as well. PTSD appears more and more to be simply "the most recent reincarnation of the psychological problems that earlier American veterans experienced under the rubric of 'combat fatigue,' 'shell-shock,' or in the Civil War era 'nostalgia,' and 'soldier's heart.'"[1]

The original gross stress reaction category in the *DSM* ignored pertinent research in at least two respects. One study based on observation of World War II veterans concluded that many stress reactions did not occur on the battlefield but, instead, erupted afterward. That study further revealed that symptoms could persist for many months or even years. The observations of persistence and delay indicated a need to recognize "delayed" and "chronic" features as components of gross stress reaction.[2] It is important to note that treatment of psychiatric casualties of World War II continued for many veterans long after their return to the states. A well-known 1946 documentary film, directed by John Huston, *Let There Be Light*, traced the treatment at a psychiatric hospital on Long Island of seventy-five veterans who sustained debilitating emotional trauma and depression from World War II combat.[3]

The backstory of combat PTSD includes the history of combat trauma over the span of many centuries, culminating in the American Civil War, the two world wars, and the Korean War.

THE AMERICAN CIVIL WAR

From 1861 to 1865 the Union Army recorded 2,600 cases of insanity and 5,200 cases of nostalgia that required hospitalization. In addition, there were 200,000 Union deserters and 160,000 cases of "constipation," which was similar to what was called "precombat syndrome."[4]

Other conditions that emerged during the Civil War were cases recorded as "malingering" plus the "irritable and exhausted heart" named by Jacob Mendes Da Costa, a Civil War physician. Some or all of these conditions may well have resulted from psychiatric difficulties, although they were attributed to other causes.[5]

In terms of sheer numbers, the Civil War was far and away the most devastating conflict in American history. Although some estimates place the number of deaths over 600,000, it is safe to say that at least 500,000 soldiers died during the four years of war, and this at a time when the U.S. population was only 35 million. By contrast, during the Vietnam War, when the population was more than 200 million, 58,000 American military lives were lost. In the deadliest war in history, World War II, approximately 405,000 American lives were lost. The American death toll for World War I was more than 116,000, and the Korean War claimed approximately 37,000 American lives.[6]

Soldiers in the Civil War suffered extraordinary physical hardships. Although this war was the first waged with modern technology (including locomotives, rifled muskets, and naval torpedoes fired from ironclad warships), the soldiers' chief mode of travel was on foot. They had little protection against the elements, especially in winter, and inadequate food and supplies. Diseases such as cholera, typhoid, malaria, smallpox, measles, scurvy, and tuberculosis ran rampant through the troops. Medical care was primitive and fundamental advances in sanitation and germ theory had not yet occurred. For every man killed in combat, two died of disease during the war.[7]

Soldiers' prebattle suffering from psychological trauma, such as fear, tension, and anxiety, is well documented. It was not uncommon for soldiers to react with terror and even paralysis during Civil War battles, which commonly consisted of fierce hand-to-hand combat. Men often reported feeling a sense of detachment in which they displayed conflicting reactions at the same time, including fury, insane excitement, hysterical shouting, and laughter. The sound and fury of battles such as Chickamauga, Chancellorsville, and Spotsylvania Court House were more horrible than observers could begin to describe in their diaries and journals. Although there were moments when civility prevailed, the battles were so frenzied that soldiers reportedly were driven to commit "acts of violence and cruelty toward their fellow men." Atrocities against prisoners of war, captured African Americans, and captured rebels were documented. Artillery fire could inflict severe losses on the troops of both sides, and battlefield scenes following combat were often sickening sights of death and destruction. Deserters, of which there were many on both sides, were occasionally summarily executed to reinforce the deadly serious warnings about desertion. One soldier summed up the experience with the words, "War is horrid beyond the conception of man."[8]

Although Civil War veterans were not examined for signs of what is now called a post-traumatic stress reaction to the traumatic incidents of disease, hardship, and violence, a recent review of the historical evidence, including personal accounts of soldiers, reveals that they suffered from the condition during and after their service. Civil War historians of the pre-PTSD era largely overlooked this evidence, and there was little reason to pay attention to the issue until well after the Vietnam War. Most Civil War soldiers, perhaps like soldiers generally, tended to say that they were "getting used to combat" and the sights, sounds, and smells of battle after the first exposure.[9] Whether these statements indicated an adjustment or hardening to the shock and horror of combat or whether they were bluster that concealed a deeper fear and horror is unclear. Most likely, they indicate a combination of the two along with whatever training the soldiers had received to prepare them for hardship and death.

Many personal accounts suggest that the stress of battle took its toll on the soldiers and that the disclaimers merely concealed inner psychiatric distress. Civil War soldiers suffered from the same fear, horror, depression, vulnerability, and fatalism experienced by combat soldiers in all wars. Civil War casualties were overwhelming. In Gen. Ulysses S. Grant's assaults at the Wilderness, Spotsylvania Court House, and Cold Harbor, there were 65,000 casualties in seven weeks. In one of those, Cold Harbor, the Union forces suffered seven thousand casualties in less than one hour. In the trench warfare that followed, which foreshadowed conditions on the western front in World War I, artillery bombardment and sharpshooters continuously besieged both sides. The men described their stress in terms of being "exhausted" or "played out."[10]

All in all, the evidence indicates that the experience and reactions of Civil War soldiers were similar to those of veterans of other wars. Although the Civil War soldiers expressed ambivalent attitudes that reflected their understanding of the hardship and horror of war, they were devoted to their unit and their fellow soldiers. This devotion, which has long been recognized as a vital feature of military life, helped them bear the hardships and suffering of war. They appear to have experienced complex reactions; they were not simply battle-hardened from the exposure, nor were they potential victims waiting to break down.[11] Even though evidence of stress reaction was available during and after the Civil War, the time was not ripe for attention and examination given the lack of understanding of mental health problems at the time.

What psychiatrists know about PTSD depends in each instance on observations and reports of symptoms. Those factors depend on the psychiatric framework and standards that exist at any given time. Every study that is undertaken necessarily relies in part on comparison of present data with data that was recorded at a time when different standards were in effect. The examination of data from the past, for example, at the time of the Civil War, involves reinterpreting data based on current standards. Substantial evidence illustrates that Civil War veterans did show symptoms of post-traumatic stress after they returned home, and contrary to some historical reports, they did receive considerable social support from their communities. Union soldiers, for example, witnessed parades and other celebrations in countless towns in the North. Confederate soldiers were generally treated well, although their homecoming was bittersweet. Civil War veterans accepted the welcomes they received with a mixture of emotions, including both excitement and boredom, as they grappled with the problems, losses, and inner conflicts of their memories and lives. They felt, as all veterans do, that those who did not go to war could not understand what they had experienced. There was no sense of the healing or reconciliation that was publicly addressed in the post-Vietnam years.[12]

In addition, the post–Civil War period saw a continuation in civilian life of the violence of wartime. Both North and South experienced a period of turmoil following the war's end. Many newspaper reports attributed the increase in crime to the veterans who had reentered society, although the evidence is mainly anecdotal. According to one source, two-thirds of the commitments to state prisons in the North were veterans of the war, and the South experienced an even worse increase in crime.[13] A study published a year or so before the United States entered World War II concluded, "War and crime are closely interwoven. The combination of a breakdown of ordinary peacetime restraints and the increased pressures of wartime existence (economic, emotional and social) is often more than the ordinary man, woman or child can withstand."[14]

The personal stories of many veterans revealed that they continued to experience fear of being killed, anxiety, erratic behavior, inability to cope with normal living experiences, sleeplessness, and other symptoms that would now be recognized as indicating PTSD. The problems of some individuals could readily be connected to wartime experiences, but others could not. Even veterans who seemed to adjust easily to their old lives continued to suffer from a wide range of physical and psychological problems related to their military service. This historical evidence challenges the idea that the veterans of any later war were unique among American veterans in suffering from delayed stress reactions to the trauma of war.[15]

Although no concept that closely resembled the present formulation of PTSD existed at the time of the Civil War—since the medical science of psychiatry, as we know it, did not exist—a variety of terms were used in describing the mental condition at the time. These terms include "the blues," "disheartened," "downhearted," "demoralized," "nervous," "played out," "worn out," "depressed," "rattled," and "dispirited." Soldiers used this and other similar language when writing to their families. When the army was deciding whether men should be given medical leave or sent home, however, other terms came into play. These included "nostalgia," "insanity," "irritable heart," and "sunstroke." The concept of insanity was still governed by the ancient Greek diagnostic system of "mania" (anxiety, agitation), "melancholia" (depression, lethargy), and "dementia" (thinking disorder).[16]

The display of psychological symptoms generally gave rise to immediate suspicion of shirking duty or malingering, which resulted in harsh treatment. Conditions that would now be recognized as legitimate psychiatric disorders were dealt with rigorously and ruthlessly. In some extreme cases, soldiers were even committed to insane asylums. "Nostalgia" was a commonly used term, both for soldiers during the war and for veterans after the war. Although the U.S. Army officially recognized psychiatric conditions at the time, in the absence of physical collapse, the condition had to be "manifest" or "pronounced" before discharge would be considered.[17]

The emphasis was on maintaining the fighting force, as it has been in all American wars, and most soldiers' efforts to be excused from combat because of mental distress were rejected. This may account for the high levels of desertion—a total of 300,000 men on both sides deserted their posts during the Civil War. Despite the general understanding that military life could wear down soldiers mentally as well as physically, physical collapse was necessary before relief would be considered.

After the war, although Civil War veterans were not completely ignored, their problems were inadequately understood and dealt with for a variety of reasons. Because of the lack of official psychiatric diagnoses and full appreciation of mental disorders, those who suffered from obvious symptoms as well as those who were involved in alcohol abuse were generally considered as lacking in courage or virtue. The medical treatment that did exist was inadequate. Moreover, purely psychological problems were seen as secondary to the physical conditions soldiers had developed, which included a full range of diseases as well as physical injuries. For the most part, a veteran who displayed only psychological symptoms, especially if he was a deserter, was viewed as a malingerer.[18]

WORLD WAR I

The prevalence of mental injury from combat trauma that arose during World War I and lasted long afterward has generally been underestimated. Psychiatric casualties were, in fact, substantial after World War I. During that war, of the nearly 2 million men who were deployed in Europe by the U.S. Army, only about 250,000 saw direct combat, more than 116,000 were killed in battle and another 204,000 were wounded. Of the 106,000 admitted to hospitals for psychiatric reasons, approximately 69,000 suffered mental injuries so significant that they were permanently evacuated from the frontlines and lost to the fighting effort. Of those who saw direct combat, the rate of psychiatric breakdown was 27.7 percent. Another 14.6 percent of the direct combatants were admitted to psychiatric facilities for some period of time. All in all, about 42 percent of the actual combat force suffered some level of psychiatric problems serious enough to warrant treatment. Overall, nearly 160,000 were out of action for some period of time because of psychiatric difficulties. The chance of being taken out of the field for psychiatric symptoms was nearly twice that of being killed in action.[19]

The knowledge that developed during the course of the war about the condition of the returning veterans should have taught lasting lessons for future application. Many of the lessons learned were forgotten during the period between World Wars I and II. In World War I, there were vast numbers of troops, and huge, unprecedented quantities of shelling took place on both sides. The sheer magnitude of shell fire produced tremendous numbers of casualties. It was not long after the U.S. entered the war before it became obvious that huge numbers of mental casualties existed. Physicians observed symptoms in the survivors that included loss of emotional control, loss of voice, unsteadiness, tremors, difficulty standing, and chronic indigestion. Most of the symptoms were attributed to physical causes. The idea of mental disorders was difficult to accept. There was, in fact, what one scholar called "a mass epidemic of mental disorders" among the fighting lines. The disorders inspired a large body of combat psychological literature. The "mental wreckage" posed totally unexpected problems for the medical profession in all the countries involved in the war. In 1915 the term "shell shock" was coined to describe the epidemic. The term soon became a matter of common knowledge and usage.[20]

Officers dealt with the problems of mental disorders at the front lines according to their own values and inclinations, depending upon the urgency of the situation. Some soldiers were shot for cowardice; others were court-martialed. In a few cases soldiers were tied to the barbed-wire lines that protected the trenches. These harsh approaches were hampered by the fact that many officers broke down as well. Military leaders, in time, had to concede that cases of mental distress were a serious cause of troop debilitation. Soldiers often stated their complaints in language similar to that used by Vietnam soldiers more than fifty years later. Once the war was over, members of the public in the postwar society were eager to move on and leave the memory of the war behind. People did not encourage veterans to remind them of their continuing mental distress. As one commentator put it, veterans were trapped between fixation and repression.[21]

The labels applied to combat stress illustrate the incomplete understanding of the condition. The label first applied by the British and French to combat stress arising in World War I was shell shock. That label, which served as a metaphor for the new type of battle that emerged in that war, developed from good faith efforts to define the nature of the psychiatric condition observed in soldiers. The new war tactics, which consisted primarily of artillery shells and other explosive devices, were the principal cause of death and injury as well as traumatic stress. It was probably inevitable that a relationship would be perceived between the actual shock to the nervous system from exploding shells and the psychiatric injury that resulted. Historians point out that certain inconsistencies should have discredited the theory. Although German prisoners of war exposed to shelling or bombing did not develop shell shock, American soldiers exposed or thought to be exposed to toxic gases labeled themselves as shell-shocked. Then, Canadian soldiers with severe head injuries from shrapnel and gunshot showed little evidence of psychosis, causing medical experts to conclude that only unwounded soldiers suffered shell shock.[22] This series of mistaken judgments seems astounding given current knowledge.

Shell-shock cases were viewed and handled during World War I in ways that revealed a muddle of evolving insights, incomplete understandings, misunderstandings, and cross-purposes not unlike the way PTSD (and MTBI) have been handled to the present time. Physicians' attempts to diagnose and treat psychiatric conditions were often confounded by overriding military and political agendas and goals. Mistaken labels for conditions were not easily relinquished even in the face of knowledge. For example, even when clinicians stopped using the term "shell shock," soldiers continued to use it.

Regardless of the label, the British learned that offering immediate treatment near the front, also known as "forward treatment," rather than evacuating a victim to England, worked far better to get the soldier back into service. In 1917 the U.S. Army surgeon general, Thomas Salmon, who had heard of the British and French experience, adopted a treatment plan that was based on forward treatment.[23] Expediency in finding a way to return soldiers to service as quickly as possible trumped the pursuit of accurate psychiatric diagnosis and treatment.

Soldiers' expectations played a role in their reaction to stress. Those who were called shell-shocked acted as though they had sustained a shock to their central nervous system. When military physicians came to recognize that concussion was not the cause of the condition, they substituted the term "war neurosis." The soldiers immediately interpreted this term to mean that they were sick. As a result, clinicians began to use the term, "N.Y.D.," which stood for "not yet diagnosed (nervous)." This indefinite term did not give the soldiers a basis for believing that they were sick and incapacitated, which would have justified release from combat duty. The impression, rather, was that they were merely tired and nervous and needed rest in order to be ready to return to duty. Eventually, the term "exhaustion" came to be used. This evolved into "combat exhaustion," which was used during World War II until it morphed into "battle fatigue."[24]

During World War I, study of the condition related solely to its impact on the conduct of the war. The concern that drove diagnosis and treatment was the fear that the military force could be seriously depleted by wholesale evacuation of soldiers if complaints of battle stress were taken seriously. Clinicians came to believe, however, that a major factor in the condition was the separation from civilian life and the desire to return to it as soon as possible. It was much later that the study of combat stress focused on the aftermath of war and the long-term consequences of veterans' inability to leave war behind and readjust fully to civilian life. After World War I, the idea of forward treatment seemed to fade with the memory of the war, and the theory that childhood trauma was the origin of mental disorders dominated psychiatric thinking. As a result, the idea of screening out—excluding—from service people who showed evidence of such trauma gained in popularity. During the Spanish Civil War (1936–39), this tactic was used along with a continuation of the forward evacuation treatment process. Forward evacuation still had the advantage of curtailing the use of malingering to escape military life. Psychiatric casualties were low, but given the dual tactics of screening and forward evacuation, no valid conclusions about the causes of the decline could be drawn.[25]

WORLD WAR II

When the United States entered World War II on December 7, 1941, much of the knowledge that had been gained during World War I about combat stress disorder had disappeared from memory. Valuable insights into the nature and origin of combat stress, the diagnosis and treatment of soldiers, and understanding of the resources and structure necessary to deal with it had either been forgotten or repressed. Although the United States had suffered much less than other nations in World War I, it was striking that, in 1942, about 58 percent of the patients in VA hospitals were World War I shell-shock cases. As Roger Spiller succinctly put it, "Ignoring experience, knowledge, and memory, the U.S. Army followed a now familiar cycle of mystification, suspicion, diagnostic confusion, competition between military and medical authorities for the power to determine how such cases fitted within the business of war, a grudging reconciliation with the unavoidable facts of combat fatigue and, by war's end, a pragmatic approach to neuropsychiatric battle casualties."[26]

In the period between the wars, medical authorities in the army had determined that psychiatric screening of the mentally unfit was the best solution for preventing an outbreak of psychiatric disorders. Some psychiatrists were convinced that screening enlisted men for mental health problems would weed out not only those with mental illness but also those who were most likely to break down under the stresses of battle. A leading military psychiatrist, William Porter, stated, "Any individual who . . . has shown an inability to adapt himself in an adult, socially-acceptable manner to the demands of ordinary life should . . . not be chosen for military training." His thinking was that people who did not do well in peacetime would not do well under conditions of stress in military life. The assumption behind the screening program that "sturdy, well-adjusted soldiers of strong character would be able to withstand the stresses of war turned out to be ill-founded."[27]

The medical screening program for World War II excluded 12 percent, or nearly 2 million, of the 15 million men examined through 1944. This number was six times the number excluded during World War I. Of all men excluded for medical reasons, 37 percent were rejected for neuropsychiatric problems.[28] Although the rejection rate for the war was many times more than that of World War I, the psychiatric discharge rate turned out to be nearly two and a half times that of the previous war.[29] It should be kept in mind, however, that combat duration for World War II was three or four times longer than in World War I and at least four times as many American troops served in the later war.[30] Research done after World War II cast doubt on the effectiveness of screening and failed to identify with certainty the specific causes of psychiatric casualties of war. Fewer than half of cases of nervous breakdown occurred overseas, and not all of those happened at the front lines. The findings suggested that a wide variety of factors, including lack of morale, contributed to psychiatric casualties. Later research has reinforced the ideas that combat stress takes many forms and that many factors in addition to specific traumatic events contribute to it.[31]

Nearly 1.4 million men suffered psychiatric symptoms serious enough to remove them from action for some period of time. In the army ground forces, more than a half million men were lost permanently for psychiatric reasons. Another 596,000 were lost to the fighting forces for periods of weeks or months. Still another 464,000 soldiers reported psychiatric problems but were not admitted and were returned to action almost immediately. As Richard Gabriel points out, these statistics do not reveal the magnitude of the problem. About 800,000 ground soldiers saw direct combat. Of these, 37.5 percent were lost to the military because of severe psychiatric problems. Another 596,000, or 74 percent, were admitted to medical facilities for psychiatric problems for periods of days to months. It seemed that virtually every American soldier in Europe was at risk for psychiatric problems. Clearly, not only the weak or timid were breaking down in combat.[32] The end of World War II produced psychiatric casualties in even more alarming numbers than World War I.[33] Peter Bourne, a psychiatric expert, chronicled the psychiatric experience of World War II and reported that, at times, the flow of soldiers out of the army on psychiatric grounds during World War II exceeded the number of new recruits being inducted.[34]

In the first few months of American involvement in the war, the few psychiatrists who were in the army reported that mental illness reports were at peacetime levels. They felt that the war was not going to produce any new problems for psychiatrists. This view soon proved incorrect. As soon as the Allies began running into strong resistance, the number of cases of mental illness increased dramatically. The rates of nervous breakdown—or war neurosis, battle fatigue, or combat stress, as shell shock had come to be called in this war—far exceeded the numbers seen during World War I. To some, the screening program appeared to have failed.[35] This remains uncertain because there is no way of knowing what would have happened to those who were screened out.

The next step in dealing with battle fatigue was instituting a forward or frontline treatment operation. This effort was aimed at discouraging soldiers from reporting symptoms in order to get out of combat and returning soldiers to combat quickly. Psychiatrists at the front lines began to view the breakdowns in a radically different way from the view that had prevailed to that point. They began to realize, as practitioners had eventually realized during World War I, that breakdowns were caused by a combination of factors—hardship, length of exposure to combat, and "unusually harrowing events which a normal personality cannot tolerate." They now abandoned the idea that predisposition was the cause and began to see it as a "normal reaction of normal individuals exposed to the extraordinary stresses of warfare." Two leading psychiatrists remarked, "'It would seem to be a more rational question to ask why the soldier does not succumb to anxiety, rather than why he does.' Psychologists acknowledged that every man had his breaking point: it was only rational to ask when he would break down rather than if."[36] Soldiers who broke down suffered what is now recognized as possible symptoms of PTSD: debilitating and chronic anxiety attacks, tremors, stuttering, amnesia, and nightmares.

Two other factors entered into the equation. One was a concern for morale among the troops. The theory was that the incidence of mental breakdown was inversely related to the strength of morale. The recognition that the nature of the bonds among soldiers is extremely important was and still is a valid observation. The other factor was an idea advocated by S. L. A. "Slam" Marshall, a former Detroit Free Press journalist who undertook the task of interviewing soldiers who had been in combat. Marshall's controversial theory was that only a small percentage of soldiers (between 15 and 25 percent) actually fired at enemy soldiers (as opposed to aiming to miss). He argued that humans had an inherent revulsion against killing other humans.[37] In Marshall's opinion, the "fear of killing, rather than fear of being killed, was the most common cause of battle failure in the individual, and that fear of failure ran a strong second."[38] This idea was reassuring to some, who felt gratified that most men remained decent human beings with an ethical sense of the value of human life, despite all their training and exposure to battle. Marshall, however, saw this as a problem of military efficiency, and his arguments led to renewed training to raise the ratio of soldiers who actually fired to kill the enemy.[39]

Marshall agreed with the morale theory and, in the course of his writing, described the forbidding nature of the solitary experience on the battlefield as follows:

The battlefield is cold. It is the lonesomest place which men may share together. . . . The harshest thing about the field is that it is empty. No people stir about. . . . Over all there is a great quiet which seems more ominous than the occasional tempest of fire. It is the emptiness which chills a man's blood and makes the apple harden in his throat. It is the emptiness which grips him as with a paralysis.[40]

Later studies that sought to validate the theory that predisposition was the major factor in causing psychiatric breakdown in combat did not produce support. The term "exhaustion" was chosen as a diagnosis for all combat psychiatric cases because it came closest to describing what the soldiers felt and did not imply mental disturbance. Remarkably, psychiatric understanding of combat stress had not advanced during the two decades that had passed since World War I. Psychiatrists had done no more than rediscover the flawed understanding of theories popular in World War I.[41]

World War II psychiatrists did learn about the epidemiology of combat stress casualties, namely, the relationship to intensity of combat and the social factors such as morale and unit cohesion. Psychiatrists also learned important information about what contributed to the vulnerability of soldiers. They learned, for example, that soldiers new to battle were more vulnerable than experienced ones but also that soldiers exposed to combat for a long time were likely candidates for breakdown. Psychiatrists found that troops in nonbattle settings, such as in garrisons, were also subject to the condition. Soldiers could have the condition in prebattle and post-battle settings as well as in direct combat. Lessons of cumulative stress and group cohesion emerged along with the concept that "everyone has his breaking point."[42]

Military psychiatrists came away from World War II with three important insights about war neurosis. First, they learned that predicting which individuals would break down was very difficult and that screening did not solve the problem. Breakdown occurred mostly because of the intensity of combat, length of deployment, and group cohesion. Second, they learned that group cohesion and morale were key factors. The third lesson was that early treatment of mental problems near the front lines worked best to return soldiers to the battlefield. They also mistakenly concluded that recovery during wartime and return to combat meant that there would be no long-term consequences.[43] The pre-

vailing view was that psychiatric disability after the war was attributable to factors that predated the war rather than the war itself. As a result, military psychiatrists devoted little time to postwar psychiatric problems after World War II.

Studies showed that most soldiers had no real sense of what the war was
about or why they were fighting. Moreover, most of them did not care to find
out. For many soldiers, the war was a "dirty job that needed to be finished as
quickly as possible so they could return home." When the war failed to end as
quickly as anticipated, dissatisfaction with army conditions increased. These
findings showed that the majority of soldiers felt a general disenchantment
with the war, a reaction that was conveniently forgotten after the conflict when
American society was attempting to construct an image of valor and sacrifice
about the "just and glorious war." Later historical research that reappraised
World War II has confirmed these findings.[44]

In the 1980s and 1990s a body of historical literature appeared that viewed
critically the "rosy interpretation" that had persisted since World War II that it
was the "good war." Historians began pointing out the flaws in that interpretation. In addition to the flaws that had been visible for some time, such as the
restrictions of civil liberties of groups of Japanese Americans, the resistance to
gains by blacks, and the rapid erosion of women's wartime gains, historians
began to see the war in a new light. That light revealed a pervasive conformity
in behavior and belief, sometimes imposed or fostered by the government, but
generally accepted without challenge by the people. "The result was to narrow
the scope of individual freedom and to reinforce the illiberal tendencies in virtually all areas of life, but especially in class, gender, and race relations." The
conditions that resulted from the war, according to this perspective, gave substance to Alexis de Tocqueville's warning in the 1830s that any lengthy war
carried with it grave risks and dangers for a democracy.[45]

These findings are important in attempting to understand the origin, incidence, and significance of the prevalence of combat trauma in World War II
and in the Vietnam War. They are also crucial in attempting to predict, based
on prior experience, what will happen with veterans of the Iraq and Afghanistan
Wars. The findings challenge the assumptions that World War II was a popular war for all, including the soldiers, and that soldiers shared the sense of mission that society and government officials proclaimed. They further dislodge
the flawed practice of predicting the future based on a comparison between

the present wars and the Vietnam War alone. The research indicates that all wars are essentially the same in important respects and that combat trauma is universal. Breakdown during wartime appears to be attributable to the trauma of war, regardless of the particular features of or political reasons offered for the war. The findings allow latitude, however, for differences in postwar PTSD based on factors including the level of support, encouragement, and positive public attitudes with regard to the returning troops.

Conversations among soldiers in the field in World War II appeared to indicate that life in the army, rather than battle conditions or separation from home, was the cause of their trauma. The lofty and patriotic ideals celebrated at home lacked meaning for the soldiers. As one soldier stated, "The plain . . . fact of the matter was that nine out of ten servicemen wanted nothing more to do with wars after their first week of training. [The soldier's] special gripes . . . were reserved for the undemocratic, stupefying, favor-ridden totalitarian nature of military life itself." Many soldiers saw the army as inefficient, often corrupt, and with policies that were arbitrary at best and stupid and unjust at worst. As they saw it, one class of servicemen (officers) got the best of everything, and the rest got whatever was left. African-American soldiers, who were in separate units, suffered discrimination, were assigned to insignificant tasks, and suffered high rates of nervous breakdown.[46]

This information about the soldiers' feelings is significant for several important reasons. It reveals a similarity in the way that combat soldiers view all wars—not just the Vietnam War or the current wars, as is sometimes assumed. In addition to placing the significance of Vietnam in proper perspective, it reinforces the idea that the stresses of combat, regardless of the location of the battlefield, are similar in all wars. That World War II soldiers experienced combat stress indicates that the condition remains basically the same even in wars that appear to originate from clear ideals and goals. The readjustment problems of World War II veterans may have been somewhat easier to manage because, for the most part, when the troops returned home, the public was enthusiastic about celebrating them and their success.[47]

When veterans returned to civilian society, however, there was some uneasiness and anxiety on the part of the general public about the reintegration of veterans, so many of whom had psychological problems and disabilities. There was concern as well about what would happen to society as a result of the soldiers' battle training. Writing about World War II, the historian Willard Waller, who was a veteran of World War I, went so far as to warn the public that veterans had "written a bloody page of history." He wrote with inflammatory language, "The veteran is, and always has been, a problematic element in society, an unfortunate, misused, and pitiable man, and, like others whom society has mistreated, a threat to existing institutions." Waller added, "Unless and until he can be denaturalized into his native land, the veteran is a threat to society." Waller recited how the army had destroyed the personality of individuals to make them suitable for being cogs in a machine. He argued that army training was training in violence and killing and that it had imparted a hardness in behavior that would make veterans unsuitable for civilian society. Waller anticipated that almost all veterans would suffer psychological problems.[48]

His words got a great deal of press and were repeated frequently. Of course, veterans were insulted by his statements and reacted negatively, although many also acknowledged that they were changed men and did not necessarily want to return to life as before. They missed the collegiality of the military in some respects, and many wanted to live in cities rather than return to small town life. Adjustment to life at home was immensely difficult for many veterans. They felt alienated from civilian life because their experiences, exhilarating in some ways, were horrifying and deadening in others.[49] This condition is commonly perceived as a universal consequence of service and postwar readjustment, including in the Iraq and Afghanistan Wars. Current research now shows that vast numbers of veterans of World War II, even those who were not eventually institutionalized in veterans hospitals, suffered long-term consequences of their wartime traumatic stress.

THE KOREAN WAR

The Korean War began just five years after the end of World War II. U.S. involvement lasted from 1950 through 1953. During early stages of the conflict, psychiatric casualties accounted for nearly one-fourth of all evacuations from the field of combat.[50] This may have been because, as in World War II, military psychiatrists were unprepared for casualties in the early months of the fighting. The psychiatrists were not the only participants who were unprepared. According to reliable sources, the military itself was also unprepared for the engagement. One historian commented that the "Korean War came as a terrible shock to the United

States." In responding quickly to the communist invasion of South Korea in June of 1950, Washington sent to Korea "one of the least professional, least motivated armies America had ever put into the field." Mass confusion reigned, and the American troops were incapable at first of confronting the North Korean and Chinese troops. Confidence and morale were low until Gen. Matthew Ridgway arrived late in 1950 to take command. A stalemate soon developed and talk of peace began as early as the middle of 1951. Two years followed, however, before the armistice was finally signed in 1953. For the troops, that meant two years of the tedium and tension of trench warfare, consisting of boredom, cold, fear, and constant patrolling. The troops' main goal was to return home as soon as possible.[51]

Although, overall, the Korean War produced fewer psychiatric casualties than the world wars, initially the rates of debilitation were greater. During the first year of the war, the rate of psychiatric casualties was 250 per 1,000 men, nearly seven times greater than the average rate for World War II. As the war continued, however, psychiatric casualty rates dropped substantially. The average rate was slightly lower than that in World War II at 32 per 1,000. The statistics do not present the whole picture, however. Of the approximately 1.6 million men who served, more than 33,000 were killed by hostile fire and another 103,000 were wounded. The psychiatric casualties who were admitted to medical facilities for treatment numbered more than 48,000, exceeding the number killed. Of the 198,380 troops who saw actual combat, 24.4 percent suffered psychiatric problems severe enough to warrant treatment.[52]

Although relatively little psychiatric literature exists concerning the Korean War, one study done at Johns Hopkins University analyzed the psychological and physiological effects of combat on soldiers. The findings suggested that soldiers needed time away from the front and officers needed training on stress-related injuries. They also demonstrated that early return to combat after psychiatric casualty was beneficial because it gave soldiers the opportunity to prove themselves and that unit cohesion reduced mental injuries. Following the study, the APA recognized combat stress by including "stress response syndrome" in the *DSM-I*.[53] The available sources indicate that the tough strategy described in the study worked well in terms of keeping fighting men on the front lines. Psychiatric casualties were only a small percentage of the soldiers evacuated from the front lines as a result. Two exceptions can be observed, however. The first was "frostbite," noted in World War I by the British as an evacuation syndrome. Evacuation syndrome, a set of symptoms that can provide a means of getting evacuated from combat, is said to be a paradox of war psychiatry. The paradox reference is that soldiers who are psychiatric casualties must be treated and often evacuated but if other soldiers begin to realize that the casualties are being evacuated, the number of psychiatric casualties will increase dramatically. Evacuation syndrome often involves more than psychological components and can encompass physical conditions such as accidents and illnesses that have a mental component, such as "accidental" gunshot wounds or getting frostbite because of "disregarding" proper precautions in freezing weather, ultimately necessitating evacuation. During the Korean War, significant numbers were evacuated for frostbite, a preventable condition, which affected thousands of Americans who experienced extremely cold temperatures.[54]

The other exception consisted of the psychiatric problems of rear-area support troops, termed garrison casualties. Support troops eventually greatly outnumbered combat troops. These troops were hardly ever in life-endangering situations, and yet they reported a significant number of psychological conditions. Their problems were attributed to separation from home, social and physical deprivations, and boredom. They lacked the means of boosting self-esteem by being actively involved in combat. Their drug and alcohol abuse frequently resulted in disciplinary actions. This noncombat cause of stress received little attention at the time, and it remains a real, but still deemphasized, feature of combat stress conditions.[55] Later studies showed that the psychiatric casualty rate from the Korean War was very high. One study, published in 1994, showed that the current prevalence of PTSD in veterans who had not sought previous psychiatric treatment was 9 percent from World War II and 7 percent from Korea. However, among those who had sought psychiatric treatment previously, 37 percent of the World War II veterans and 80 percent of the Korean War veterans were currently suffering from PTSD. Another study reported in 1989 showed that 54 percent of a group of psychiatric patients who had been in combat in World War II met the PTSD criteria, and 27 percent were still suffering at the time of the study.[56]

This is not the end of the story as far as Korea is concerned. The phenomenon of garrison casualties that existed in the Korean War later became a dominant type of psychiatric casualty of the Vietnam conflict.[57] The psychiatric problems of support troops stem from immediate stress during wartime rather than from post-traumatic stress in readjusting to society after the war. Although efforts to reduce psychiatric casualties eventually worked militarily in the Korean War, the reasons for their success are uncertain, and clearly the main focus was still on returning troops to battle rather than on long-term mental health. Although knowledge of combat stress disorder increased on a piecemeal basis as the war progressed, the comprehension of its lessons came slowly and sporadically. Even as some understanding developed, military leaders failed to transmit their new knowledge to those who led future military operations. There was little continuity in the way military psychiatrists handled the disorder in the intervals between wars. Prior mistakes were often repeated at the beginnings of subsequent conflicts, and the military proceeded with the principal goal of maintaining an effective fighting force. Although that goal is expected, it should not be the sole consideration in treating combat stress that occurs in the course of war. Nonetheless, the demands of diagnosing and treating an individual soldier's PTSD were then and still are subject to the military's priority to maintain the fighting forces. To a large extent, the same uncertainties continue to exist and controversies rage on regarding psychiatric treatment versus returning to combat.

THE EARLY WARS: CIVIL WAR THROUGH KOREA

Every major American war has brought with it large numbers of psychiatric casualties. The symptoms gave rise to a litany of colorful names, some of which hinted at aspects of the disorder but none of which struck home. For example, the name in the Civil War was "soldier's heart" or "nostalgia." The disorder became "shell shock" in World War I and "battle fatigue" in World War II. After the Vietnam War and until it entered the *DSM*, it was known as "post-Vietnam syndrome." As political scientist Richard Gabriel observed, "Even a cursory reading of the accounts of battles over the ages provides examples of men manifesting various forms of psychiatric and emotional symptoms brought on by the fear and stress of war."[58] For a variety of reasons, including misunderstanding of the symptoms and their causes, the conditions that were observed were not identified as signs of psychiatric illness. The primitive state of medical science may account for earlier misunderstandings of the import of symptoms, especially during the Civil War. In addition, very little attention was paid to the plight of the ordinary soldier until midway through the twentieth century. The forgetting—or ignoring—of what was learned in the course of each war about mental illness cannot easily be excused. No doubt one reason for the lapses was the extreme inconvenience of psychiatric breakdown during wartime. Given the demands on the military to fulfill the expectations of government leaders and the public, it is no wonder that mental breakdown was unwelcome at the front lines—even more than physical injuries, which did not undermine morale or threaten solidarity to the same degree as mental illness. Accordingly, treatment was geared mainly to returning the soldiers to combat as quickly as possible. One way of discouraging the reporting of psychiatric problems was shaming the victims by labeling them as cowards, a characterization that frequently led to severe punishment. In later times, the diagnosis led to verbal abuse and efforts to discourage any complaints that would diminish troop strength. The concern with psychiatric symptoms was solely on their interference with the conduct of the war. What happened after discharge was paid little attention at the time of the Korean War.

Several features of descriptions of combat stress in the early wars are noteworthy. One is that, until very recently, the concept of moral injury stemming from the requirement of killing enemy combatants and others was simply not considered a mental disease. Another feature that did not receive attention was the potential conflict of interest of psychiatrists assigned to the military. Military psychiatrists were rarely criticized if they elevated the military's needs above those of the individual patient. As a result, from the Civil War through the Korean War, there was a lack of clear understanding or vision on the part of political and military leaders about the causes of psychiatric casualties that occurred in large numbers in each war. Little or no effort was made to uncover the causes, to understand the underlying problems, to treat the individual soldiers with a view to restoring their health, or to provide a meaningful transition to civilian life. Even Korean War veterans, who fought in a war for which the United States was ill-prepared, managed on their own to reintegrate into society as veterans of earlier wars had done. Few Korean War veterans speak today about combat stress or psychiatric problems stemming from the war. A major factor in this, of course, is that no officially recognized condition existed at that time of Korea. Long-range studies, however, are revealing many late-in-life mental health problems of veterans of the Korean War. It is apparent that, whether or not symptoms are identified and dealt with at the time, they surface sooner or later.

4

The Politics of PTSD
Vietnam

The Vietnam War is commonly described as unique among American wars. It has been said, for example, that it was "an aberration of America's military experience."[1] But some military historians disagree. For example, Roger J. Spiller, who taught for twenty-five years at the U.S. Army's Command and General Staff College in Fort Leavenworth, Kansas, argues, "Convenient as such a judgment might be, it cannot withstand scrutiny. Except insofar as any historical event is unique, our military experience in Vietnam was hardly unusual. The same is true of PTSD."[2] The truth may lie somewhere between these two points of view. To make a fair assessment of Vietnam, one must separate fact from fiction and reality from myth. It is also crucial to recognize that the assessment of any war is bound to change over time. What may have seemed significant during or immediately after a war is not necessarily what seems significant a decade or two later. The consequences of war unfold gradually over time, and the events that follow a conflict influence the assessment of the outcome. In analyzing the Vietnam War, I necessarily confine myself to the aspects of the war that relate to the development of PTSD.

The Vietnam War was the second longest war to date and certainly one of the most unpopular wars in American history. It had a pronounced impact on American society, which at the time was riding the crest of a tidal wave of social and cultural change. The war shared many features in common with all wars, including the world wars and the Korean War, which in some respects foreshadowed it. From the present vantage point, the combat experience of military personnel in Vietnam looks far more similar to than different from the experience in prior wars. This is readily apparent when the wars are viewed from the troops' perspective. The social, economic, and political factors that shape any war tend to recede into the background in the face of exploding bombs or gunfire.

One of my purposes is to examine how the incidence of combat trauma in earlier wars, notably, the world wars and the Korean War, should have taught lasting lessons that would have helped those in charge create policy to deal effectively with combat stress during and immediately after Vietnam. That did not happen. Despite hastily drawn conclusions at the close of the Korean War that lessons had been learned and carried out, the lessons regarding combat stress had to be learned all over again in the Vietnam War. Even a cursory examination of the outbreak of PTSD among Vietnam veterans in the decades following the war bears out that assessment.

BACKGROUND

The Vietnam War and the five-year period that followed it represented a watershed, not only in American political and social life, but also in psychiatry, especially in war psychiatry. The antiwar movement began in earnest around 1965 and peaked in 1968, and the period of political upheaval lasted throughout the war and beyond. When American troops were finally withdrawn from Vietnam in 1975, the social unrest that had been brewing during the war overflowed as the returning veterans ran into obstacles when they reentered American society. The protest movement of the 1960s and 1970s was the product of a coalition of interest groups, including unions, students, suburban leaders, and political leaders. This movement also encompassed political, racial, and cultural forces. The same forces, along with a group of psychiatrists, eventually united in support of the veterans, who were struggling to regain their footing in society. Although the story of the war and its aftermath has been told many times for many purposes, it remains incomplete. I address how the various groups eventually coalesced after the war to change the way psychiatry viewed mental health casualties of war and traumatic stress in general.

The adoption of PTSD in the *DSM* reflected a giant step forward. Traumatic stress began to take its place as a public health problem rather than merely as an individual problem or as an obstacle for the military to surmount. Before the Vietnam War, combat stress had been considered a problem only because of its immediate impact on war efforts, not because it was a continuing or chronic condition that hampered readjustment to civilian life. At the time the war began the consensus in the psychiatric community was that soldiers who recovered from an episode of combat stress would not suffer long-term consequences.[3] Observers assumed that the psychiatric disability that appeared after a war was related to preexisting conditions rather than the effects of war.[4] As a consequence, military psychiatrists had devoted little attention to postwar psychiatric syndromes, and when they did, they did not connect them to the combat experience. The post–Vietnam War period produced a major shift in thinking in light of the explosion of social and psychiatric problems that the returning veterans brought with them.

Compared with previous American wars, the Vietnam War was not a combat intense conflict. The amount of actual combat was relatively low overall, and when combat did occur, it tended to be brief. The number of psychiatric casualties was also low at the beginning, but increased to higher levels during the Tet Offensive of 1968. Paradoxically, as the intensity of combat fell off during 1970 and 1971, the psychiatric casualty rate continued to climb. The military called these later casualties "disorders of loneliness," which sounded very much like the earlier "nostalgia" terminology—another example of the convenient practice of finding a name for psychiatric problems that avoids acknowledging the fact that war causes mental injury and illness. Although, at the beginning of the war, evacuations for psychiatric reasons amounted to only 6 percent of total evacuations, the rate had increased to 50 percent by 1971.[5]

Over a ten-year period, only 10 percent of the 2.8 million men who served in Vietnam actually engaged in combat with the enemy. The total number of psychiatric casualties was about 35,200 soldiers. The total number killed by hostile enemy action was 45,735. When these numbers are considered relative to the number who actually engaged in combat, 16 percent were killed and 12.5 percent were psychiatric casualties.[6]

THE AFTERMATH

Fifteen years after the United States withdrew from Vietnam, a public health survey reported that 480,000 (representing 15 percent) of the 3.15 million

Americans who had served in Vietnam suffered from service-related PTSD. Beyond that, nearly 1 million (between a quarter and a third) of all the veterans of the war displayed PTSD symptoms at one time or another.[7] Although the data is not precise, estimates of PTSD cases range generally from a half million to a million and a half, which would mean roughly 16 percent to as much as 48 percent of the total force suffered psychiatric problems at some point after the war. Although the Vietnam War produced more cases of PTSD than any other war in American history, it must be kept in mind that the formal PTSD diagnosis that gave shape to the symptoms did not exist before 1980, five years after the final U.S. withdrawal from Vietnam.[8]

It seems surprising that such a major shift in psychiatric thinking about the traumatic stress condition came out of a war during which so few psychiatric conditions were reported. Not until after the Vietnam War ended and the United States withdrew from Vietnam was the prevalence of the condition recognized. It is logical to ask why military leaders and psychiatrists failed to recognize the condition during the war. Was the condition the same as or different from that previously designated by other names in earlier wars? Had military psychiatry been in denial about the disorder during this and previous twentieth-century wars? What part did substance abuse play in masking symptoms during the war and contributing to the high rate of PTSD that was visible after the war?

To what extent were the delayed symptoms as much a product of the social and economic situations faced by veterans as they were the result of combat trauma? Did the formal creation of the concept of PTSD spawn more claims than otherwise would have appeared? It is well to recognize that symptoms as well as treatment of combat stress vary from culture to culture.[9]

One point was clear. The focus in 1980, several years after the withdrawal and return home of U.S. soldiers from Vietnam, was no longer on dealing expeditiously with psychiatric casualties in order to return soldiers to combat as quickly as possible. That need was long past. The focus instead was on helping returning veterans solve their medical and psychiatric problems as well as their legal problems. The broader goal of the psychiatric community was to help them regain their places in society or, better still, to help them be better off than they were before the war.

As American involvement in the Vietnam War deepened during the 1960s, the need for soldiers escalated. Many soldiers doubtless were drawn from the ranks of people who were not well educated or otherwise equipped to have secure places in society in the first place. The factors involved in raising a conscription army or a volunteer one, and the demographics of the body of recruits in each, warrant closer study with respect to predisposition to readjustment difficulties.

It would be a mistake to overlook the fact that, in building an army, whether volunteer or conscript, a large number of enlistees may have preexisting problems or deficiencies that could contribute to readjustment problems after their military service. Although recruiters commonly conduct basic screening in the enlistment process, such as checks of criminal history or psychiatric and medical history, they do not investigate the recruits' social or economic backgrounds. Indeed, whether a volunteer army suffers fewer psychiatric casualties than a conscripted army is open for debate. More than 25 percent of the troops who served in the U.S. military during the Vietnam War were drafted, but the vast majority—nearly 70 percent—were volunteers.[10] By way of contrast, America's present forces in Iraq and Afghanistan are all volunteers. However, many reservists who did not anticipate active service in combat when they enlisted have been deployed and redeployed in Iraq and Afghanistan. Volunteering for combat duty during wartime and volunteering for reserve duty in peacetime present very different situations. The standards for recruiting troops during the Vietnam period were deliberately lowered to fulfill the necessary personnel requirements. The lower standards doubtless had an effect on the number of returning veterans with readjustment problems.

The traumas that caused PTSD in returning Vietnam soldiers had happened months or years in the past; this made the stressors more difficult to identify and connect with symptomatic behavior. The shift in focus from the immediacy of treatment for military purposes to long-range treatment for rehabilitation and reintegration into society was significant. Although the *DSM-III* criteria did not specify a duration for symptoms, in 1987 the *DSM-III-TR* required a one-month recovery period following the first appearance of symptoms. If the symptoms persisted for more than a month, the condition could be considered PTSD. Clearly, the emphasis had changed. In future wars, however, the main concern could easily shift back to returning soldiers to the battlefield to meet personnel requirements. In the current wars, in fact, there is concern about mental health both in relation to wartime service and to postdeployment adjustment. In the case of Vietnam, other behaviors, such as acting out and substance abuse, masked the high incidence of psychiatric problems, and military psychiatrists largely overlooked combat stress during the war.

The authors of the *DSM* decided to write a general definition for the disorder rather than a combat-specific or even Vietnam War–specific diagnosis in order to create a category of broad application. Writing a more general diagnosis was consistent with prior practice and tended to avoid the claim that the disorder category was not organic or that it was the product of political lobbying for a particular group. The general diagnosis also brought combat PTSD within the psychiatric mainstream. Had the original category been limited to combat stress, or at least to traumas of that magnitude, the diagnosis could have been refined in the future through research and study using a discrete body of information drawn from relevant experience. The attempt to create a one-size-fits-all category, so broad that it included natural disasters, accidents, and human misconduct occurring in both military and civilian settings (e.g., sexual assault and other crime victims, employees who are wrongfully terminated, and, more recently, jurors who have sat on murder cases with graphic evidence), may have undermined the structural integrity of the diagnosis in the long run. Certain crucial features of combat stress do not exist in civilian environments.

That traumatic stress was reclassified because of political and social pressure and negotiation does not undermine its legitimacy. The APA should be aware of and attentive to social and economic change, as well as new information about medical and psychiatric conditions. Opinions of people outside the psychiatric profession are important. The *DSM* is, after all, meant to be a working document that is effective in dealing with real-world situations. If the *DSM* is not the product of scientific evidence and research exclusively, however, it should not purport to be such.

The story of how PTSD emerged out of the Vietnam War experience suggests several themes. The first theme of the war relates to the basic elements of the war itself, which ran from 1961 to 1975. The second theme is the way the war and the veterans were portrayed in American popular culture. The media portrayal affected the policies that developed as much as the realities of the war did. The third theme, relating to the campaign to adopt PTSD, began in 1975, when American military involvement in Vietnam ended, and continued to 1980. During that period, a coalition of forces worked toward a common goal of adding a traumatic stress syndrome variously called "post-Vietnam syndrome," "traumatic war neurosis" or "post-combat disorder" to the *DSM-III* (or perhaps of restoring a former diagnosis in a new form). The effort of the coalition of representatives from psychiatry plus various social and political interest groups and people in the anti–Vietnam War effort culminated in the inclusion of the disorder, eventually called PTSD, in the *DSM-III*.

The societal impact resulting from the formal adoption of PTSD continues in force to this day, just as cultural shock waves from the Vietnam period continue to reverberate through American society. The public skepticism about prolonged, ambiguous wars; the populist democratic movement that was incubated during the Vietnam period; and the cynicism about government that persisted after the war are vigorous forces in American political life. The Vietnam period is an important reference point in American history. The first theme occupies this chapter, and the second and third themes follow in the next chapter.

PSYCHIATRIC DIMENSIONS OF THE WAR

The Vietnam War is sometimes viewed historically as roughly consisting of three segments. The advisory segment, during which American advisers were assigned to Vietnamese field units, ran from 1961 to 1965, although a few Americans were there even earlier. During that period, the United States had very few combat troops in the country and suffered almost no psychiatric casualties. The second phase was the period of active combat running from 1965 to 1969. This phase witnessed escalating U.S. involvement and large numbers of combat troops deployed but with few reported psychiatric casualties. The final phase began in 1969 when the United States and South Vietnam agreed that the United States would begin withdrawing troops. This led to a long period of negotiations and withdrawal, which ended in a peace accord in 1973. This phase consisted of winding down and withdrawal during which there were fairly large numbers of psychiatric casualties. By April 1975 the last American troops had been withdrawn.[11]

The Vietnam War was fought in the midst of a civilian population. Some of the civilians were friendly and some hostile, and American soldiers often had trouble knowing the difference. The technology employed by combatants was advanced and destructive, but at the same time, a great deal of the fighting took place at night in harbors teeming with small boats and enigmatic occupants or in hostile and alien jungles, in small-scale increments. Americans fought against an enemy that was largely unseen but always watching, an enemy that seemed to know the Americans' slightest movements.[12]

The story of the war, "a guerilla war, an insurgent war, fought without clear military objectives and no front line, with some constraints on freedom of military action,"[13] has been told and retold many times over. Its repercussions and reverberations are endless and timeless.

Before assessing the role of military psychiatry in the war, it is worthwhile to note the general background features of individual soldiers' personal combat experiences.

VIEW FROM THE GROUND: PERSONAL ACCOUNTS
OF VIETNAM VETERANS

The combat trauma to which soldiers were exposed during the Vietnam War varied greatly depending on the nature, purpose, and timing of their deployments. Some troops saw intense combat on a regular basis, and others saw very little. Many soldiers adapted easily to the rhythm of daily exposure to combat, but others adapted poorly. Although the Vietnam War was marked by distinct geographical, topographical, and cultural conditions, the common features of the war tended to override the distinctive ones. Whether battle was waged on a mountaintop, in the jungle, or afloat in the Mekong Delta, the danger that enveloped soldiers resembled that of earlier wars. Although some soldiers experienced symptoms of PTSD while on active duty in the war zone, others were not aware of PTSD symptoms until returning home.

JAY: Jay spent his year in the jungle. He faced the risk of death or injury every day. Jay described his mission as follows:

> I was with . . . 101st Airborne. Our mission was to seek out the enemy and destroy them. We were on the ground . . . transported from one location to another out in the boonies. The only time you saw a plane was for supplies. Otherwise, you just stay out in the jungle all the time. You set up your own camp . . . your unit . . . your platoon. . . . Basically you have artillery support from a base somewhere around you. . . . You are maybe four hundred to five hundred meters from them. Your job is

sweeping to see what you can find on foot. . . . The foot patrol . . . looking for Vietcong. When you're on a mission, all the Vietnamese look alike. You don't know who the enemy is. That's what brought on my PTSD too . . . taking somebody's life . . . somebody that I don't know and who doesn't deserve to die.

You go into the village . . . and sometimes you just have to shoot. Your job is sweeping . . . and they're in the village. If command tells us they believe the enemy is in the village, we suspect everybody. . . . We can't pick and choose. . . . Some innocent kids get killed too by mistake. . . . When you take a kid's life or a mother's life or father's life, and you see the kids cry for a parent, it's very disturbing. . . . I've seen a lot of that. You can't question your orders when your mission comes down. . . . When battalion command says for your platoon to do this, this is what you do. If you don't, they lock you up. . . . We did this all the time . . . going from village to village. It was our routine. We did the same thing every day. Half the time, we didn't know what day it was. There were no days off . . . unless you were sick or wounded.

Although destruction was everywhere, one death made a lasting impression on Jay:

I lost my only real close friend. . . . I was really close to him. We had incoming fire. . . . They were shooting mortars and rockets at us. One must have landed three to four meters from him in an open strip. . . . It ripped him apart. We put sandbags all around. When the incoming fire started, everybody started running. You had to crawl too. We all started running to get back and everyone made it except him. He was the last one and got ripped. I could see his body all messed up.

Once the rockets are coming in, they're like raindrops. There's nothing you can do until you get air support so you call in for air support . . . and the helicopter comes. The Cobras shoot rockets. Once they get there the enemy backs off. The enemy tries to catch you off guard. They know you are there under cover. You don't see the enemy. They usually attack at night . . . especially when it's raining. This incident was a big one. . . when I lost my best buddy. It was early in my service. Up till then, you have a lot of fear until your first contact. It's funny to say, but you got so much fear, but then, when something happens, you turn brave. It's like you've used up all your fear, and then you have nothing else left.

RON: Ron's experience in the navy lasted until late 1973. Five years later, with his life still in disarray, he enlisted in the army. Although his experience in Vietnam did not involve intense combat, his deployment was characterized by excruciating tension spiked with traumatic episodes. He used drugs throughout his time in the service and for years after his discharge.

While he was in the navy, from September 1971 to the fall of 1973, Ron was assigned to small boats in the Mekong Delta in what was called Operation Market Time. According to Ron, this assignment involved

the patrolling of the rivers and coastline. . . . Vietnam had huge harbors . . . and they all had to be patrolled. People fished every day in small . . . and large fishing boats. There were tons of boats. Many of the boats were carrying supplies . . . or arms . . . down from the North to soldiers in the South. We'd pull alongside a boat . . . train our 50s on them and go in and search. If they had too much of anything, it was naturally considered that they had contraband. . . . You never knew when you might get shot.

Once at 3:00 in the morning, I had jumped in my bunk so exhausted, and all of sudden, I heard a bam and then another one. They blew me out of my bunk and slammed me against the other side. I couldn't hear anything. It was like my body went and then the rest of me caught up with it, and that's when I couldn't hear. The place was full of smoke and on fire. We got the ammo up because if that ignites, you're done. . . . With all the tension and danger, it took me all these years to find myself again. We'd be told to have a joint. . . . You'll feel better . . . and you do. . . . That and liquor. . . . Booze with opium. We'd get it in Thailand and the Philippines opium dens. You had to pay the MPs [military police] to let you know which dens would not get raided. If you were a hardhead and didn't, you went to the brig.

Even leave time had its downside. Although the Philippines was a popular destination for leave time, it did not offer an escape from violence.

The Philippines was a very dangerous place. It was one of the worst things I saw in Asia. We went there for what they called damage repair. They tell you don't wear watches, rings . . . wear nothing. It was just a village with bars. . . . When the sun started going down, there were so many people in this place. It was like when ants give birth and there are so many on the ground. There was jungle just like Vietnam, and the Communists tried to coax you off the strip into the jungle. They'd grab you. One time, I spent the night sleeping it off outside, and in the morning, I watched the navy guys pulling two bodies out of the river . . . which they called the shit river because of all the stuff floating in it. They had been decapitated. They were Filipino soldiers, but they had all American stuff and weapons. After I was home, I got diagnosed with PTSD. I was still addicted.

These accounts of combat stress and danger demonstrate the high level of daily trauma that many soldiers experienced. Jay was able to get into the rhythm of combat and, as a result, experienced few symptoms of PTSD while he was in country. Ron's experiences, in contrast, pushed him beyond his limits. Both were disabled by psychiatric illness and unable to cope with civilian life for years after returning.

SOCIAL VALUES DURING THE WAR

Social values in the United States changed dramatically during the 1960s. Compared with the previous decade, it was a time of great freedom. Attitudes of respect and deference to authority figures broke down. Among many people in middle- and upper-level social and economic groups, the war became enormously unpopular. Many eligible young men took steps to avoid the draft. According to one historian, "The draft worked as an instrument of Darwinian social policy. The 'fittest'—those with background, wit or money—managed to escape. Through an elaborate structure of deferments, exemptions, legal technicalities, and non-combatant military alternatives, the draft rewarded those who manipulated the system to their advantage." Medical and psychiatric exemptions were also exploited. The standards pertaining to recruits' intelligence were relaxed to enable the military to meet its personnel needs. Needing additional troops, the military took urgent measures, including the establishment of a program called "Project 100,000" which ultimately took in some 350,000 soldiers over the course of five years from 1966 to 1971.[14]

During the initial buildup for the second phase, military psychiatry was in place with ample resources. Based on the Korean War experience, the military understood the need for psychiatrists, and the psychiatrists, for their part, recognized their function within the military. The psychiatrists' response to the medical and psychiatric complaints of troops—both combat and support—in Vietnam is revealing. Some psychiatrists had no trouble adhering to military priorities, which called for treating soldiers for the purpose of preparing them to return quickly to their assigned duties. This required psychiatrists to avoid getting too deeply involved in individual problems. Others were uneasy about carrying out that limited role.

Disturbing ethical conflicts arose during the Vietnam War. Some psychiatrists openly questioned whether they could, in good conscience, rapidly treat combat fatigue or use patients' guilt about deserting their comrades and their loyalty to their units as leverage in encouraging them to return quickly to combat, where they might soon be killed. Military psychiatrists in Vietnam came under severe criticism from their civilian colleagues who dismissed the old justification that whatever helped the military helped the individual. Some critics even accused military psychiatrists of ethical corruption.[15]

Although it is common knowledge that drugs, especially alcohol, play a role in virtually all wars, never before had drug use so permeated a war as it did in Vietnam. By the mid-1960s, the drug culture, especially the marijuana culture, had become solidly established in the United States. It should, therefore, have been no surprise to anyone that American troops used drugs extensively in Vietnam. Psychiatrists observed, and the military acknowledged, that marijuana played a major role in relieving tension, reducing anxiety, and creating a source of bonding among troops. Officially, the military opposed the drug use and made efforts to stop it. But, unofficially, at the combat and support troop levels, it was tolerated, permitted, and, according to many sources (including the veterans whose personal stories appear in this book), even tacitly approved. By mid-1970, a heroin epidemic was also well under way in Vietnam. Heroin was widely available and inexpensive. One estimate was that one-fifth of the U.S. Army was addicted to narcotics. In 1971 more soldiers were evacuated for drug use than for injuries. The drug problem was difficult to treat, and to some extent, "the Army didn't want to know about it," according to N. M. Camp, a young physician working with the army in Saigon.[16]

Many controversies about the impact of the extensive drug culture among the troops in Vietnam remain. One involves a question about whether the abuse contributed not only to serious postrelease problems in veterans, but also to the growing drug culture in the country as a whole by creating a generation of drug users. Another is whether the soldiers were truly addicted or whether they abandoned heroin use upon their return to the states. A third is whether the drug abuse undermined the effectiveness of troops in combat or whether it was limited to off-duty periods. The military generally preferred to accept whatever interpretations minimized the impact of the rampant drug abuse on troop performance. That naive (or perhaps disingenuous) interpretation is difficult to support based on the many accounts that indicate otherwise, not to mention logic and common sense.[17]

According to military reports, combat stress casualties failed to materialize during the war. As early as 1966, two Pentagon physicians reported that psychiatric casualties were lower than in any previous war. They attributed this result to the one-year combat tour of duty, the ample rest and relaxation, shortness of battles, and high morale. They felt that the problem of combat exhaustion had been overcome and that the sense of hopelessness that had prevailed in past wars did not exist.[18]

These evaluations appear even more baffling now than they must have appeared to informed observers who were close to the action at the time. Psychiatrists in Vietnam understood that "things were not quite as they seemed, and Vietnam was not the same as previous wars." They observed that the twelve-month rotation undermined rather than augmented unit morale and loyalty. Every soldier was governed by his private calendar, and he counted the days until his release. As a result, "he sees himself as fighting directly for his own survival." This phenomenon was actually given a name—short-termer's syndrome, a term that referred to the reluctance of soldiers to risk their lives when their time was nearly up.[19]

Several factors further confused the mental health picture. Psychiatrists saw the development of an increased rate of psychosis in U.S. Army troops. The number of cases, like the psychiatric problems, peaked after active combat.[20] Another factor was the high incidence of what were described as "character disorders" or "acting out." As the proportion of conscripts in the army increased in the late 1960s, the volume of character disorders as revealed in misbehavior increased. Because the army chose not to attribute this misbehavior to psychiatric disease, the cases were handled administratively and did not appear in the statistics. Some psychiatrists wondered whether character disorders were typical of Vietnam, just as shell shock was typical of World War I and combat exhaustion of World War II. Acting out was interpreted as evidence of the soldiers' sense of alienation from the war and confrontation with the "tragic absurdity" of risking their lives for what was increasingly viewed as a meaningless military exercise.[21]

Although various theories were offered to explain the low rate of psychiatric casualties, none was validated at the time. One theory was that stateside psychiatric screening had been effective. Another was that the psychiatric casualties were not diminished as reported but, instead, were concealed in the vast amount of substance abuse as well as in the cases of acting out. One historian posited that a lack of group cohesiveness plus disillusionment with the war alienated soldiers from the military and the unit and resulted in "regressive alternative groups" based on race, alcohol or drug consumption, delinquent or hedonistic behavior, and countercultural lifestyles. The prime motivational factors for soldiers became personal survival, revenge for deaths of friends, and enjoying the unleashing of aggression.[22]

Based on the period of U.S. military involvement, which represents only one segment of the Vietnam experience, some tentative conclusions emerged. A leading military psychiatry historian, Franklin Jones, concluded that the Vietnam experience revealed the limits of the World War II–type psychiatric treatment policy in a low-intensity, prolonged, and unpopular conflict. Jones reasoned that prevention must be the focus in such conflicts and that unit social cohesion is essential in order to minimize substance abuse. He suggested that a previously used treatment program for nostalgia might be a workable model. That program concentrated on social factors that gave soldiers a sense of health and mastery of weapons.[23]

Many factors may have contributed to the huge numbers of psychiatric disorders that eventually appeared after the war. The war was low in intensity but prolonged and vastly unpopular. A significant percentage of the forces were conscripted soldiers rather than volunteer soldiers. The traditional group morale did not exist. After training, recruits were shipped separately to Vietnam on commercial jets rather than in groups on military aircraft. Soldiers were rotated frequently during their tours of duty, and the fact that the tours were one year promoted an ethos of survival rather than victory. This was the first war in which rampant drug abuse, much of it tolerated, if not tacitly sanctioned, by the military, was a problem. The war was fought, often with little visible progress, with vague and changing goals, in an alien environment. Soldiers had great difficulty distinguishing hostile combatants from friendly or neutral citizens.[24]

The stage was set for the first highly visible post-combat trauma epidemic to begin, and it did almost immediately upon the soldiers' return. Eventually, through the efforts of Vietnam veterans groups and a group of psychiatrists, the first steps toward recovery began. In 1975, the year in which American involvement came to an unceremonious end, two army psychiatrists offered future predictions for veterans. They wrote, "One may predict that, after a latency period characterized by relief and relatively good functioning, typical stress response symptoms may appear. . . . We are predicting general and delayed stress response symptoms."[25]

Protests against American involvement in the war began as early as 1965 and lasted until the last troops were home in 1975. The postwar period from 1975 to 1980 was marked by continued unrest as Americans watched the South Vietnamese government fall into the hands of the North Vietnamese. With the principal source of tension gone, the United States, under the Jimmy Carter administration, began dealing with an assortment of issues raised during the war, such as pardoning draft evaders. For many veterans, however, the process of reintegrating into society took years or even decades. For some, it has not yet come to a close.

The long and debilitating war had taken its toll, not only on the war's survivors, but also on society as a whole. The bitter experience left a bad taste in everyone's mouth. Many veterans had difficulty getting help for their psychiatric and substance abuse problems, and many found themselves involved with the criminal courts. In July 1967, a handful of Vietnam veterans had marched in protest in New York City under the banner of Vietnam Veterans Against the War (VVAW). They urged Vietnam veterans to unite in order to bring the troops home and American involvement to an end. This small and disorganized group eventually would become a major force in the campaign to persuade the APA to recognize combat traumatic reaction in the *DSM*.

5

The Campaign for PTSD

The next theme, the portrayal of the Vietnam veteran in popular culture, played a role in the successful campaign to recognize PTSD. The campaign process, which relied on both fictionalized and real images of the Vietnam veteran, contributed to a shift in the recounting of war history from the generals' perspective to the perspective of ordinary soldiers in the trenches and supply lines.

Starting in the late 1960s, the media began portraying Vietnam veterans as unique in American history for their widespread suffering from readjustment problems. According to this portrayal, the problems that veterans faced initially stemmed from an unprecedented war against an uncertain enemy that was difficult to discern from friendly civilians. The enemy used ordinary people, including women and children, as shields and assassins, leading directly to the killing of innocent civilians. In addition, American combat troops lacked traditional group solidarity and morale because of the one-year tour of duty imposed by existing military policy. The further deterioration of discipline that resulted when troops eventually turned to drugs to help them bear the hardships contributed heavily to difficulties in readjustment. Moreover, the quick return to civilian life after a tour, without transition time for unwinding, as had been typical in prior wars, heightened the problems. Once at home, veterans were, at best, ignored by the civilian population and, at worse, blamed and rejected, even by veterans of previous wars. The readjustment problems were further exacerbated by drug or alcohol addiction, high unemployment rates, divorce, suicide, crime, sickness caused by exposure to Agent Orange, and, of course, pervasive symptoms of PTSD.[1]

This popular cultural portrayal distinguishes the experience of the Vietnam veteran from veterans of previous wars using the nature of the war itself. According to this portrayal, Vietnam veterans were unable to readjust to civilian life because they were neglected and mistreated, not only by the government, but also by the citizenry. Although this popular perception of the Vietnam veterans first emerged in the late 1960s, it was further defined in the early seventies and continues to be widely accepted today. In fact, with some modifications, it has regained new life during the Iraq and Afghanistan Wars as the paradigm used in predicting the prevalence of PTSD in the returning veterans from the current wars. Many commentators mistakenly use the commonalities between these wars and the Vietnam War as the model for predicting future wars, just as the Vietnam War has become the standard for measuring and shaping the current view of combat PTSD. The portrayal of the Vietnam veteran that emerged at the time gave its subject an "almost mythic stature—the 'survivor-as-hero'—who fought under insane conditions in Vietnam and then rebuilt his life in an ungrateful America."[2]

Various theories exist as to how the popular cultural portrayal of the Vietnam veteran developed. One theory, offered by a sociologist, Jerry Lembcke, is that political jockeying by the Nixon administration and the antiwar forces shaped and nourished the image-making fostered by the media. Lembcke also points to the some of the major indicators of PTSD, such as flashbacks, survivor guilt, and feelings of alienation from others, as having origins in the media portrayal more than in science. Both ideas are worthy of attention because they suggest that the *DSM* category for PTSD has cultural, social, and political origins and significance as well as medical and psychiatric significance and origins.[3]

Lembcke's theory, in short, is that the characterization of the Vietnam veteran as psychologically damaged arose from the Nixon administration's effort to combat the antiwar forces while explaining away the antiwar position of many Vietnam veterans. The media picked up on this theme and popularized the idea that huge numbers of Vietnam veterans were suffering from symptoms of psychiatric disorders. Thinking about the veterans within a mental health framework caught on in popular culture despite the lack of solid statistical support for the administration's theory at that point. The media's framing of veterans issues led to the later labeling of the symptoms and conditions with psychiatric terminology as mental health professionals picked up on the media and political portrayals and used them in the campaign for PTSD. As Lembcke puts it, a "mode of discourse" was discovered "that enabled authorities to pathologize the radical political behavior of veterans opposed to the war, and thereby discredit it, while simultaneously appearing sympathetic to the plight of veterans and maintaining their own anti-war posture."[4] The stage was set for the appearance of PTSD in a leading role.

Other aspects of the media portrayal of Vietnam veterans developed over time. They included the veterans' sense of alienation from society together with lingering survivor guilt stemming from their safe return. A side effect of the portrayal was to project the well-known phenomenon of civilian discomfort with returning war veterans onto the veterans themselves. As a result, the idea of civilian discomfort was turned on its head and a different cultural image was created—that it was the veterans who felt discomfort with civilian society rather than the reverse. In the end, the memory of the war itself was rewritten according to the portrayal of the Vietnam veterans. The history of the war was rewritten to be "a war that was lost due to betrayal on the home front" rather than "a war that was lost to a small, underdeveloped Asian nation." Initially, veterans appeared in popular imagery as abused and neglected figures. Later, they emerged as heroes despite all the controversial elements of the war, including the large number of civilian casualties.[5]

With respect to the Vietnam War itself, during the height of American participation in the 1960s, most accounts reported that veterans were readjusting satisfactorily back home. Many efforts had been made to see that jobs were available in the public and private sectors. The GI Bill provided for continuing education. The print media reported frequently on the welcoming receptions that the returning veterans received. Vietnam veterans were characterized favorably as compared with Korean War veterans.[6] That view changed in the late 1960s, however, when the veterans began to be described as unappreciated, troubled, rejected, and blamed for the war.

The crisis in public confidence in the economy from 1970 to 1972 also played a role in the way civilians perceived veterans. The release from service of about 1 million soldiers in 1970, exacerbated by a cooling of the economy, made unemployment a serious problem. These factors combined to stimulate a host of measures to solve the major problems of Vietnam veterans, including drug screening, drug treatment, an enhanced GI Bill, and a proclamation of Vietnam Veterans Day in 1974. With these efforts, the unemployment rate for veterans settled to pre-1969 levels. Reports showed extensive use of the GI Bill. Studies showed the veterans had higher median income levels than their civilian peers. Vietnam veterans garnered little media attention during 1975 and 1976, but in 1977 they appeared in headlines. Veterans organizations called again for the country to "come to terms" with Vietnam.[7]

The prevalence of PTSD in Vietnam veterans and other individuals was the subject of great uncertainty after the disorder's official recognition. Estimates of incidence among Vietnam veterans ranged from 500,000 to 1.5 million. As of 1978, however, only some 95,000 veterans had been deemed disabled for psychiatric or neurological reasons. By contrast, as of 1946, more than 450,000 World War II veterans were receiving disability benefits for neuropsychiatric diseases.[8]

Discussion of the concept of PTSD was not limited to veterans alone during the 1970s. Several magazine articles commented on the traumatic consequences for individuals who evaded the draft, and one even raised the possibility that the entire population of the country was suffering from a type of PTSD or guilt syndrome related to the Vietnam War and their avoidance of the draft.[9]

Although, overall, Vietnam veterans have received services that are at least equivalent to those received by veterans of past wars, the image of victimhood and neglect remains an open subject. Vietnam veterans continue to be used as a reference point for other subjects of psychiatric stress disorder, including a wide variety of trauma victims.[10] It may be that the coincidence of a vastly unpopular war occurring during a period of significant social and cultural change in America touched a nerve in society, setting off a series of moral and ethical, political, and social reverberations. The phenomenon changed the way Americans view the military, mental health, law, government and politics, and many other institutions.

THE CAMPAIGN FOR PTSD

The experience of American troops in the Vietnam War was instrumental in redefining the role of psychiatry in American society, changing the popular perception of mental health, and, as some historians would argue, contributing to the creation of a new "consciousness of trauma" in Western society. The story of the triumph of the coalition that spearheaded the move to include PTSD in the *DSM* is complex and involves social, political, and medical elements. Four main factors contributed to the success of the campaign: the bitter aftertaste of the debilitating war and the persistence of the antiwar movement; the politics of both veterans affairs and American psychiatrists; the dynamic of new developments in American psychiatry; and the legacy of the Holocaust as embodied in survivors.[11] The long and debilitating war had fomented not only disruption, unrest, and rebellion within American society, but also a social and political environment that remained conducive to change. Any hope that may have existed in 1946 in the wake of World War II that America would enjoy a long period of peace, stability, and prosperity had been shattered by the brooding omnipresence of Cold War tension.

One person who, by chance, played a pivotal role in the movement to obtain official recognition of PTSD was Sarah Haley, a social worker at the VA hospital in Boston. During her first morning at the hospital in September 1969, she interviewed a new patient, a Vietnam veteran, who appeared to be highly agitated and anxious. He related a story about being part of a company in Vietnam that, in March 1968, had killed a large number of women and children in the village of My Lai. A short Associated Press story had appeared earlier that month in a newspaper, revealing that an officer, William Calley, had been charged for the deaths of civilians in the same incident, which was later to become known as the My Lai massacre. On the day the veteran appeared at the hospital, however, neither Haley nor any of the VA staff knew about the short news report or the episode. A full story reporting the details of the episode was published two months later, in November 1969. Haley later assumed that the initial AP story had triggered the anxiety reaction that brought the veteran to the hospital.[12]

The veteran told Haley that he had not fired any shots during the massacre, but that afterward, several of his platoon members who had participated had threatened to kill him if he told anyone about it. He said that he had "unraveled" a few days before coming in and that he believed he was in danger. Unlike other, more seasoned, staff members, Haley believed the man's story. At the time, operating under the *DSM-II*, mental health professionals in the United

States assessed Vietnam veterans using diagnostic criteria that contained no specific entry for PTSD or any of its predecessors, such as gross stress reaction, which had appeared in the *DSM-I*, much less any entry for war-related trauma. VA physicians did not routinely collect details of combat experience as part of the histories they obtained. Many of them assumed that veterans who were agitated or anxious about their war experiences suffered from a psychiatric condition that originated in circumstances other than combat.[13]

Some psychiatrists, however, still considered war neurosis valid despite the elimination of gross stress reaction from the *DSM-II*. Some, including psychiatrist John Talbot, had published an article urging the readoption of gross stress reaction. Others, including psychiatrists at the Boston VA, asked for military histories and combat experience for their patients and considered these experiences to be significant. In 1971 Haley provided a scheme of rating therapists on the Boston VA facility treatment staff for the local VVAW chapter to use in referring veterans to the facility. The purpose was to alert the chapter concerning therapists who would be receptive to considering PTSD and those who would not.[14]

As the movement to convince the *DSM* committee to recognize combat stress gained support, a startling incident captured national attention. In April 1971, a young Vietnam veteran named Dwight Johnson, who had been awarded the Congressional Medal of Honor by President Lyndon Johnson two and a half years earlier, was shot and killed by a liquor store clerk as he attempted to rob the store at gunpoint. Johnson had been cited for heroism when he "went on a rampage" after the entire crew of a tank he had been riding in was killed in an ambush. The lone survivor of the attack, he subdued the enemy and single-handedly destroyed the ambushing forces. Despite the initial acclaim after the incident and securing a public relations job with the army, Johnson was unable to hold employment and was assigned to a VA hospital. He was diagnosed as suffering from "depression caused by post-Vietnam adjustment problems." He left the VA hospital in March 1971 and never returned. His name later reappeared in the news—and in court—after the liquor store robbery.[15] A year later the *New York Times* published an article by Dr. Chaim F. Shatan called "Post-Vietnam Syndrome," a term that made psychiatrists uneasy but captured public attention. Shatan predicted that the syndrome often appeared some nine to thirty months after the return from deployment in

Vietnam. The fact that a heavily decorated soldier could engage in such criminal conduct and end up this way shocked the public and drew attention to Vietnam veterans' issues in a dramatic way.[16]

In addition, a group advocating recognition of traumatic stress in Holocaust survivors supported the Vietnam veterans' group in pursuit of recognition in the *DSM*.[17] Holocaust survivors clearly were victims of terror, whereas combat survivors were victims in one sense but perpetrators in another. Despite their different outlooks, however, the two groups found common ground in advocating the inclusion of traumatic stress in the *DSM*.

Work to have PTSD formally recognized continued throughout 1974, and eventually key people in the National Vietnam Veterans Research Project (NVVRP) met in 1975 with leaders of the movement to incorporate a combat PTSD category in the *DSM*. Encouraged by the possibility of success, a working group began gathering evidence to persuade the *DSM* committee. The working group called the proposed disorder "post-combat disorder." (It was also given a label of post-Vietnam syndrome.)[18] After considering concentration camp survivors and other victims of trauma, the working group began thinking in terms of a more general diagnostic category of which post-combat disorder would be one example. Later in 1975 the working group was integrated into the process of writing the *DSM-III*, which extended into 1976 and 1977. The final draft included a diagnosis under the name of "post-traumatic stress disorder," which consisted of virtually the same criteria as the working group had agreed upon. The disorder eventually was published in the *DSM-III*.

The diagnostic category approved was general and covered a wide spectrum of traumatic causes of the stress reaction. Despite the unique features of combat stress, there was some benefit to having a single all-inclusive category. A major benefit was that military psychiatrists and their patients were no longer considered to be outside the mainstream of psychiatry. Instead, they were part of a standardized model that encompassed all types of traumas befalling civilians, including accidents, natural disasters, and intentional human actions. In the view of some historians, the original post-Vietnam syndrome, which applied only to combat neurosis, acquired greater status and authority by being joined with all sorts of civilian trauma—a new unitary kind of trauma.[19] From my perspective, this represents an odd twist of fate because, as the disorder and its legal uses have evolved over time, the situation has more recently been reversed. Today, combat stress is widely viewed as authentic, whereas some traumatic stress claims by civilians are viewed with skepticism.

What can one conclude about the process by which PTSD found its way for the first time into the official registry of mental disorders? A cynic might argue that PTSD is little more than a social concept, one that was contrived and promoted by the lobbying power of a handful of psychiatrists who joined antiwar activists and the veterans' movement to advance the interests of Vietnam veterans. A more generous perspective suggests that, by bringing the real problems of Vietnam War veterans to the forefront, the APA came to recognize and acknowledge a disorder that was "more than the sum of its diverse parts" (despite the symptom overlap with other disorders)—one that could stand on its own. The psychiatric profession views a novel formulation of a disorder as merely acknowledging a disorder that was always there but was simply not clearly identified and articulated. This sociological approach recognizes that the complex process does not discredit the end result.[20]

A major question at the time PTSD was adopted in the *DSM* was what constitutes a normal response of soldiers to combat (and of other survivors to other types of traumas). In accordance with the psychiatrists who believed that the patient's combat and other war experience was a relevant factor for diagnosis of the disorder, whether it was called war neurosis, post-Vietnam syndrome, post-combat disorder, or PTSD, the committee decided to define the cause or stressor as stemming from a war experience rather than from particular aspects of the individual soldier's background and psychological makeup.[21]

To answer the question of how to define and describe the disorder, the proponents of the recognition of PTSD asserted and the committee decided that soldiers disturbed by combat trauma were not abnormal. They reasoned that it was normal to be traumatized by the abnormal events that can occur during wartime.[22] A crucial question remaining concerns the point at which a normal reaction crosses the line into the abnormal, that is, the realm of mental illness. That question and others, such as what types of trauma qualify as stressors, remain unsettled, as definitions have undergone numerous changes in subsequent editions of the *DSM*.

The adoption of PTSD represented the official psychiatric recognition that the emotional distress of combat trauma, among other traumas, was worthy of diagnosis and treatment. This was a significant development because the *DSM* is a vital diagnostic tool for psychiatrists and patients. In that respect, it represents the official pronouncement of who is mentally ill and who is not at any given time. It is important for other purposes as well, in particular, for courts and judges. Although it does not control legal determinations, it is a necessary reference point for some decisions, such as for the insanity defense, and is looked to by courts as the authoritative statement of psychiatric disorders.

In the wake of the successful campaign to include PTSD in the *DSM*, some mental health professionals declared that the debate over Vietnam had been depoliticized by the endorsement of combat PTSD. They believed that the vast majority of Vietnam veterans had integrated seamlessly into society and were already leading productive and emotionally stable lives. In their view, veterans were not "walking time bombs" or "invincible robots." In their view, only a small (albeit significant) number of veterans was suffering from debilitating symptoms of PTSD, and now those few would be able to receive the help they needed.[23]

OUTLOOK ON VIETNAM

Another theory as to why the Vietnam War produced so many PTSD casualties was suggested by Lt. Col. David Grossman, author of the well-known book *On Killing*.[24] Lieutenant Colonel Grossman suggested that a major contributor to PTSD may be the military mandate that a soldier must kill enemy soldiers as well as civilians who pose serious threats. The moral injury that results from carrying out this command can contribute to developing PTSD. Several factors may come into play in given situations. One factor is group leadership and morale. In past wars, mature older comrades provided leadership, a situation which boosted the morale of younger soldiers. In addition, a high level of morale was derived from the presence of trusted friends who had shared the experiences of training and combat and from constant praise and assurance that the soldier was doing the right thing. Lieutenant Colonel Grossman explains that Vietnam was a teenage war, in which both leaders and followers were teenagers. The horrors of combat were internalized at a stage of life in which soldiers were highly vulnerable.[25]

Soldiers in a war on foreign soil, regardless of age, are vulnerable in many respects. In addition to anxiety about their own physical and mental health, they likely have concerns about their families and other relationships left

behind. This means that combat PTSD, unlike PTSD acquired in a civilian setting, always strikes its victims when they are at their most vulnerable. The fear
of death or injury is compounded by the potential for moral injury and general anxiety. Vietnam was a "lonely war" with individuals arriving and leaving
alone, rather than with their units, after a one-year rotation cycle. Each of these
features of the war contributed to lower morale among the troops.

Another factor is the adherence by all parties to codes and conventions of
warfare, such as the Geneva Convention. Lieutenant Colonel Grossman called
Vietnam a "dirty war" in which troops killed women, children, and civilians.
Still another factor is the presence of limitations on exposure to a combat zone.
Vietnam, Grossman argues, was an "inescapable war"—an endless war with
invisible enemies and no ground gains. Fourth is an orderly transition home
after a successful campaign to a warm and admiring welcome. In Grossman's
view, the transition home for most Vietnam veterans was abrupt and without
a cooling off period, their welcome was not warm and admiring, and they had
nothing to show for their efforts on the battlefield.[26] The pullout was viewed
as a defeat and as depriving soldiers of fulfillment for their sacrifice. The extensive drug use in Vietnam intensified the disorderly readjustment to society.
Lieutenant Colonel Grossman also argued that conditioning that raised the
soldier's firing rate from 15 percent to 90 percent may have contributed to the
incidence of PTSD because, although it trained soldiers to fire quickly by overcoming or bypassing their natural reluctance to kill other humans, it may have
increased the chance of long-term psychic damage. Killing, even under these
circumstances eventually is likely to take a toll, psychologically, on soldiers.[27]

Questions may remain as to whether any of the analyses, including
Grossman's, can account fully for the surge of PTSD and criminal behavior
that followed the war in light of evidence that psychiatric casualties are prevalent in all wars, even when those casualties are incorrectly attributed to other
causes. It may be that PTSD did not surface during the war essentially because
the political and military leaders did not acknowledge mental injury as a valid
consequence of war. Moreover, no PTSD category existed and no culture supported or encouraged the reporting and seeking of treatment for mental injury.

The inclusion of PTSD in the *DSM* together with sweeping cultural change
in the United States that made society and courts receptive to claims of traumatic stress were significant later on. Moreover, the fact that Vietnam was the

first war in which both the media and historians focused more on the experiences of ordinary soldiers than on military leaders and their strategies played a role in creating a receptive climate for claims of war trauma and injury.

Chapter 6 will follow the Vietnam veterans to their next battleground—the criminal courts.

Vietnam Veterans in the Dock

Shortly after midnight on August 22, 1977, Charles Heads, a Vietnam veteran who had been a letter carrier in Texas for seven years following his service in Vietnam, arrived at his sister-in-law's house in Shreveport, Louisiana. Heads was searching for his estranged wife, who had left his family home four days earlier. After receiving no response to his repeated knocks on the doors and windows, he kicked in a door leading from the carport and entered the house. He was armed with a pistol. The first person he encountered was his brother-in-law, who was standing at the end of the bedroom hall, also armed with a pistol. The exact sequence of events is not clear from the trial evidence, but at some point Heads began firing his pistol down the hallway until he had emptied it of bullets, despite his brother-in-law's pleas to stop shooting and leave. Heads then ran to his car, retrieved a rifle from the trunk, and returned to fire several more bullets, one of which struck his brother-in-law in the eye and killed him.[1]

The case gained the attention of the national media. One account contained this colorful account:

> The fog rolled in over the field . . . like a smoking cloud of napalm. The tall grass slumped lazily in a Mekong funk. The humidity squeezed a grunt's temples and wouldn't let go. Charles Heads watched the tree line silhouetted against the sky and without warning, was tragically transformed. . . . Heads was back in Vietnam, a marine ready for combat. The

man before him wasn't Lejay, his brother-in-law, but a dangerous Viet Cong. Heads pulled a rifle from his car, shot Lejay through the eye and then maniacally stalked the ranch house as though it were a straw hooch. When the police arrived, they found him standing silently, slowly coming out of his trance, unable and unwilling to resist.[2]

The State of Louisiana charged Heads with first-degree murder, a death penalty offense. After a trial in May 1978, a jury found him guilty. His insanity defense failed for lack of evidence. Although his lawyers offered evidence of his intense emotional state, they could not establish that he was provoked to the point of rage, as required by state law to qualify for a manslaughter verdict. After a death penalty hearing, the jury recommended life imprisonment. According to Heads's lawyers, the insanity defense at the first trial failed because the examining psychiatrists had not found evidence of any recognized mental disorder. PTSD was not yet in the *DSM*. Although Heads's lawyers suspected their client's behavior might be connected to his war service, Heads denied any connection and his lawyers never argued the point.[3]

The APA had not officially recognized PTSD at that point, and no one involved with the case had heard of the disorder, although the campaign to introduce it into the *DSM-III* was under way. Before 1980, the combat stress defense had been presented several times in court.[4] For example, World War II veterans used this defense, although, despite media reports that veterans experienced psychological disturbances after returning home, they were largely unsuccessful in establishing a causal relationship between war stress and criminal behavior.[5]

After he was sentenced to life imprisonment, Heads appealed, and the Louisiana Supreme Court affirmed the conviction.[6] The U.S. Supreme Court agreed to hear the case based on a claimed error in instructing the jury by the trial court. The Court vacated the conviction and remanded—sent the case back—to the state court for further consideration. On remand, the Louisiana Supreme Court reversed the conviction and ordered a new trial.[7] By the time the case was retried in 1981, PTSD had been included in the *DSM-III*, and lawyers in twenty-four cases had used the disorder in seeking acquittals or reduced sentences.[8] While preparing for Heads's second trial, his lawyers learned about the potential court uses of PTSD. They structured their new defense around evidence that Heads suffered from PTSD, that his Vietnam experience was connected to his PTSD, and that his disorder was related to the killing. PTSD, therefore, was used as a bridge to connect Heads's Vietnam War experience with the killing. The new formal acknowledgment of PTSD provided insight into psychological aspects of the case that had not been explored before.[9]

Heads's lawyers learned that, during his nine months in Vietnam, he had been in a Marine Corps force reconnaissance battalion near Da Nang. In the course of his deployment, he had gone on many patrols in small teams, his sergeant had been killed by a booby trap, and he had been shot twice in the stomach during an ambush. Because of his wounds, he had been declared physically unfit and honorably discharged. Since his return home, he had experienced a great deal of trouble readjusting to civilian life because of memory impairment, survivor guilt, sleeplessness, recurring painful memories, and at least one dissociative state, in which he felt disconnected from his surroundings and had reverted to a combat mode. His psychiatrists diagnosed him with PTSD.[10]

The description of PTSD in the *DSM* provided a theory of legal relevance for admitting into evidence testimony about Heads's life, including his childhood, work history, Vietnam experiences, readjustment difficulties, and lack of a serious criminal record, as well as testimony by other veterans regarding their Vietnam experiences and reactions.[11] The trial strategy was to present three PTSD experts who had examined Heads, witnesses to corroborate the pertinent facts in his life, and detailed testimony about the events before and during the shooting ambush. Heads, the final defense witness, testified, "It was like I was being controlled. . . . I was on; I could not have stopped."[12] The defense presented the theory that Heads had experienced a dissociative state before the night in question, the physical conditions at the scene of the shooting were Vietnam-like, he was under emotional threat of losing his wife and family, and as a result, he was "on automatic." After the shooting, Heads had stood by quietly, holding his weapon, while police arrested him.[13]

After a two-week trial in the fall of 1981, the jury of twelve returned a unanimous verdict of not guilty by reason of insanity, concluding that Heads could not distinguish right from wrong at the time he shot the victim. The Heads case was one of the first occasions when an insanity defense based on the *DSM-III* formulation of PTSD was successful in a capital case. Since then, PTSD has been used frequently as the basis for insanity defenses, although the success rate is not high.[14]

WHAT THE CASES REPRESENT

Most of the reported cases involving claims of PTSD by Vietnam veterans occurred between 1980 and 1985. The legal literature on the criminal uses of PTSD by Vietnam veterans concentrates on a body of four or five dozen criminal cases. Although precise statistics on the role of PTSD in criminal dispositions of Vietnam veterans are not available, one commentator stated that, in its first five years of use, the PTSD defense helped some 250 Vietnam veterans obtain acquittals, shorter sentences, or reduced penalties, such as drug, alcohol, and psychiatric treatment instead of jail.[15]

No statistics exist on the number of times that claims of war-related PTSD have persuaded prosecutors to reduce criminal charges, juries to convict defendants of less serious charges, or judges to give lower sentences. Moreover, PTSD probably would be mentioned in reported cases only when it was involved in an issue on appeal, since decisions focus on the issues. Based on estimates of court involvement and readjustment problems in the National Vietnam Veterans' Readjustment Study (NVVRS), discussed later, most Vietnam veterans who were arrested probably went to court for nonviolent, drug-related or domestic charges. PTSD may well have been raised during preliminary stages or negotiations in those cases. The cases that follow illustrate the ways in which PTSD was raised on the record in criminal proceedings. They also illustrate the ways in which claims were framed in terms of PTSD criteria and the types of criminal behavior that were allegedly caused by war-related PTSD. Finally, they provide a glimpse at how judges and juries received and dealt with PTSD claims and the role of PTSD in the outcome. These examples shed light on how veterans of the current wars may fare with PTSD claims in criminal matters.

When veterans first used PTSD in court, they had little success. This may have been attributable to lack of knowledge and skepticism about the relatively new theory of defense. It may also have been because the Vietnam War was unpopular. With the passage of time, however, veterans had more success as the theory became more accepted in the court system and generally known throughout society and as the public memory of the war receded into the past.

VIETNAM VETERANS IN THE COURTS

Although a considerable amount of anecdotal material exists alongside individual criminal case reports with regard to the criminal conduct of Vietnam veterans, reliable statistics are scarce. Despite the common belief that huge numbers of Vietnam veterans ran afoul of the law in the years following the war, solid numbers are hard to find. Estimates exist, however, as to how many Vietnam veterans have suffered or still suffer from PTSD. One comprehensive source recites a commonly given estimate that between 500,000 and 1.5 million Vietnam veterans in the United States have suffered from PTSD. The wide range of numbers in that estimate, which is based on studies, surveys, and media reports, raises questions about its accuracy. One report on the prevalence of PTSD estimates that 30 percent of male Vietnam veterans and 26.9 percent of female veterans have suffered.[16]

Apart from estimates of PTSD diagnosis and treatment, estimates of veterans' involvement in criminal behavior are less conclusive, and many are based on observations made immediately following the war. For example, one 2010 article reports, "Surveys conducted in the early 1980s indicated that Vietnam War veterans in the United States suffering from PTSD displayed a high rate of criminal behavior compared to that of the general population."[17] The source of that statistic, however, was a study done many years before, which concluded, "There was a significant relationship between combat role factors, exposure to stressors in Vietnam, and criminal behavior after returning home from the war."[18]

That study from the 1980s further suggested that

among Vietnam veterans with PTSD, what predisposes the onset of a criminal act is a changed psychological state of being that we have termed the survivor mode of functioning which operates as a behavioral defense mechanism. In this psychological state the veteran responds to conscious or unconscious manifestations of the anxiety disorder by reverting to the class of behaviors learned in combat which were connected with survival. In this altered state of being, the individual may then commit a violent or non-violent crime depending on predominant symptom dynamics of PTSD and the idiosyncratic nature of his experiences in the war.[19]

Just as it is important to acknowledge the role that combat stress may play in criminal behavior, it is equally important not to overstate that role or make it appear that criminal behavior resulting from PTSD is inevitable and widespread.

One source asserts that combat veterans with PTSD have a propensity to commit crimes. It is commonly repeated that in 1992, about one-seventh of the inmates in federal prisons were military service veterans and that approximately 10 percent of those veterans likely suffered from combat-induced PTSD. Another report states that in 1994, 127,500 veterans, representing approximately 10 percent of the population of all the state prisons, were incarcerated. The NVVRS found that 480,000 male veterans returning from Vietnam had developed PTSD and that almost half of this number had been arrested or jailed at least one time, 35 percent had been arrested more than once, and 11.5 percent had been convicted of a felony.[20] These numbers alone, however, do not necessarily indicate that proportionately more veterans suffering from PTSD are incarcerated than are other groups of people.

Generally absent from the equations used to calculate these statistics is partial PTSD (also called subclinical or subsyndromal PTSD). Partial PTSD exists when one or more of the disorder's diagnostic criteria are present and observed, but some crucial features are missing.[21] Even though a diagnosis of PTSD is not made if all criteria are not met, people with partial PTSD certainly may experience similar consequences as those with PTSD. In addition, the lack of a diagnosis may mean the veteran will not receive treatment, and therefore, the symptoms suffered may be acute or chronic. Although this configuration of PTSD-like illness or injury clearly cannot be considered in PTSD statistics because it is not diagnosed as PTSD for treatment or insurance purposes, it may have a significant impact on behavior, including criminal behavior.

Despite the imprecision of post-Vietnam figures, individual case studies are valuable because they show the range of the legal uses of PTSD and how courts deal with PTSD as a defense. Vietnam veterans' experiences in criminal courts can be instructive, especially when combined with the actual experiences of Iraq and Afghanistan veterans to date. Given the greater awareness of PTSD presently, PTSD statistics should soon be abundant. The cases that follow illustrate the full range of potential uses of PTSD and how the PTSD criteria are related to various kinds of criminal behavior. The cases are generally categorized as being either unplanned violent or explosive offenses (such as murder, attempted murder, or assault) or planned nonviolent crimes (such as drug conspiracies and tax fraud).

THE NVVRS

The NVVRS may provide a basis for predicting what is likely to happen to veterans from Iraq and Afghanistan over the course of time. However, it cannot be used to predict how many criminal cases will result or what the specific consequences will be for individual veterans. The NVVRS was published in 1990 and was based on a four-year (1984–1988) study of Vietnam veterans that was mandated by the U.S. Congress in 1983. It drew on samples of veterans and nonveterans who represented three major groups of interest. The first group consisted of Vietnam theater veterans, that is, people who served on active duty in the U.S. armed forces during the Vietnam era, August 5, 1964, to May 7, 1975, in Vietnam, Laos, Cambodia, or the surrounding waters or airspace of these three countries (the area involved in military operations, or "Vietnam theater"). The second group was composed of Vietnam-era veterans, that is, people who had served on active duty in the U.S. armed forces during the Vietnam era but who did not serve in the Vietnam theater. The third group consisted of people who did not serve in the military during the Vietnam era. This group was matched to the theater veterans on the basis of age, sex, race/ethnicity (for men only), and occupation (for women only).[22] The NVVRS provides a workable framework for examining selected cases and the most accurate overview of PTSD in Vietnam veterans together with a full range of adjustment difficulties, including family discord and criminal offenses.

Some of the findings of the NVVRS are relevant to the present and future status of Iraq and Afghanistan veterans. A majority of Vietnam theater veterans successfully reentered civilian life and experienced few symptoms of PTSD or other adjustment problems. However, a substantial number—480,000—of the male veterans returning from Vietnam (15 percent of 3.14 million) developed PTSD by the time the study ended in 1988. As noted earlier, almost half (about 240,000) had been arrested or jailed at least once, 35 percent had been arrested more than once, and 11.5 percent had been convicted of a felony. Theater veterans were especially likely to engage in violent behavior. Of the approximately 7,200 women who served, 8.5 percent were diagnosed with PTSD. The rates of PTSD for both male and female theater veterans were drastically higher than rates for comparable era veterans. Nearly one-third of male theater veterans (more than 960,000 men) and more than one-fourth of female theater veterans (more than 1,900 women) were found to have had the full-blown disorder at some time during their lives. That meant, the study concluded, that about one-half of the men and one-third of the women who had ever had PTSD still had the disorder at the time of the study. That conclusion suggested that PTSD could be a chronic, rather than acute, disorder.[23]

Many other findings that bear on PTSD were described in the report. Not surprisingly, the report suggested a strong connection among the presence of PTSD, the presence of other disorders, and difficulty readjusting to civilian life. The findings confirmed that, even beyond the painful symptoms of PTSD, the lives of Vietnam veterans with PTSD were profoundly disrupted. The veterans suffered problems in virtually every aspect of their lives. Generally speaking (because there were variations for race, ethnicity, and other factors), male veterans who had been exposed to high levels of war-zone stress were significantly more likely than their civilian counterparts (and to a lesser extent, their Vietnam-era counterparts) to report lower levels of life happiness and satisfaction, higher levels of social isolation, higher prevalence of homelessness or vagrancy, higher levels of active hostility and violent behavior, and higher levels of criminal arrests and imprisonment. Female veterans did not experience the same problems, except in the area of social isolation.[24]

Among theater veterans, males exposed to high war stress were much more likely to be arrested, convicted of felonies, and incarcerated.[25] Many of the readjustment problems experienced by theater veterans involved disadvantages in life conditions, such as homelessness, relationship instability, alcohol and drug abuse, lower educational achievement, and lower income (accompanied by higher risk of unemployment nationally). All of these conditions obviously combine to create greater social and economic vulnerability and greater risk of criminal behavior. Common sense dictates that the combination of homelessness, unemployment, and alcohol or drug abuse will increase the likelihood of criminal arrest and prosecution, regardless of military status. When an underlying psychiatric problem, such as PTSD and its symptoms, is added to the mix, the risk is even greater.

The NVVRS reported that, although PTSD was the "most severe form of reaction to a traumatic life event," it was "not considered a mental illness but a natural reaction to an overwhelmingly stressful, even catastrophic, event."[26] The report, therefore, takes a side in the dilemma I posited earlier: Is PTSD a normal reaction to abnormal stress or an abnormal reaction to normal stress? The position put forward in the NVVRS is consistent with the idea that PTSD should be considered a mental injury of war rather than a mental illness. Of course, the *DSM* uses trauma in the sense that it is an "abnormal" life condition and classifies PTSD as a psychiatric disorder, but a disorder can result from either injury or illness.

The report found, in addition, that PTSD had a substantial negative impact on the lives of spouses, children, and others living with veterans. Finally, it confirmed other reports that "very substantial proportions" of Vietnam veterans with readjustment problems had not used the VA or any other source for their mental health problems, especially during the twelve months just prior to the report's publication.[27]

The short- and long-term prevalence of PTSD in Vietnam veterans remains the subject of controversy and dispute. In 1988, the same year that the NVVRS was completed, another study conducted by the Centers for Disease Control (CDC) reported its finding that only about 15 percent of veterans had had PTSD and only about 2 percent still suffered from the disorder. The NVVRS had found that 31 percent suffered PTSD and 15 percent still had it—seven times the CDC's estimate.

In 2006 a group of researchers led by Dr. Bruce Dohrenwend published a reanalysis of the NVVRS data. The Dohrenwend study, published in August 2006, showed rates of PTSD that were considerably lower than the NVVRS results. Dohrenwend and his researchers, however, did something that neither the CDC nor the NVVRS did. They created a test for measuring for veterans' probable severity of exposure to war-zone stress. To create this test, they analyzed military personnel data along with data from military archives and historical records. Using this information, they concluded that the NVVRS had overestimated and the CDC had underestimated the PTSD rates among veteran. They found that 18.7 percent of all Vietnam veterans—what they termed a "substantial" number—suffered PTSD at some point and that, as of 1990, 9.1 percent of all Vietnam veterans still suffered PTSD.[28]

Whether the NVVRS figures or those of the Dohrenwend study are used, the conclusion is clear that PTSD was and still is after all these years a major problem for Vietnam veterans. The following examination of the court cases focuses on the type of criminal behavior involved in the crime, its relationship to the *DSM* diagnostic criteria for PTSD at the time of the behavior itself, the claimed role of PTSD in the crime, and the way the participants in the legal system addressed and resolved the PTSD factor in deciding the case.

CRIMINAL CASES: THE INSANITY DEFENSE

Most of the available cases—those on which an appellate decision or media report exists—were reported between 1980 and 1985. Generally speaking, the cases that reached the appellate level were cases in which defendants were precluded from presenting the PTSD defense and the result was unfavorable to the defendant. I use the term "defense" in the broadest possible sense, referring not merely to uses that, strictly speaking, would be legal defenses, such as the insanity defense or self-defense, but also to any issue that is asserted by a defendant at any stage of a criminal case to avoid conviction or minimize a penalty. This use of the term includes relying on evidence that tends to show that the government has not proved the requisite mental state (such as intent or recklessness) at the time of the crime. It also includes evidence used to reduce the sentence imposed by the court, especially in the penalty phase of a capital case, or information presented in posttrial proceedings (such as a motion for new trial or a habeas corpus petition) to give the defendant another opportunity. On each occasion, the defendant has appealed some ruling of a trial court that he claimed was wrong and adverse to his interests and legal rights. Defendants in some post-Vietnam appeals were successful in getting court-ordered legal relief; in others, they failed. In the three cases that ended at the trial level—*State v. Heads*, *State v. Felde*, and *State v. Mann*—Heads and Mann were successful but Felde remained convicted.[29]

Categorizing the criminal cases is difficult because it is not always clear how PTSD was raised as a defense in court. In addition, when medical or psychiatric matters are addressed in court, proponents talk about them in legal terms rather than as medical or psychiatric concepts. While expert witnesses commonly refer to psychiatric concepts and sources, particularly the *DSM*, they must relate their testimony to the legal requirements that govern the situation. For all these reasons, psychiatric terms in the *DSM* for symptoms of PTSD may be expressed in nonpsychiatric language in the courtroom. The ways in which PTSD is taken into account in trials are not always explained thoroughly by trial courts. The reason is that juries in criminal cases announce their verdicts orally without elaboration in court, and judges sometimes do not provide detailed explanations of their decisions in criminal cases. In view of the considerable range of PTSD symptoms and the lack of specifics in criminal case reports about how the disorder came into play in particular cases, researchers often categorize cases in terms of the behavior involved—explosive criminal, nonviolent, or compulsive behavior, for example. Most cases involving PTSD involve violent or compulsive behavior.

I will begin with *United States v. Tindall*, which concerned a large-scale drug-smuggling operation carried out by fifteen people, some of whom were veterans who had served together in Vietnam. PTSD was successfully argued as an explanation for the nonviolent criminal conduct involved in this case, based on expert testimony about the "action addiction" of the defendant, Michael Tindall. Tindall had received two Distinguished Flying Crosses, two Bronze Stars, and thirty-two Air Medals during his year as a helicopter pilot in Vietnam. His lawyer used footage from well-known movies *The Deer Hunter* and *Apocalypse Now* to persuade the jury that, even if Tindall did smuggle drugs into the United States during the six-year period in which he participated in the scheme, he should not be held responsible for those actions. According to the defense theory, the war had turned Tindall into an "action junkie" who was unable to resist opportunities to engage in thrill seeking. The PTSD defense was stretched further than it had been before to apply to someone whose avocations included diving off cliffs, skydiving, stunt flying, and exploring underwater caves.[30] According to testimony at trial, the stress reaction that caused him to revert to combat behavior was his psychological devastation after his application for a pilot's license was rejected. His disorder caused him to use survival methods common to Vietnam and to become part of a dangerous paramilitary drug-smuggling operation that included fellow combatants in Vietnam. The jury found Tindall not guilty by reason of insanity in September 1980.[31]

In *United States v. Krutschewski*,[32] the defendant, Peter Krutschewski, Tindall's copilot in Vietnam, was the organizer and manager of another drug-smuggling operation. His claim of PTSD was not successful, and he was found to be sane. Krutschewski's expert witness testified that his illness rendered him incapable of forming the criminal intent necessary for the offense with which he was charged—organizing and supervising a drug-smuggling operation. The witness did not change his opinion based on the fact that Krutschewski collected $500,000 from his marijuana smuggling enterprise. The government psychiatrist contradicted the defense expert, saying that his examination revealed "no evidence of mental illness to such a degree to imply a Vietnam insanity defense." It did not help that Krutschewski had said in a newspaper interview before the trial that if he were found guilty on any of the five counts, in the first stage of the jury trial, he would plead insanity and claim that he suffered from Vietnam syndrome. Krutschewski was convicted and received a ten-year jail sentence.[33]

Explosive behavior was involved in *State v. Mann*. Michael Mann, a Vietnam veteran, was charged with three counts of attempted murder and was successful with his PTSD defense. Because the *Mann* case was not reported in a court opinion, my information comes from a journal article that reported the factual details. In late December 1982 Mann, a double amputee and unemployed veteran, attended a party in rural Wisconsin. During the party, Mann opened fire with a .357-magnum revolver, causing critical injuries to the hosts, Robert and Patricia Freed, plus another person. Mann claimed that he attended the party in order to sell his revolver because he needed money. He testified that he became upset during an argument about the sale price and that, when he turned to leave, he felt a blow on the back of his head. Freed's version of the story was entirely different. He told the police that he asked Mann to leave because he was harassing his wife. On the way out the door, Mann went on a shooting spree. Whatever the circumstances, the shooting ended when a guest wrestled the gun from Mann. At that point, according to the guest, Mann resisted at first but went completely limp after the weapon was grabbed from him. Mann said he remembered little after feeling a blow to his head other than a vision or dream of being back in Vietnam.[34] He reportedly told a lawyer he had called that "I'm in the hospital and I don't know why. They tell me I shot someone, but I don't remember and I'm scared."[35]

At trial in 1983, Mann claimed that he was not criminally responsible for his actions, even though he admitted that he had committed the shootings. His defense was based on his suffering from PTSD arising from his Vietnam service. After a five-day trial with thirty-eight witnesses, the jury deliberated less than ten minutes and took only one vote before reaching a unanimous verdict that Mann was not guilty because he was a victim of PTSD. The jury determined also that his PTSD at the time of the shooting caused his conduct.

The insanity defense based on PTSD also prevailed in *New Jersey v. Cocuzza*.[36] Cocuzza was a Vietnam veteran with a post-military history of job-related and marital problems. He was charged with assaulting a group of police officers in a park with a large log he carried as if it were a rifle. Although little information is available about this case, an article in the *Criminal Law Bulletin* reported that, at the time of the incident, Cocuzza was "engulfed in a delusional flashback in which he genuinely believed he was once again in the jungles of Vietnam and perceived the police officers to be enemy soldiers who were following him. It appeared that the defendant was vaguely re-experiencing an incident in which his patrol had been ambushed and a friend killed."[37]

At trial, Cocuzza's wife testified that he had suffered periods of depression, punctuated by episodes of excessive drinking, explosive violence, and recurrent nightmares during the preceding two years. According to the bulletin article, medical experts testified at trial that although "'he knew the nature and quality of his acts' in the sense that he was attacking someone, it was equally clear that he 'did not know that those acts were wrong' since, in his mind, he was not attacking police officers but rather was attacking enemy soldiers. The defendant was accordingly found to be not guilty by reason of insanity."[38]

On the other hand, the PTSD defense failed in the case of *State v. Felde*. The defendant, Wayne Robert Felde, was a Vietnam veteran who was charged and convicted by a jury of the murder of a police officer in 1978. He was sentenced to death, and his conviction was upheld on appeal.[39] In an earlier case, a few years after his return from a tour in Vietnam in 1969, Felde had been convicted of shooting an ex-convict to death in Maryland. An appeals court had reversed this earlier decision and ordered a retrial. On retrial, Felde pled guilty to manslaughter and assault and received a twelve-year sentence. After being denied parole in 1976, he escaped from prison and fled to Louisiana, where the second incident occurred.[40]

After Felde's mother died in October 1978, Felde learned that police were looking for him. On the night of October 20, he was observed drunk and in possession of a handgun in a bar in Shreveport; he was apparently attempting to commit suicide. The police arrived and searched him but failed to find his gun. He was arrested for intoxication and placed in the backseat of a police car. On the way to the jail, he pulled his gun. During the struggle over the gun, four shots were fired. One bullet ricocheted and struck a police officer, who died as a result. Felde escaped the car but was captured soon after. Two years later, he was tried for first-degree murder.[41]

His defense lawyer notified the state that "part of Felde's defense would concern mental defects caused by a Vietnam delayed-stress syndrome and also possibly caused by Felde's exposure to . . . Agent Orange." Expert testimony at the trial indicated that the defendant suffered from chronic PTSD. Dr. John Wilson, an expert for the defense, testified that the earlier Maryland killing confirmed his diagnosis of PTSD. Wilson also testified, when asked why Felde pulled a gun, "If he pulls a gun, it means he wants to kill himself. . . . It is a security piece, his last bit of security." Wilson equated Felde's experience of being tracked by the police with his experience walking through fields with land mines in Vietnam. During the trial, Felde refused to listen to testimony about himself, and because he was ordered to remain in the courtroom, he covered his ears at times.[42]

The prosecutor argued that, although he did not question that Felde had a form of PTSD, the defendant did know right from wrong and there was no evidence that he had actually attempted suicide. The jury found Felde guilty of first-degree murder. In the penalty phase hearing, Felde told the jury that it should recommend the death penalty. After deliberating only a half hour, the jury announced that it was recommending the death penalty. Despite the verdict, the jury stated, "We, the Jury, recognize the contribution of our Vietnam veterans and those who lost their lives in Vietnam. We feel that the trial of Wayne Felde has brought to the forefront those extreme stress disorders prevalent among thousands of our veterans."[43]

Neither the trial court nor the Louisiana Supreme Court doubted that Felde had PTSD. The problem was that his PTSD was not enough to meet the stringent standards of the test for legal insanity. Felde testified that his dissociative reaction did not begin until after he had pulled the gun on the police officer and fired the first shot accidentally. The jury was faced with a dilemma. If Felde had been sane when he pulled the gun and first fired it, would a subsequent dissociative state during the events that followed excuse the killing? The jury apparently answered that question in the negative, and the Supreme Court upheld its finding as reasonable.[44]

In his final statement to the court, Felde said, "Like many other vets, I know what Vietnam did to me. . . . Critical wounds do not always pierce the skin, but enter the hearts and minds and dreams that are only begging for help so badly needed."[45] Since the trial ended, Felde has attempted suicide on several occasions.[46] In cases in which the PTSD defense has been argued successfully, such as *Heads* and *Mann*, the defense lawyers built an elaborate structure of facts concerning life experience and war experience to convince juries of the similarity of the stressful conditions surrounding the war trauma, the circumstances of the explosive crimes and a believable dissociative state. Since having PTSD is not, in itself, enough to prove a causal connection to a crime, lawyers must muster sufficient facts to support the claimed defense.[47] When the PTSD defense fails, some critics attribute the lack of success to inadequate legal representation. Others point out that the PTSD defense was not well established in the early 1980s and that, since that time, PTSD has become widely accepted, not only in the psychiatric and legal communities, but in society in general.

PTSD BEYOND THE INSANITY DEFENSE

Although the use of PTSD for the insanity defense has attracted the most attention, the disorder has been used for many other purposes in criminal cases. One use is in plea bargaining with prosecutors during the early stages of a criminal prosecution. Occasionally, prosecutors have been persuaded to go forward with lesser charges in return for guilty pleas and recommended sentences that might include a treatment program. In *State v. Gregory* the prosecutor agreed to lesser charges and a lenient sentencing recommendation when the veteran entered his guilty plea.[48] Gregory had entered a bank while heavily armed and held customers and employees hostage for several hours. He fired his gun frequently but did not injure anyone. He eventually released all the hostages. As the result of a plea agreement, he was released to receive outpatient treatment at a local VA center.[49]

Another use of PTSD in criminal cases is to support a claim that the government has failed to prove a mental element in its case.[50] The most important is to support a claim of diminished capacity, that is, a claim that the defendant was not mentally capable of committing the crime.[51] Although diminished capacity is a defense in some jurisdictions, in most jurisdictions it operates as a claim that the government has failed to meet its burden of proving the mental element of a crime. The claim can be made even when the defendant has not offered any evidence of diminished capacity at trial, in which case it stands or falls depending on the adequacy of the government's proof. The defense, in either form, involves the issue of the defendant's capacity to form the requisite intent for committing the specific crime or, in layman's terms, the mental element of the specific crime. PTSD is well suited to this defense because it deals with mental capacity at the time of the crime and not the ability to discern right from wrong, which is part of the insanity defense. The diminished capacity defense may simply reduce the conviction to a charge that has a different—diminished—mental state as an element, but it can also result in an outright acquittal. This defense, if successful, does not result in commitment to a mental institution, as is the case with the insanity defense. Reported cases involving diminished capacity are scarce because, if successful, generally the defendant is acquitted of the most serious charge and convicted of another with a lesser mental element. The court record may not reflect precisely what happened during the plea negotiation phase of the case.[52]

Vietnam veterans have commonly used PTSD as a mitigating factor in the sentencing phase of a criminal proceeding, including the penalty phase of a capital case. In *State v. Spawr*, in which William James Spawr, a Vietnam veteran was convicted of attempted assault, the trial judge rejected a suspended sentence. The Tennessee Supreme Court, however, ordered another sentencing hearing to consider probation in response to Spawr's appeal.[53]

Finally, PTSD has been raised frequently in the course of post-conviction proceedings, such as motions for new trial, parole hearings, and habeas corpus petitions. *State v. Jensen* provides an example of a long-delayed use of PTSD in a case involving Shawn Jensen, a Vietnam veteran.[54] The Arizona Supreme Court granted the defendant's petition for post-conviction relief when the veteran came forward with a new claim of war-related PTSD. Jensen had been convicted of a criminal offense ten years earlier. The Supreme Court sent the case back to the trial court for a hearing on whether the failure to claim PTSD at the trial in 1973 would have had any impact on the conviction or sentence. Based on the defendant's evidence, the trial court found that it would have made a difference. The court noted that PTSD did not exist as a disorder in 1973, and so no diagnosis could have been made. The court also found, "While there is an overlapping of the common terms as shell shock used after World War I and battle fatigue used after World War II, the Vietnam War was a different type of war and that the stress to the military was of a more intense and different nature." The court further found that the defendant had probably been suffering from PTSD since 1973, the year of his original trial.[55]

PTSD IN THE POST-VIETNAM YEARS

After the Vietnam War, veterans and their lawyers saw considerable, although not universal, success in obtaining recognition of PTSD as a legitimate defense. Although the psychiatric condition of combat stress that is now called PTSD was still an unknown quantity through the end of the war, it became common knowledge after it was included in the *DSM* in 1980. Its use in cases involving Vietnam veterans introduced it into popular culture as well as the legal system. By the end of the 1980s it was well established in the criminal justice system as a valid disorder that could, under appropriate circumstances, affect human behavior in meaningful ways. Lawyers around the country began using it in civil as well as criminal cases.

These were ground-breaking years for veterans claiming PTSD, who fought an uphill battle to survive after returning home, just as they had fought to survive in the theater of war itself. Once the disorder was firmly established in the legal culture, the path was clear for future veterans and others to draw on PTSD as a defense. The use in court by Vietnam veterans secured its place in the legal system. The *DSM* adoption and use in the post-Vietnam years gave an official name and status to a cluster of symptoms that had appeared throughout the history of warfare. The creation of the diagnostic category, therefore, became self-fulfilling in a real sense, channeling complaints and claims into one category.

Other changes occurred to legitimize the veterans' use of PTSD as a defense. The Vietnam War and its aftermath were pivotal events in American society in several respects. A new sense of individualism and independence from government emerged from that period. Soldiers and veterans could now claim they were not perpetrators of actions on behalf of their government but, instead, were victims of war machinery—victims just as surely as the Vietnamese people were victims.[56] This framing of the events supported the idea of survivor guilt and would have been nearly impossible after any earlier American war, even though many soldiers in all wars have felt a certain alienation from the government that ordered them to fight. A growing acceptance of the culture of victimhood, along with acceptance of the consequences of trauma, in the society as a whole made such claims more acceptable. It is difficult to imagine a veteran of World War I or II or even the Korean War publicly proclaiming himself to be a victim of his government's illegal or immoral war. Any development that acknowledges the toll on human lives and leads to better care for soldiers who suffer combat stress is beneficial. Whether soldiers and veterans should consider themselves victims depends on circumstances, however. Certainly, classifying as trauma victims soldiers who have committed actions that inflict injury or death on others remains a highly controversial idea. Whether the cultural changes that emphasize the study of trauma and victimhood are positive developments because they reflect sensitivity to human suffering or negative because they focus on human vulnerability rather than human strength is an open question. Undue focus on vulnerability that ignores the capacity of people to grow from stressful and demanding experiences is misplaced. Whether service in the military should be viewed as a fair political or moral duty or an unfair burden is an important issue in our twenty-first-century democracy. The concept of the citizen-soldier, so long an integral tradition in American society, appears to have fallen by the wayside in the last century.[57]

The next chapter will discuss how PTSD has emerged in the era of the Iraq and Afghanistan Wars. There is no question that claims of PTSD symptoms are more prevalent during the current wars than they were during the Vietnam War. The concept of PTSD has now had three decades to become widely understood and established. PTSD has been treated positively in the media, and veterans of the current wars continue to have public support. Most soldiers and veterans know about PTSD, although some may still be hesitant to claim it. As a result, PTSD claims by Iraq and Afghanistan veterans likely will have widespread acceptance in society as well as in the courts

PART III

IRAQ AND
AFGHANISTAN

7

Breeding Ground for PTSD
Iraq and Afghanistan

The mental stress of soldiers and veterans deployed to Iraq and Afghanistan is receiving an unprecedented amount of media attention. Reports come, not only from professional journalists and citizen journalists, but from firsthand accounts of participants on the ground published in video postings, in blogs, and on social networks. Numerous research studies and surveys evaluate this aspect of today's ongoing wars. The personal stories of veterans are my starting point.

VIEW FROM THE GROUND: PERSONAL STORIES
Art described his first day as a Marine in Kuwait:

> On my first day, we drove in pulling guns with our trucks. After the first mile, we got our first firing mission. We had six guns in our unit and probably shot five rounds each. We didn't know what we were firing at. . . . About six miles in, we saw what we had hit. Mostly it was buildings, but there were some bodies. . . . It hit me when we had to pick them up. They were Iraqi soldiers. It wasn't bad when we were just driving by. You could see and smell it but kind of get over it. It was when we stopped and they told us we had to collect everything. We had to line up and cover the bodies. . . . It was different then because you touched them. That's the first time I had ever seen a dead body except in a funeral. The first thing you think of is 'better them than me.' Then you realize that their mothers wanted them to come home just like my mother wants me to come home.

121

Art said that after the first combat experience, the soldiers began to question their mission.

I think what got to me was when I started to question why . . . because everybody was saying it's just for the oil. . . . The nights got real long after that. We were so close to the shore that you could hear the radio calling for naval gunfire. . . . You could hear the ships fire a round and hear them land. . . . The next day you could see the holes in the ground, and you got these Iraqis walking up to us for food, and we have to feed them . . . and you can't sleep at night because you have to watch them. That's when it really got to me. The first time, I thought I was ready for it, but I wasn't. . . . How can you be ready for it? . . . If you haven't been there, you can say you understand, but you can't.

I'm 100 percent sure I'm not alone in this. . . . One guy . . . they sent back to the ship. He just froze and was no good to anybody. That was one of the main reasons why I didn't want to say anything. When they sent him back, everybody started talking about him. I didn't want that to be me. There was nothing in our training about killing and the psychology of it. They didn't train you about the effects of what happens when you [kill someone]. They just train you to shoot a weapon. . . . In the artillery, you shoot over your own guys. They probably figure you won't see and it won't hurt you. We didn't know we'd have to clean it up. We had to cover up the bodies and line them all up. . . . I just looked at it and wondered why . . . ? What for?

Alan's combat experience was in Iraq. He envisioned a career in the military, but his alcohol problem ruined that. He was in a rehabilitation program while he was in the Marines. The rehab staff tried to help, but he was eventually discharged four months early. During his seven months in Iraq, conditions were bad. Insurgents were everywhere, schools were blown up, and the people were afraid of Americans. The troops were mortared almost every night; ambushes were common. Alan's platoon worked to win over the civilians while avoiding getting shot.

Alan recalled, "I was on point every time we went out on patrol. I volunteered. . . . I didn't want to be anywhere else on the patrol. I had to make sure we weren't walking into an IED [improvised explosive device]. We worked with bomb units. Every time we'd see an IED we'd cordon off the area and wait for them to show up. . . . The main thing they tried to teach us was that complacency kills." The tension and anxiety took a toll on Alan.

Ray was deployed twice to Afghanistan. The first time was on September 11, 2001. "We heard about 9-11 on the radio, and it was a shock to us. Once the war started, my life got easier . . . because it was just nonstop training. . . . It's hard to explain how those four years felt like a lifetime."

His role as a sniper was not what he expected. "You're not kicking doors down, and you're not face to face with people. . . . You still go . . . on missions. The sniper may sit for two or three days and watch. . . . It was an amazing job. I loved it. It's just overly romanticized in the movies."

Ray still feels deeply guilty about several deaths that he thinks he could have prevented had he not opted out of a mission. He learned later that his sniper skills had been desperately needed to save the lives of several soldiers. He believes that "because I was a glory hound, I passed up where I was supposed to go and maybe my parents would be mourning . . . instead of their parents." He learned later that the soldiers trapped by enemy fire had been calling for him.

Linda felt in constant danger during her deployment to Iraq

because we were supplying the infantry. I had an ammunition truck. My friend, the only girl out there with me, had her fuel truck. We had the most dangerous ones. If you got hit, you were done. We didn't have a lot of encounters, and I was never able to shoot back because we couldn't see the people shooting at us. . . . If you can't see, you can't shoot. In a way, I'm glad because I didn't want to shoot anyone. I think that would mess me up even more. . . . I almost had to when we had mortar rounds shot at us and I was on top of the truck.

Linda recalls,

My girlfriend was in an accident when her truck driver flipped over the truck. She was pretty badly injured. We drove her back to the base. Her leg was broken. Later, she had the choice to go back home or to come

back. She came back to us. . . . I said like 'Oh my God, I was lost without you.' I was the only girl while she was gone. . . . It was kind of
depressing for me. . . .

I have a lot of intense dreams and nightmares. I have dreams all the
time of my gun not working. My counselor says that is very common.
I've had dreams that I've gotten shot in the leg. I can actually feel them
in my dreams, which is weird. I'll wake up and my leg feels weird. . . .
Right after I got back, I heard a plane going over and I had to look up
because it sounded exactly like a mortar round. I knew I was in a safe
place, but my reaction was to look and make sure. I knew there was
something wrong, but I didn't say anything until I got out of the service
and got to the VA. I was scared at times, but I don't think I had PTSD
there. When I got back, it was a whole different story.

During Dax's eight-month tour in and around Afghanistan on ship, he was
not "in direct center line of fire," but he was "there for [his troops]." "In my
first Iraq tour, my company and 'Force Recon' pushed through the berm
between Kuwait and Iraq and fought all the way to Tikrit." After that tour, he
reenlisted before his four year commitment was up. He was slated to be an
instructor for the school of infantry, but that plan changed. "My Marines came
and asked me to do a third tour of combat because they said they felt safer
with me beside them . . . so I went with them. . . . I was planning on making
it a . . . lifelong career, but due to the injuries I received on my third tour, I was
medically retired."

In Iraq, "we saw a lot of explosions . . . a lot of getting blown up. . . . My
wingman [and I] were the . . . best gunners in the company. . . . Death was a
constant presence. At one point, our vehicles ran into a 'killbox' [heavily protected enemy territory] and were pummeled by gunfire and rocket propelled
grenades." Although Dax and his wingman survived the attack, Dax realized,

Most people get a sense of being afraid of dying, and adrenaline kicks in.
. . . I didn't have that fear because I had realized at that point . . . I was
dead; I just wasn't dead yet. . . . I knew . . . there was no way humanly
possible I should have made it through that, and because of that I literally had a gray spot of hair . . . in the middle of my head, come up within

twenty-four hours. . . . I realized . . . that I was not gonna survive that, and I'd come to terms with that. My only plan was to take as many of them with me as I could. I was OK with it.

Dax sustained a serious shoulder injury repairing a 450-pound 25-millimeter gun during the attack and later had shoulder surgery.

After Dax was treated for damage to his feet from cellulitis, his vehicle commander asked him to return to the gunner seat, even though he had not even begun recovering. During his third tour, on July 25, 2004, Dax sustained serious injuries when he "quite literally got blown up. I had three land mines . . . that were stacked . . . on top of each other [go off underneath my vehicle]. . . . Shrapnel hit my helmet and took a piece out of it. . . . It broke my spine in two places and caused me to receive chronic disc [degeneration], meaning my discs are pretty much eating themselves up because they can't support anything after that amount of explosion." Beyond the chronic degenerative injury to his spine, Dax received other injuries, including TBI and hearing loss.

The combat experiences of these veterans varied greatly as to intensity and trauma. The causes of their PTSD doubtless can be traced to different sources. Some coped effectively during combat exposure whereas others struggled to adapt. The background that the stories provide is essential as a foundation for the next sections, an overview of significant insights into the mental health consequences of these wars.

RAND CORPORATION STUDY

In 2008 the Rand Corporation, a nonprofit research organization, published a comprehensive report on the scope of mental health and cognitive conditions that troops face when returning from deployment to Iraq and Afghanistan, the costs of these conditions, and the adequacy of the care system.[1] At the time the study was completed, 1.64 million military service members had been deployed in support of the wars. More recent estimates, in 2011 after ten years of war, place the total numbers at more than 2 million troops deployed in both theaters since September 11, 2001.[2]

The Rand study was guided by three overarching questions: (1) What is the scope of mental health and cognitive problems faced by returning troops? (2) What are the economic costs of these mental health and cognitive conditions to the individual and society? (3) What are the existing programs and services available to meet the health-related needs of service members with PTSD or major depression? A related question pertained to the gaps in veteran services and what steps could close them. The Rand study, in brief, found that rates of PTSD, major depression, and TBI among veterans were relatively high when compared with the U.S. civilian population. The survey sample reported substantial rates of mental health problems within the preceding thirty days. Specifically, 14 percent were positive for PTSD and another 14 percent for major depression.

Based on deployment figures as of October 2007, Rand estimated that 300,000 individuals were suffering from PTSD or major depression at the time of the survey. About half of those who met the criteria for PTSD and major depression had sought medical or psychiatric help for a mental health problem during the past year, about the same proportion as in the civilian population. The Rand report conceded that reserve units and those who had left military service were underrepresented in the study and that both groups may be at higher risk for these conditions. Rand also found that "too few" of those who sought help received high-quality care and that many barriers to getting treatment existed, including concern for lack of confidentiality and fear of harming military-career advancement or civilian job potential.[3]

CHARLES HOGE, MD, 2004 STUDY

An influential article in 2004 by Col. Charles W. Hoge, MD, and published in the *New England Journal of Medicine*, reported that the prevalence of PTSD in Iraq War veterans could be as high as one in five, depending on the frequency of firefight participation.[4] Using a broad definition of PTSD, this study found that 18 percent of an army study group that had been deployed to Iraq and 19.9 percent of a marine study group also deployed to Iraq tested positive for PTSD. When a strict definition was used, the percentages dropped to 12.9 and 12.2 percent, respectively.[5] Responding to the Hoge article, Dr. Matthew J. Friedman observed,

There is reason for concern that the reported prevalence of PTSD of 15.6 to 17.1% among those returning from Operation Iraqi Freedom or Operation Enduring Freedom will increase in coming years, for two reasons. First, on the basis of the findings of the Fort Devens study [a study on the Gulf War reported in 1999], the prevalence of PTSD may increase considerably during the two years after veterans return from combat duty. Second, on the basis of studies of military personnel who served in Somalia, it is possible that psychiatric disorders will increase now that the conduct of war has shifted from a campaign for liberation to an ongoing armed conflict with dissident combatants. In short, the [existing] estimates of PTSD . . . may be conservative.[6]

HOGE AND SEAL STUDIES, 2009

Other recent estimates have produced predictions of PTSD as high as 20 percent in soldiers and 42 percent in reservists returning from the wars.[7] A 2009 study by Colonel Hoge and others, published in the *Journal of the American Medical Association*, reported, "19.1% of soldiers and Marines who returned from OIF [the Iraq War] met the risk criteria for a mental health concern, compared with 11.3 % for OEF [the Afghanistan War]." Further, "31% [of Iraq veterans] were documented to have had . . . at least 1 outpatient mental health care visit within the first year postdeployment."[8]

A study by Karen H. Seal and others found that 36.9 percent of separated Iraq and Afghanistan veterans enrolled in the VA health-care program had been diagnosed with mental health disorders, and more than 40 percent either had mental health disorders or were found to have psychological or behavioral problems or both.[9] Many other studies and reports, including reports by multiple mental health advisory teams (MHATs I- VI), corroborate the findings as to the anticipated prevalence of mental health problems among veterans returning from the current wars.[10] That the MHAT studies were conducted shows an encouraging level of attention to mental health issues.

STANFORD STUDY, 2009: A DYNAMIC MODEL

According to the 2009 Stanford study, the rate of PTSD among soldiers and marines deployed to Iraq may be as high as 35 percent, if one takes into account combat deployments plus time lags. The report states that the estimated rate is about double the rate from the raw survey data. The doubling is attributable to delayed onset, the time lag between the PTSD-generating event and the onset of symptoms, and to the fact that many of the service members surveyed will face additional deployments.[11] Although the prediction may be inexact because of underlying assumptions and other factors, the study provides valuable insights into the future mental health condition of the soldiers. The Stanford researchers also concluded that multiple deployments raise each individual's risk of PTSD, while lowering the total number of cases. The greater number of individuals exposed to combat, however, the greater the total number of those with PTSD. In other words, the configuration of PTSD within the group would be different. The data also suggested that reservists show symptoms sooner than active-duty soldiers, and civilians tend to report symptoms sooner than military personnel.[12]

PTSD begins to affect a veteran's life as soon as symptoms occur, regardless of whether the veteran ever reports the symptoms or received a PTSD diagnosis. Mental health resources will be needed at the VA and elsewhere in society when the veteran seeks help or is ordered to get help. Clearly, this disorder will affect, not just mental health resources, but also society and its institutions, including the courts.

As noted, partial PTSD, in which one or more symptom criteria is absent, still constitutes a threat to veterans who are attempting to adjust to and cope with civilian life and to those in close contact with those veterans. In addition, PTSD symptoms that are not recognized or diagnosed can still present huge obstacles to success in life. There may be a significant gap between the number of veterans predicted to have PTSD and the number who are evaluated at all, much less treated. It is commonly estimated, for example, that the majority of people in the general U.S. population who suffer from mental health problems do not receive treatment for many reasons, including the serious stigma attached to such problems as well as access to health-care treatment. Even if veterans do seek and receive treatment, PTSD symptoms may come and go over long periods of time, and full remission may not occur.[13] These considerations are important for treatment purposes, and they are also important for purposes of understanding the potentially huge impact on America's legal, social, and economic resources. It is essential that PTSD be viewed as a public health problem, not just an individual mental health problem. Mental health workers who deal with veterans suffering from PTSD know that veterans rarely present themselves with direct reports of symptoms. They show up for a wide variety of reasons that include other injuries or illnesses, alcohol or drug problems, domestic problems, and family violence, along with a plethora of other problems, including criminal arrests for operating under the influence, assault, theft, homelessness, minor assaults, or encounters with the police. Some patients show up for treatment at a critical juncture of their lives, such as at retirement. Veterans of all wars commonly show up at VA hospitals or community centers at unpredictable times and for unpredictable reasons. Moreover, new consequences of PTSD, and therefore new symptom patterns, may be developing. For example, information is currently emerging about how PTSD might contribute to or cause dementia.[14]

Researchers acknowledge that many other factors can affect the behavioral health of troops, such as demographics (e.g., age, gender, marital status), environment (weather, uncertain future deployment), expectations about the length of the war and the soldier's role (e.g., combat, noncombat, reserve, active), experience in different segments of the military operation, and time of return to civilian life. The Stanford study noted that because waivers of enlistment standards are increasing and pre-combat training for recent army recruits is decreasing (allowing more recruits with personal problems to enlist), more recent recruits may be more vulnerable to PTSD than those surveyed earlier. The researchers also observed that, for unknown reasons, members of the Army Reserve and the National Guard accounted for more than half of the suicides among Iraq War veterans to date, a startling figure because these groups represented considerably less than half of the total forces deployed in that theater.[15] This study is a valuable contribution to the understanding of PTSD and psychiatry's capacity to predict how many veterans of these wars are likely to suffer from the disorder.

BARRIERS TO MENTAL HEALTH CARE FOR VETERANS

A 2008 Pentagon investigation turned up several well-known barriers that discourage soldiers and veterans from obtaining the mental health care they need. They include the heightened stigma within the military against seeking help from mental health providers, poor access to military providers and facilities, and disruption in care when soldiers are transferred. Despite efforts to reduce the stigma, it remains pervasive and prevents many soldiers and veterans from seeking care. The Pentagon report found that the procedures in place were not adequate to overcome the stigma.[16] Another study reported that half of the subject-soldiers believed that seeking mental health care would harm their careers and that more than 60 percent believed they would be viewed and treated less favorably by their leaders and unit members.[17] This barrier appears to be attributable to the failure to change attitudes and practices within the military.

In addition, treatment facilities are incapable of providing adequate care, especially in view of increased need. Shortages exist in numbers of active-duty and other mental health care professionals within the services. The Pentagon task force report indicated insufficient continuity of care, gaps in service, inadequate treatment plans, inadequate monitoring of patients, and insufficient help to family members. Without sufficient monitoring, service members can terminate treatment unnoticed.[18] This barrier is attributable to poor funding of the military's mental health service. Mental health monitoring and treatment do not have sufficient priority among other military services to be better funded.

Another barrier has a *Catch-22* dimension to it. The government can deny VA health-care benefits to soldiers who have preexisting mental health conditions or who were discharged on less-than-honorable terms. When veterans who suffer from PTSD are diagnosed with personality disorders, they become ineligible for mental health care benefits. To be eligible, they must show that their prior existing conditions were aggravated or made worse by military service, a difficult burden. Moreover, episodes of poor behavior, such as drinking or drug abuse, resulting in punishment can result in discharge on a less-than-honorable basis. When that happens, the veterans may lose benefits for combat stress—even though such behavior commonly accompanies or results from PTSD.[19] The federal government has passed legislation and implemented programs to deal with veterans issues since the Afghanistan and Iraq Wars began. One example is the Veterans' Mental Health and Other Care Improvements Act of 2008 (Veterans' Mental Health Act).[20] Before the Veterans' Mental Health Act, in 2007 Congress passed the National Defense Authorization Act for Fiscal Year 2008.[21] The federal government has also conducted studies on the problem of military mental health care, including the Pentagon task force report discussed previously, that have revealed barriers to professional care, such as the stigma of seeking help for mental health problems.[22]

ESCALATING MILITARY SUICIDE RATES

The increasing rates of military suicides are receiving extensive attention, not only from the media, but also from the military. Because PTSD is seen as an

important factor in military suicide, most authorities view the escalating suicide rate as a sign of pervasive inadequacy in dealing with PTSD problems.[23]
If any lingering doubts exist about the authenticity of PTSD as defined in the
DSM, the statistics on military suicides constitute hard evidence of emotional
and mental distress resulting from military service during wartime and its
destructive role. Despite variations in the studies, universal agreement exists
that the number of suicides has steadily grown since 2001 to a shocking and
unacceptable level.

The annual army suicide rate, which is viewed by some experts as an indicator of the prevalence of PTSD, has more than doubled since 2001, culminating in a thirty-year high in 2008.[24] The number of suicides among
active-duty soldiers in the army in 2009 was 160, exceeding the record total of
140 in 2008. The total was only seventy-seven in 2003. During June 2010,
the monthly total of army suicides hit a record high of thirty-two.[25]

From the invasion of Afghanistan in October 2001 until the summer of 2009,
the U.S. Army lost 761 soldiers in combat. During the same period, a higher
number of U.S. soldiers—817—died by taking their own lives. According to
one military source, the surge in suicides is a vexing problem that baffles and
frustrates army officials despite "deploying hundreds of mental-health experts
and investing millions of dollars." According to an army spokesperson, one-
third of the suicides were committed by soldiers who had not been deployed,
renewing uncertainty about the causal relationship between the suicides and
combat experience. Significantly, army leaders report that "broken personal
relationships seem to be the most common thread linking suicides."[26]

Research indicates that it may take as many as three years for a soldier to
recover from the stress of a one-year combat assignment. One psychologist
observed that the military is in a dilemma: "'We train our warriors to use controlled violence and aggression, to suppress strong emotional reactions in the
face of adversity, to tolerate physical and emotional pain and to overcome the
fear of injury and death. . . . These qualities are also associated with increased
risk for suicide.' Such conditioning cannot be dulled 'without negatively affecting the fighting capacity of our military.'"[27] In a special Pentagon report released
in 2010, the military asserted that nearly four-fifths of army suicides were committed by soldiers who had been deployed one time, thus casting doubt on multiple deployments as the prime factor. The report placed blame on a lowering

of recruiting and retention standards plus failure of commanders to recognize or heed their soldiers' high-risk behavior. As to the first factor, the pace of deployments has forced an increased number of enlistment waivers that would have kept people out of the service and misconduct waivers that would have forced soldiers to leave service. The report also found that 60 percent of suicides were committed during the first enlistment period, usually four years. Significantly, the soldier who typically commits suicide is "possibly married, couple of kids, lost his job, no health care insurance, possibly a single parent."[28] Because so many Iraq and Afghanistan veterans fit this profile, this is a serious societal problem.

Although the surge in suicides began to garner attention in the media in 2006, an article in the *New York Times* in August 2009 ignited public discussion and provoked a response from the military, the National Center of PTSD, the National Institutes of Health (NIH), and mental health organizations. The article focused on the stories of four veterans from the 145th Transportation Company who committed suicide after returning home.[29] In their responses, the NIH and the army reminded the public that in 2008 they had initiated a five-year study of mental illness in the army titled the "Study to Assess Risk and Resilience in Service Members" (STARRS). That study is planning to cover depression, anxiety disorders, and PTSD in addition to suicide.[30]

TWO WATERSHED EVENTS: SEPTEMBER 11 AND PORTER V. McCOLLUM

Two events connected with the wars in Afghanistan and Iraq heightened the American public's awareness of PTSD. The first was the September 11, 2001, attacks on the World Trade Center and the Pentagon, which led to the invasion of Afghanistan. Not only has PTSD been acknowledged as a cause of mental distress of many victims who survived the attacks, but it also affected the workers and volunteers who participated in the response efforts. Numerous studies were conducted in the years following the attacks. In one study with nearly 12,000 participants, 51 percent met threshold criteria that warranted a clinical mental health examination. A subset of the participants was closely examined, and 13 percent of that subset met full PTSD diagnostic criteria.[31] Although actual numbers are not clear, one study showed that 12.4 percent of the rescue and recovery workers aided victims on 9/11 suffered from PTSD. So did 6.29 percent of the police officers and 21.1 percent of the unaffiliated volunteers.[32] Those would be high percentages by themselves, but they do not take into account the surviving victims at all levels of exposure, including those who escaped the buildings.

The importance, for my purposes, of these studies and media accounts is that they heightened awareness of PTSD among the general public. Since all Americans shared the shock and horror of the events, they hardly doubted the fact that huge numbers of victims and rescue workers were traumatized and eventually suffered from PTSD. If PTSD had any more ground to cover as far as public awareness and acceptance were concerned, it gained the necessary exposure during the events and aftermath of the September 11 attacks.

The second event was in November 2009, when the U.S. Supreme Court decided the case of *Porter v. McCollum*.[33] *McCollum* was an appeal of a decision on a habeas corpus petition in which a Korean War veteran challenged his confinement in prison. After George Porter, a Korean War veteran, was convicted of murder and sentenced to death in Florida, he sought habeas corpus relief in the state courts, alleging that his attorney had provided ineffective assistance in failing to raise as mitigating evidence his outstanding war record and his PTSD at sentencing. Failing to obtain relief, Porter turned to the federal courts. The District Court's grant of relief was reversed by the Eleventh Circuit. The U.S. Supreme Court reversed, concluding that the sentencing decision should have taken account of the PTSD that Porter claimed occurred because of his war service. The Court noted that combat service had traumatized and changed the veteran. Although the Court did not rule on PTSD as a defense of the crime but only as mitigating evidence in sentencing, the case is significant because it represents a pronouncement from the high court that PTSD is a valid disorder and a crucial factor to take into account during the judicial process—even based on war experience that took place decades earlier. That PTSD contributed largely to the U.S. Supreme Court's reversal of a sentence for murder lends the disorder legitimacy.

Never before in history has such extensive and in-depth information about a psychiatric disorder been within the grasp of every individual who has access to the media. Not only is every member of the military familiar with PTSD, the general public knows about it as well. However, many problems continue to exist with effective prevention and treatment. They include the failure to eliminate MST and substance abuse from the military, inadequate preparation for transition to civilian life, continued political reliance on military action without taking into account the huge and predictable toll of both mental health and physical casualties, and the stigma of disclosing mental health problems within the military.[34]

A PERFECT STORM: PTSD IN IRAQ AND AFGHANISTAN

What insight can we gain about current PTSD problems by applying the criteria that David Grossman used to assess the Vietnam War to the Iraq and Afghanistan Wars? As for group leadership and morale, the present picture is considerably more favorable than in Vietnam. In America's all-volunteer army, troops are deployed in regular army or reserve units that have trained together. Soldiers in general are older than those drafted for Vietnam, and many reservists are older still. Young members of the armed forces in these wars have an ample supply of mature men and women as leaders and role models.

Ambiguity prevails concerning adherence to traditional codes and conventions of war. Soldiers in Iraq and Afghanistan face similar difficulties as the Vietnam forces did in distinguishing combatants from civilians. In Afghanistan, the Taliban combatants are part of the civilian population, and after attacking, they disappear into the civilian population of towns and villages. The need to scrutinize civilians as potential enemy combatants is significant. As to the third feature, the present U.S. forces operate in an environment in which potential hazards are everywhere and combat exposure is virtually unlimited. The new methods of insurgency warfare rely heavily on roadside bombs and rocket-propelled grenades (RPGs), discharged by civilians as well as combatants.

Today's veterans may not be better off than Vietnam veterans were with regard to the fourth factor, orderly transition home after a successful campaign. Multiple deployments cause considerable stress. Each deployment brings a new disruption and prevents normal life from resuming. Although troops are well received within their communities, the public tends to be generally disengaged from the war effort. Polls taken in 2011 indicate that the public is weary of the war and impatient about delay in bringing it to an end.[35] The reentry of veterans is complicated by the personal economic and employment problems that plague many Americans.

Many factors, including increased firepower on all sides; protracted duration of the war; pace of deployments, including multiple deployments; and the constant exposure of nearly all troops to combat conditions, contribute to escalating rates of PTSD. Other factors that contribute are the leadership's unclear or shifting objectives, increased survival rates after injury because of advances in medical technology, difficulties in identifying enemy combatants from noncombatants, and shaky public support at home, along with economic and social obstacles to smooth transitions to civilian life. The fact remains that the features of war itself—including displacement from home, morally conflicting duties and their consequences, risk and anxiety, sleeplessness, and witnessing devastating injuries and deaths—cause mental stress to rise to the breaking point in many individuals.

No amount of screening, conditioning, or resilience training will eliminate psychiatric casualties. Certain measures will help maintain the fighting forces and treatment may lessen its impact, but there is no ultimate panacea for war's toxic impact on the human soul and body. This discussion provides a backdrop for examination of criminal cases involving veterans of Iraq and Afghanistan.

8

The War at Home
Veterans in Criminal Court

When Jessie Bratcher, a twenty-six-year-old veteran of the Iraq War, was arrested for murder in August 2008, he freely admitted that he had shot and killed José Medina. The only question for jurors when he was tried fourteen months later was whether they should find him guilty but insane because of the trauma he had suffered in combat during his deployment in Iraq.

Jessie's is a classic story of combat PTSD and its deadly consequences. When he was a high school student in rural Oregon, he had a reputation for being a peacemaker. He would never initiate a fight but would try to "cool the parties down." He was a good student and had never been in trouble with the law before serving in the military. In 2002, at the age of twenty, he joined the Oregon National Guard. He was feeling a "surge of patriotism and a value plan to get an education." By the end of 2004 he was in Iraq, one of four hundred soldiers from the Third Battalion, 116th Armored Cavalry Regiment, from eastern Oregon. The regiment troops had retrained as infantry before their eleven-month deployment. Jessie was assigned as a machine gunner.[1]

In Iraq, Jessie took the U.S. rules of engagement seriously, even memorizing them. He had trouble with other squad members when he refused to shoot at people he could not readily identify as enemy combatants. On one occasion, he refused to fire on civilians whom his unit engaged. On another occasion, he filed a report that conflicted with other reports about an incident in which men from his unit shot and killed an Iraqi civilian who was armed but not acting in a hostile manner.[2] His platoon sergeant confirmed that the other reports were covering up the incident but that Jessie was telling the truth. After that incident, the others in his unit bullied him, so his sergeant assigned him to another squad with a close friend, John Ogburn.

As Jessie's new unit patrolled ninety-six villages around Kirkuk in Humvees and on foot, it was in constant danger of roadside bombs and insurgent attacks. Jessie witnessed Ogburn, a turret gunner in a Humvee, being crushed to death in a rollover accident when an Iraqi truck veered into the patrol convoy. After the accident, Jessie withdrew from the other soldiers. Several weeks later, a roadside bomb exploded near his Humvee in the same area where his friend had been killed. Jessie's personality changed markedly after his friend's death, and he seemed not to care what happened.[3]

When Jessie returned to Oregon in November 2005, "he was hostile . . . more or less towards everyone." His grandfather, with whom he lived, had raised him and cared a great deal about him. He observed that Jessie's "'attitude was hostile. More or less towards everyone. . . . And [he] wanted guns. I didn't like it . . . He wasn't peaceful.' He asked his grandson to move out." The men in his reserve unit noticed the difference in his behavior and his peculiar stare. Jessie went to the Boise VA for help, but benefits were denied because his PTSD symptoms were considered too mild. His symptoms worsened over time, and in the spring of 2007, he went to a psychotherapist. He reported flashbacks involving his friend Ogburn to the psychotherapist. He also told her that he was depressed, angry, and irritable and that he frequently camped in the woods and set up military perimeters around his campsites.[4]

After Jessie saw the psychotherapist, he had a second evaluation by the VA and was found 70 percent disabled. When he lost his job as a stock clerk at a grocery store, he was found unemployable and his disability rating went up to 100 percent. At the age of twenty-five, he was diagnosed with PTSD and began receiving treatment and disability pay of about $32,000 per year. His life began to improve, and he kept his VA appointments. He started a serious relationship with a woman named Celena. When she became pregnant, he was excited about becoming a father, and they made plans to get married. One night, however, Celena told him that she was not sure the child was his. She said that two months earlier, on a night when he was at his VA appointment in Boise, she had gone out drinking with a girlfriend. That night she had met a man, and he had raped her.[5]

This news set off a bizarre chain of events, which culminated with the murder of the alleged rapist and Jessie's subsequent arrest. When Celena told Jessie about the rape, he was beside himself with grief. During the course of the evening, he exhibited bizarre behavior, including putting the barrel of his AK-47 in his mouth. The morning after their talk, he purchased a .45-caliber semi-automatic handgun and ammo and drove to Medina's home. Jessie had a conversation with Medina, in which Medina first denied knowing Celena. Then he claimed that "it was sex, not rape" and that he would take responsibility. Jessie pulled the gun from his back pocket and shot Medina ten times as Medina ran away. The victim was hit in the buttocks, hip, waist, shin, and head. Jessie claimed that, during the shooting, he had a flashback in which he was in Iraq.[6]

During the nine-day trial, the jury heard from many witnesses. The defense attorney told the story of a soldier, once peaceful, who experienced danger and death, was changed by war, and returned to his hometown struggling to reconcile his war experiences with his prior civilian life. Jessie Bratcher was the first Iraq War veteran in Oregon and among the first veterans in the United States to offer a defense based on PTSD in a murder case. The prosecutor opposed the insanity defense, suggesting that Jessie was faking his condition. The prosecution expert, however, concluded that Jessie was legally insane at the time of the crime, in part because of Jessie's accounts of his flashback during the murder in which he felt an IED blast and saw dead Iraqi bodies.[7]

The psychologist called by the defense as an expert witness supported the insanity defense. Although Jessie offered to plead guilty to a charge of manslaughter by reason of insanity and face hospital treatment instead of prison time, the prosecutor refused. The second prosecution expert was troubled by Jessie's memory lapses and exaggerations. He found it suspicious that Jessie reported every symptom of traumatic brain injury and was unconvinced by Jessie's claims of flashbacks. He testified, contrary to the defense claims, that Jessie had never fired his weapon in combat, had not been shot at during his first patrol, and had seen no dead bodies except that of Ogburn. Jessie's platoon sergeant, who was called as a state's witness, testified that Jessie was trained to respond automatically to threats with force. In his closing argument, the defense attorney argued that the case was a Shakespearean tragedy in which "everyone loses."[8] After two days of deliberation, the jury found Jessie legally insane because of his PTSD. The judge placed Jessie under the supervision of

Oregon's Psychiatric Security Review Board for life and committed him to the Oregon State Hospital.[9] Although the Jessie Bratcher case was undoubtedly one of the first successful PTSD insanity defenses to murder by an Iraq or Afghanistan veteran, it would not be the last.

HOMICIDES INVOLVING VETERANS

Media reports are a major source of information about criminal cases involving Iraq and Afghanistan veterans because few court opinions are available at this point in the reintegration process. According to one *New York Times* report, dated January 13, 2008, more than 120 Iraq and Afghanistan veterans had been charged with homicide as of that date. Although no statistical conclusions were possible at that time, the article claimed that a considerable amount of violence had occurred in the states because of psychiatric problems resulting from combat deployments.[10]

The *Times* article reported that three-quarters of the veterans involved in the crimes were still in the military at the time of the homicides and more than half of the cases involved guns. The remaining homicides were stabbings, beatings, strangulations, bathtub drownings, and vehicular homicides. One-third of all the homicide victims were spouses, girlfriends, children, or other relatives. One-quarter were fellow service members, and the remaining victims were strangers. Thirteen of the veterans committed suicide after the killing, and several others expressed a death wish or attempted to commit suicide. Only one case involving criminal behavior by a female veteran was included. The report stated that, in many of the cases, combat trauma and deployment stress along with other factors such as alcohol abuse and domestic discord appeared to "set the stage" for the criminal problems. In some of the cases, however, there was no apparent connection between combat service and the criminal behavior.

The *Times* report included a statement by Robert Lifton, the physician who played a major role in persuading the APA to include PTSD in the *DSM* in 1980: "When they've been in combat, you have to suspect immediately that combat has had some effect, especially with people who haven't shown these tendencies in the past." According to another *Times* article, the military keeps track only of cases committed on its bases, and the Justice Department, the FBI, and the VA do not keep track of crimes committed by veterans after their return to civilian life at all. [11]

In a commentary in the Nieman Reports, Matthew Purdy stated that the January 13 *Times* article had noted that the homicides were "an extreme manifestation of dysfunction for returning veterans, many of whom struggle in quieter ways, with crumbling marriages, mounting debt, deepening alcohol dependence, or more-minor tangles with the law."[12]

A controversy erupted over the January 13 *Times* report and its social implications. The author of a *Newsweek* article expressed concern that the report perpetuated the myth that all returning veterans were "crazed and unstable." He noted the Pentagon's criticism that "lumping together different crimes such as involuntary manslaughter with first-degree homicide" was questionable and wrote that the increase in wartime numbers might be attributable to "an increase in awareness of military service by reporters since 9/11." [13]

The APA responded to the controversy stirred up by the January 13 *Times* report with an article reporting independent research into the homicides included in the *Times* in an effort to clarify the association between combat exposure and post-deployment violence. In more than 80 percent of the cases (included in the *Times* article) studied, the APA was able to find significantly more information about the perpetrator than in the *Times* article. The APA's findings are worth repeating because they deal directly with the connection between war, PTSD, and crime. The APA determined that 53.7 percent of the offenders were between eighteen and twenty-four years of age and 85 percent were under thirty. Where race and ethnicity were known, the majority (54.4 percent) were Caucasian, 23.5 percent were Hispanic, and 22.1 percent were African American. Of the offenders, 62.8 percent were army veterans and 30.6 percent were marines. More than 90 percent had served in Iraq, and 10.7 percent had served in Afghanistan. Eleven offenders (9.1 percent) had been deployed overseas twice during current hostilities, and five (4.1 percent) had deployed three times.[14]

The victims included strangers (35.2 percent), friends or acquaintances (23 percent), spouses or girlfriends (18.8 percent), children (8.3 percent), and others or unknown (14.7 percent). Handguns were the most often used weapon among the veterans, as they are among the general population. More than half of the charges in the 121 arrests or convictions involved first-degree murder. Seven veterans had been acquitted, and 30 percent of the cases were still pending. By mid-2008, when the article was written, no veterans had received a not guilty by reason of insanity acquittal, although combat exposure appeared to influence the disposition of one case. More than one-fifth involved vehicular homicide, and all but one involved substance abuse.[15]

The APA authors also evaluated the cases for evidence of psychiatric symptoms. Although diagnosis was impossible based on the limited information available, the researchers found significant psychiatric symptoms related to PTSD, antisocial personality disorder (ASPD), substance abuse, or some form of psychosis in all but seven of the cases. Only four of the veterans showed psychotic symptoms. PTSD symptoms were reported in eighty-five of the 121 cases. The researchers noted that, in general, they focused on any evidence that the veterans had returned from combat "disturbed" or "changed." On this score, they noted that those who had close contact with the veterans, such as friends, family members, attorneys, or even judges, referred to symptoms, including nightmares, insomnia, intrusive thoughts, survivor guilt, hyperarousal, hypervigiliance, intense anger, depressed mood, and suicidal ideation in connection with the veterans. Thirty-four percent of the veterans displayed only PTSD symptoms, an additional 19 percent displayed PTSD and substance abuse, and 17 percent displayed PTSD and ASPD together. The APA researchers observed that thirty-nine of the veterans (32.2 percent) demonstrated significant symptoms of ASPD. To determine ASPD symptoms, they examined the nature of the crime: Was violence committed for material gain? Did the killing occur during the commission of a felony? Was the veteran involved in other criminal activity? Did he demonstrate a callous disregard of others, or lack remorse? They found that 17 percent of the veterans showed ASPD symptoms, another 17 percent showed PTSD along with ASPD, and one veteran showed substance abuse with ASPD.[16]

Finally, the researchers evaluated the strength of the relationship between the perpetrator's violent act and combat experiences using a seven-point scale in which "1" represented no relationship and "7" represented the strongest relationship (meaning that the act would likely not have been committed "but for" combat). The APA calculated the mean rating as 5.2, indicating a very significant association between the crime committed and the combat experience. More than half of the veterans were rated "6," and fewer than five veterans got a "0" rating. The researchers concluded that the prevalence of PTSD symptoms in this sample of 121 veterans who were charged with or convicted of homicides of various types far exceeded the prevalence found in other samples of returning veterans. They noted that this "finding appears to be consistent with prior research that suggests that PTSD mediates the frequency and severity of violent behavior among combat veterans." They pointed out, however, that a substantial minority displayed no symptoms of PTSD and seemed to demonstrate signs of habitual criminality.[17]

The APA report concluded, without specific reference to the sample of homicides, that social support is a strong protective factor against PTSD. The researchers wrote that if the public misinterpreted the news reports of violent veterans, the "already immense public health problem" represented by PTSD could become even less manageable. They observed that it "would be terrible for the public to conclude erroneously that returning veterans are inherently dangerous." That is why, they noted, veterans advocacy groups emphasized that the homicides in the January 13, 2008 *Times* article yielded an estimated 8.6/100,000 homicide rate in the veteran population, in contrast to the 29.3/100,000 among American men aged eighteen to twenty-four.[18]

The *Times* article, as illuminated by the APA study, demonstrated what could happen when veterans returned from war unprepared to reenter civilian society. Although the cases that I will discuss are not statistically significant because they were not organized and analyzed as part of a rigorous study, they evidence the plausible connection between military combat, PTSD, and criminal behavior—the connection between the violence of war and violence in society. They further highlight many warning signs that could serve as useful alerts to psychiatrists and civilian and military leaders concerning factors that can contribute to or trigger violent reactions.

TYPES OF CRIMES

The homicides charged to veterans of Iraq and Afghanistan through early 2008 fell into five categories. The veterans I will discuss all displayed symptoms of PTSD prior to their criminal activity.

The first category consists of vehicular homicides, which typically involve substance abuse and reckless behavior. The second consists of homicides involving strangers as victims in which a motive is identifiable. The third consists of murders in which the victim was a person with whom the veteran was involved in a nonintimate relationship. This category covers a broad range of relationships, including casual acquaintances, work and military colleagues, friends, and family members. Obviously, different factors may be involved with each subcategory. In some, the victim was simply in the wrong place at the wrong time, whereas, in others, the victim was an active participant in the events that led to the homicide. The fourth category consists of crimes against people with whom the veteran was intimately involved, such as spouses and partners. Domestic violence or child abuse was often a factor in homicides in this category. Finally, the fifth category consists of murder-suicides.

The factors involved in the first category, vehicular homicide, are relatively easy to identify. At the other end of the spectrum, the fourth and fifth category killings involve elements that are more difficult to discern. Those crimes seem incomprehensible and irrational; murder-suicides (and suicides) are rarely well understood or resolved satisfactorily.

Whether any of these homicides would have been committed in the absence of combat stress is impossible to say. The presence of this elusive "but for" factor is always uncertain—and sometimes the "but for" factor is entirely missing from PTSD-related criminal activity. A similar sample of ordinary civilian homicides, entirely unrelated to PTSD, might produce similar categories. The daily occurrence of homicides in American society should not distract from analyzing combat-related homicides. It may be that, with proper screening, training, and transitioning to civilian life, some of these homicides, at least, were preventable.

VEHICULAR HOMICIDES

Vehicular homicides represent about one-fifth of the veteran-committed homicides. In one of these cases, Lucas T. Borges, who served as a marine in Iraq, was convicted of second-degree murder and received a twenty-four- to thirty-two-year sentence. After spending six months in Iraq at the beginning of the war, Borges "came back different, like he was out of his mind," his mother said. Upon his return from Iraq, he was assigned to a maintenance battalion at Camp Lejeune, North Carolina, and he developed an addiction to inhaling the ether used to start large internal combustion engines in the winter. His sister believed that he developed the habit to relieve the anxiety that plagued him after his war experience. According to his lawyer, the Marines were aware of his substance abuse problem as well as his past drug addiction but failed to remove him from a job in which he had access to his drug of choice and to provide the necessary drug treatment.

In November 2003, four months after his return from Iraq, Borges was caught inhaling ether in his car at Camp Lejeune. Military officials impounded the car, which contained several ether canisters, and sent Borges, who threatened to kill himself, to the mental health ward. While the officials were pursuing Borges's dismissal from the service, "they processed him out, handed him the keys to his car, and his supervisor said, 'If you're not careful, you're going to kill somebody.'"[19] When he retrieved his car, Borges discovered that the ether containers were still in it. After getting high, he drove east down the westbound lane of a state highway and collided head on with the victims' car, killing the teenage daughter of another marine who had served in Iraq and seriously injuring four other people.

In another case, once Anthony Klecker returned from eight months in Iraq, he was unable to sleep, he had panic attacks, he suffered flashbacks, and he found bar fights unavoidable. Desperate for sleep and relief from his problems, he drank heavily. One morning, his parents found him curled in a fetal position in his closet. On another morning, he was found slumped over the wheel of his car in the driveway. Klecker's problems culminated with a drunk-driving accident in which he caused the death of a sixteen-year-old high school cheerleader. Until the homicide, the soldier had refused to acknowledge the depth of his problem, but he has since been diagnosed with severe PTSD. According to Klecker, "I was imprisoned in my own mind."[20]

Klecker was among the first marines to fight from Kuwait to Baghdad and on to Tikrit. He endured ambushes and firefights as the gunner on the rear Humvee in a First Marine Division convoy. On one occasion, he fired a warning at a man in farmer's robes running toward his convoy. Suddenly, a white van came hurtling up the road. He fired another warning and followed with several bursts of machine-gun fire at the van. He assumed that he killed all the individuals in the van, but he did not know whether they were innocent Iraqis or insurgents. He felt proud of his actions initially, but over time, he began to feel pangs of doubt and shame—"shame about if I did the right thing or didn't."[21]

After his Iraq tour, Klecker shipped out to Okinawa, where he began drinking heavily. When he returned home, his panic attacks, nightmares, and insomnia worsened—as did his drinking. He accumulated arrests for drinking and fighting. He hit bottom on October 6, 2006, when he drunkenly drove into a highway divider, which dislodged and trapped another driver, the sixteen-year-old high school student. The student was killed when a tractor-trailer rammed her car.

After the incident, Klecker received a full veterans disability rating for combat stress. At his trial for vehicular manslaughter, the judge accepted his lawyer's request for special treatment on the basis that the war contributed to his crime. After only a year in jail, he was moved into an intensive inpatient program at a veterans facility to deal with his drinking and combat stress. Although he was a model patient for a while, he ran into problems during a hiatus between programs and was forced to leave because of rules violations. When the court ruled that he could not serve his sentence at home, he returned to prison for nineteen months.[22]

It is obvious that, in both Borges's and Klecker's crimes, PTSD played a major role in the deaths that occurred. Both men developed substance abuse problems in the course of their deployments to Iraq. Both developed PTSD symptoms (although it appears that Borges had not been diagnosed, even after his substance abuse was known) and relieved those symptoms by turning to or deepening their substance abuse. The substance abuse led directly to the motor vehicle homicides that they committed. Borges was charged with a more serious crime than Klecker and suffered more serious consequences as a result. Klecker was given special treatment at sentencing because of his PTSD, whereas it does not appear from available facts that Borges relied on his combat PTSD symptoms as a defense. In both cases, military experience in Iraq appears to be the contributing factor to the deaths of innocent victims.

HOMICIDES OF STRANGERS

Like vehicular homicides, murders in which strangers are the victims are often fairly straightforward, mainly because they do not involve the entanglements of human relationships. In these crimes, the roles of victims are generally clear and simple, and the factors that account for the crimes are reasonably apparent. One classic example is the case of Matthew Sepi, a twenty-year-old Iraq combat veteran whose case involved a stress-related response to a perceived threat.

Late one night in the summer of 2005, Sepi headed to a convenience store in a seedy Las Vegas neighborhood where he had settled after returning from

Iraq. Plagued by nightmares about an Iraqi civilian killed by his unit, he needed alcohol to sleep. He was anxious about lurking danger in the neighborhood, so he tucked an assault rifle under his trench coat to protect himself. He paid a stranger to buy him two tall cans of beer, his self-prescribed treatment for his PTSD, and started home. Two men, later identified as gang members, both large and armed, stepped out of the darkness to confront Sepi. Later, in an interview with police, the veteran said he saw the butt of a gun, heard a boom, saw a flash, and "just snapped." As a result of the incident, one gang member was dead and the other was wounded. Sepi fled, "breaking contact" with the enemy, as he later explained to police. With his rifle raised, he continued home, loaded 180 rounds of ammunition into his car, and drove until the police approached. "Who did I take fire from?" he inquired. He added that he had been ambushed and then instinctively "engaged the targets." Although the police were sympathetic to his situation, they arrested him. Sepi, a Navajo, had joined the army at the age of sixteen, with permission from his mother. He saw intense action in Iraq and found the war "mind-bending." His infantry company, when it arrived in April 2003, was assigned to clear resistant strongholds north of Baghdad. "Me and my buddies were the ones that assaulted the places. We went in the buildings and cleared the buildings. We shot and got shot at," he said.[23]

After a year of combat, Sepi returned to Fort Carson, Colorado, where life seemed dull and regimented and the soldiers drank heavily. After he was arrested for underage driving under the influence, he was ordered to complete drug and alcohol education and counseling. Feeling lost after his discharge, he lived in a room in a rundown area of Las Vegas and survived with menial jobs. His alcohol counselor recognized his PTSD symptoms—adrenaline rushes, jumpiness, nightmares, and excessive alcohol use. Although his counselor directed him to get help from a VA hospital, Sepi did not follow through because of his twelve-hour shifts at a bottling plant.[24]

When Sepi's public defender asked him about his war experiences, she learned about one incident in which his unit singled out the wrong house during a mission. Assigned to search about a hundred targets, they set off C-4 plastic explosives at each address to stun the residents into submission. They entered the yard of one house and found an Iraqi sitting in his car. When he got out of this vehicle, the soldiers realized that he was on fire. He stumbled around the yard, collapsed, and died. Afterward, Sepi and his unit discovered it had been the wrong house. The image of the dying man haunted Sepi.

Law enforcement officials accepted Sepi's story of self-defense in the Las Vegas incident, in part because both victims were gang members. Sepi's lawyer worked out an arrangement by which the charges would be dismissed after he successfully completed the substance abuse and PTSD treatment programs. He did complete his treatment and learned how to deal with his anger, sadness, anxiety, and guilt. He no longer owns guns, and he is employed.[25] Sepi's case represented a classic overreaction to a threatening situation. The charges against him were dropped and he has since been successfully rehabilitated in part because his case was handled in a thorough and sensitive manner.

In a bizarre case taking place in January, 2005, Andres Raya, a former marine who spent seven months in combat in Iraq, entered a liquor store in Ceres, California, with a semiautomatic rifle under his poncho and demanded that the clerk call 911. He waited outside, and when the police arrived, he began firing, killing one officer and wounding another. As he fled, he was shot and killed by the police. Although he apparently had never been screened for or diagnosed with PTSD, his father believed that his son suffered from the disorder. Raya began screaming in his sleep after he returned from war. "After Iraq," his father said, "he wasn't Andy anymore."[26] An autopsy found cocaine in Raya's system. Investigators speculated that the nineteen-year-old veteran wanted to die in what police call "suicide by cop" because he faced redeployment and didn't want to return to combat. Why Raya behaved as he did remains unclear, although his crime included elements that are common to the crimes of people with combat experience—substance abuse, access to weapons, desperate and impulsive behavior, suicidal impulses, possible depression, and PTSD symptoms.

NONINTIMATE RELATIONSHIP HOMICIDE

James Gregg, a national guardsman who served in combat in Iraq, was convicted of murdering an acquaintance in July, 2004. His insanity plea based on PTSD was rejected. Although his war experience was taken into account by the trial court during sentencing, he received a prison sentence of twenty-one years. His conviction was affirmed on appeal.[27] Gregg joined the National Guard at the age of eighteen, while he was studying at a technical school with the goal of becoming a diesel mechanic. His combat engineering company was deployed to Iraq in the spring of 2003. After building a bridge across the Tigris River, his company took on infantry duties. Gregg estimated that he searched more than ten thousand vehicles and fired more than a thousand rounds. A psychologist who treated him said that Gregg found checkpoint duty unbearable. Iraqi civilians would bring their dead or wounded to the checkpoint and would blame those at the gate for what had happened. He began to contemplate suicide and volunteer for dangerous missions. His superior officer instructed him never to hesitate when he perceived a threat because "if you hesitate, you're dead."[28]

After returning to South Dakota following his discharge, Gregg began drinking heavily to ease his stress. On the evening of July 3, 2004, he was spending time on the Crow Creek Reservation with friends. He was drinking heavily. At one point in the evening, he engaged in a physical fight with two other men concerning the attentions of a woman who had rejected him.[29] Later, Gregg drove to the neighborhood where one of the men lived. When the man opened the door to his truck, Gregg shot and killed him. Gregg testified at his trial that he thought the man was going for a weapon and started shooting to stop him, as he was trained to do in combat.[30]

He fled the scene, and when a SWAT team tracked him down, he pointed the gun at himself. In response to his lawyer's question at trial about why he wanted to kill himself, Gregg replied, "Because it felt like Iraq had come back. I felt hopeless. . . . I didn't want this to happen. I never wanted to shoot him . . . never wanted to hurt him. Everything happened just so fast. . . . It was almost instinct that I had to protect myself."[31] Gregg's lawyer presented PTSD as a defense. Mental health experts for the defense testified that "PTSD was the driving force behind Mr. Gregg's actions." After having suffered a severe beating, they said, he experienced an exaggerated "startle reaction," when the man reached for his car door. In one courtroom exchange, the prosecutor asked Gregg whether military trainers try to strengthen soldiers' minds. Gregg replied, "They actually break down your mind. . . . They break down your mind, and then they try to build you back up." "Into a killer?" the prosecutor asked. "Yes," Gregg answered.[32]

The jury found Gregg guilty of second-degree murder but not first-degree murder, leading the trial judge to remark that Gregg had "dodged a bullet, so to speak." Although the judge openly took into account Gregg's combat experience, he indicated that neither Gregg's military service nor his PTSD warranted "downward departures" from the federal sentencing guidelines. The judge sentenced him to more than twice the mandatory minimum sentence. Gregg reportedly has been placed on suicide watch in prison several times.[33] Gregg's appeal, which was turned down, raised no claim about combat PTSD.

Whether or not Gregg deserved a different result based on his defense at trial or more leniency in sentencing based on his PTSD symptoms, a connection between his combat experience and his crime is evident. The use of PTSD as a defense failed to persuade the jury and judge enough to produce a result like Sepi's. The factual circumstances of the two cases, however, are very different, and Gregg did not have the benefit of so many favorable circumstances. Unlike Sepi, Gregg took the initial aggressive action and went looking for his victim. His victim was not an armed gang member preying on innocent victims. Criminal cases turn on their facts, and legal defenses are no stronger than the evidence that gives them credibility in the eyes of jurors and judges.

INTIMATE RELATIONSHIP MURDERS

Murders that stem from intimate relationships tend to generate a great deal of media attention; murders by veterans in this category are no exception. Even though the percentage of such murders committed by veterans within the January 13, 2008, *Times* report is less than one-fifth, which is less than other types of homicides, such as murders of strangers (35.2 percent) or murders of friends and acquaintances (23 percent), murders taking place within intimate relationships receive far more coverage. Perhaps the conflicting emotional entanglements, the vulnerable victims, or the fascination with details of romantic relationships turned bitter generate interest. Another compelling factor is the plight of victims trapped in situations in which they are powerless to escape from violence. When veterans return home with PTSD and other mental illnesses, the first battleground is often the home. The troubled veteran, plagued by nightmares, anger, anxiety, depression, or hypervigilance, often takes out his problems on those close at hand or turns to substance abuse within the home. Family members may be the only people who know about the problems and the only ones in a position to get help for the veteran.

If a relationship becomes strained, either for reasons that existed at the time the veteran returned, such as an impending breakup, or for reasons that develop after the return, the situation can become perilous. Often economic pressures or alcohol abuse heighten the veteran's stress. It is not surprising that the home is the place where the stress, frustration, and turmoil of readjusting to civilian life play out. The potential victims need protection, and the veteran needs outside help to cope with varied, complex problems. Although many of the violent situations have taken place in the homes of veterans who have been discharged, some have taken place on or near military bases while combat veterans are still in the service.

Sgt. William Edwards's murder of his wife, Sgt. Erin Edwards, in July 2004 is a case in point. Not long after the couple returned to a Texas army base early in 2004 after separate deployments in Iraq, William violently assaulted Erin. The four-year marriage had been troubled, and after a year in Iraq, Erin Edwards had gained enough confidence to end it. She had told her husband that she wanted a divorce. When they had a disagreement about a custody arrangement, he beat her violently. She privately arranged for transfer to a New York base, pressed charges, and obtained a protective order. She sent her children to her mother's home and received assurance that William would not be permitted to leave the base alone. Although William had been confined to the base, he repeatedly left it unescorted. Erin returned to court to make the protection order permanent. Her husband assured the court that he would not touch her physically. She stated in court that she was transferring and moving with the children. This was the first time her husband had heard about her plans, and he was visibly upset. The following morning William Edwards skipped his anger-management class, slipped off the base alone, drove to his wife's house, and, after a struggle, shot and killed her before killing himself. An investigation later revealed that necessary steps had not been taken to confine William Edwards to the base.[34]

The Terrasas case provides another example. One evening in December 2002, Sgt. Jared Terrasas was drunk and angry following a telephone conversation about the looming war in Iraq. Venting his anger, he struck his wife. He was arrested but then was deployed to Iraq. The pending domestic violence prosecution was delayed until his return. On his return, he pleaded guilty to the charge and was ordered to participate in a sixteen-week batterer intervention program run by the Marine Corps. After a few classes, Terrasas was deployed again to Iraq, despite the Lautenberg Amendment, a 1996 statute that forbids offenders convicted of domestic violence misdemeanors from carrying firearms, with no exception for military personnel. When he returned, he completed the batterers program but admitted to police when they responded to a domestic argument that he suffered from "postwar traumatic syndrome." Apparently, he did not seek mental health counseling. Several months after returning from his second deployment, Terrasas was charged with the murder of his seven-month old son, who died of a brain injury. After a plea agreement, he was sentenced to seven years in prison for felony child endangerment, although he did not admit abusing his child.[35]

These examples of PTSD-related murders demonstrate how irrational behavior can result from relationship stress that, under normal circumstances, might be resolved without violence.

MURDER-SUICIDES

The Edwards case, discussed previously, is a classic example of a homicide followed by suicide. Based on the available information, it is difficult to find distinguishing features between intimate murders followed by suicide and those not followed by suicide. Because many veterans who commit murder may have had undiagnosed or partial PTSD rather than diagnosed PTSD, in some cases individual mental health factors have not been assessed closely enough to explain the suicides.

The perpetrator of another murder-suicide, Sgt. Jon Trevino, a medic with a history of mental health problems, including PTSD, was repeatedly deployed to Iraq and Afghanistan. Although his prognosis indicated that his PTSD was treatable and that he could handle his job as an aeromedical evacuation technician in a war zone, he had trouble dealing with the carnage that he experienced. When he returned from his second deployment to Iraq, he acknowledged having "serious problems" dealing with his wife and feeling "panicky or anxious." He was immediately restricted from operational duty and treated. His wife's family noted, however, that he was profoundly changed and that he acted threatened and paranoid. His behavior was erratic, and his temper was unpredictable. He struck his wife at least once before the fatal incident. Finally, his marriage frayed, and his mental health substantially deteriorated. He burst in on his wife one night in 2006, shooting and killing her, and taking his own life, all in front of her nine-year-old son.[36]

Although no statistics on homicides charged to veterans have been released since January 2008, the *Washington Post* reported in mid-2009 that the rate of violent crimes in the hometowns of veterans who served with a Fort Carson, Colorado, combat brigade were exceptionally high. The report indicated a murder rate among veterans of the brigade that was 114 times that of Colorado Springs, a city adjacent to Fort Carson.[37]

In view of the lack of statistical information at this time concerning the total number of homicides and other violent crimes committed by or charged to veterans and the lack of sound comparative statistics with nonveteran populations, it is not possible to reach firm conclusions. It seems likely that additional violent crimes, including homicides, have been charged or committed since January 2008. However, exaggerating the risk of violence by returning veterans, as has happened in the past, is not appropriate. Neither is it appropriate to ignore the evidence of violent criminal activity involving veterans of the Iraq and Afghanistan Wars because, regardless of comparisons with respect to nonveterans, individual cases point to serious problems attributable to the combination of combat, PTSD, and criminal activity.

The dynamics of domestic violence homicides and murder-suicide in domestic situations have been the subject of numerous studies and a great deal of literature.[38] Intimate homicides occur in civilian society among people who have had neither military experience nor PTSD. In those instances, they result from other causative factors. It is unlikely that homicides that arise in the military setting are exclusively the product of combat PTSD. If combat PTSD is a triggering or contributing factor in the causal mix, however, the homicides are a relevant subject. Estimates of current rates of PTSD range from 20–35 percent or even higher, and indications are that these figures will continue to grow over time.

These compelling personal stories of homicide and murder-suicide reveal clear evidence of combat stress. In some situations, such as vehicular homicide or stranger homicide involving overreaction to perceived threats, alcohol abuse and hypervigilance are obvious factors. For crimes against spouses, partners, and children, the impact of PTSD is part of a complex pattern but, nonetheless, clear and unmistakable. There can be no doubt that the stresses involved in the cycles of deployment, combat, return, and redeployment have contributed heavily to development of mental health problems, notably PTSD, and ultimately to criminal behavior, which too often is violent.

Early indications are that PTSD will be extensively used in connection with criminal defenses involving Iraq and Afghanistan veterans. So far, some veterans have been successful in demonstrating the contributory or causative role of PTSD whereas others have not. The court system does not traditionally welcome mental health excuses or defenses for crimes committed. The increased awareness of the results of combat PTSD, however, may result in greater acceptance and understanding.

9

Women's War

The Faces of PTSD

The role of women in war has undergone dramatic changes during the Afghanistan and Iraq Wars. Nearly 214,000 women are on active duty, and since 2001, approximately 240,000 women (about 11 percent of the military) have been deployed to war zones.[1] When these figures are compared with the number of women who served in Vietnam—7,500—and the number of women who were deployed to the Gulf War in the early 1990s—41,000—the historic dimension of women's role today is apparent.[2] In today's wars, one of every ten U.S. soldiers in the war zones is female. Moreover, as of 2009, "More women have fought and died in Iraq than in all the wars since World War II put together."[3] In addition to suffering injuries and death, an unprecedented number of women have been exposed to higher levels of stress than they have ever experienced before in wartime. Not surprisingly, as the opportunities for women have expanded and diversified so have the risks of death, injury, and suffering.

Although the Pentagon still technically bans women from serving in ground combat, the nature of the current wars places women directly in the line of fire. Women typically carry out dangerous missions, including driving or guarding combat patrols or convoys, raiding houses, searching and arresting insurgents, and other jobs that expose them equally with men to enemy fire, grenades, and explosive devices.[4] The growing number of female soldiers deployed brings with it new, important, and serious problems. One such problem is that, not only are female soldiers exposed to the same combat trauma as men, they are also exposed to military sexual trauma.

Although the total number of women deployed has increased substantially, women are nearly always a small minority in their platoons and companies. As a result, women are relatively isolated and vulnerable to abuse within the dominant male culture that still prevails in the services. Military culture has not yet matured to the point at which an infrastructure is in place to offer protection, to encourage and process complaints fairly, and importantly, to prevent MST. Suffering sexual abuse at the hands of men who serve as their superior officers is a critical problem. Victims are left feeling like they have no one to report the abuse to and nowhere to turn. The dual stress of combat and sexual trauma is wreaking havoc on female soldiers and producing record levels of PTSD in women.[5]

The focus of this and the next chapter is on the burdens that women, both military and civilian, bear in modern warfare that involve courts and the criminal justice system. These burdens include the domestic violence that results from the readjustment problems of their military spouses as well as the stress of exposure to combat conditions and the persisting problem of MST.

HOW COMBAT PTSD AFFECTS WOMEN

Women are traditionally affected by PTSD secondarily, as partners of deployed soldiers and veterans. While their partners are deployed, they are on their own to face the personal, economic, and social challenges of caring for themselves and their families. They also encounter problems when their partners return, often with physical or mental health disabilities. Beyond that, homecoming, while a respite from anxiety and uncertainty, brings stress and strife that often erupts in domestic violence.

Second, PTSD affects women by means of the combat stress of war. As greater numbers of women serve in combat zones, they face hardship, trauma, and stress on a variety of fronts as soldiers and later as veterans. They often confront the stress of combat while trying to manage their relationship and family problems from a distance. Combat exposure can be traumatic for women for all the same reasons as it is so for men.

Finally, PTSD affects military women who experience sexual trauma during their service. Many female (and some male) soldiers endure the trauma of sexual abuse—ranging from harassment to sexual assault. As an extension of that problem (and almost serious enough to being considered a category of stress and trauma in itself), they face bureaucratic obstacles to reporting the abuse, achieving justice, and securing safety in the future. The hurdles are often so high that they are discouraged from reporting their MST. If they choose to report those who abuse them—sometimes their superior officers—they face verbal abuse and humiliation as well as risk to their military careers and, thus, their livelihood.

One caveat is important. It would be a disservice to women in the military to overemphasize the victimhood role of female soldiers and veterans. Beyond question, women handle their assignments with equal or greater competence, courage, and determination. They are by no means easily victimized.[6] Military culture, however, has not yet changed sufficiently to guarantee them the basic safety, dignity, and respect they are due. Physical and sexual abuse of women is a serious global public health problem, especially in wartime, and exposure within the military is no exception. Before discussing these multiple exposures to PTSD, a brief look at the prevalence of the disorder in women is relevant.

PREVALENCE OF PTSD IN WOMEN

Differences exist in the prevalence of PTSD in men and women. Many survey studies done by epidemiologists, whose field is the health of populations, reveal that PTSD in general is twice as common in women than in men.[7] In addition, differences exist in the type of traumas that cause PTSD in men and women, the way the disorder presents itself, and the conditions that accompany it.

A comprehensive review of 290 studies conducted between 1980 and 2005 appeared in the *Psychological Bulletin*, a publication of the APA, in 2006.[8] According to that APA publication, males experience more traumatic events than females in the services, but females are more likely to meet diagnostic criteria for PTSD. Female soldiers, however, are more likely to have experienced sexual assault and childhood sexual abuse. Sexual trauma may cause more emotional suffering and is more likely to contribute to a PTSD diagnosis than are nonsexual traumatic events. The review also noted, "PTSD may be diagnosed more in women in part because of the criteria used to define it. Cognitive and emotional responses to traumatic events make a diagnosis of PTSD more likely. So even though men may experience more traumas, they do not seem to have the same emotional responses, such as fear or anxiety, with respect to traumatic events."[9]

The authors of the review noted that one reason why men may not fit the current diagnostic criteria of PTSD is that their symptoms may manifest themselves differently. Males were less likely to report anxiety or depression but more likely to report behavioral problems, such as irritability, anger, violence, or drug abuse.

Another report on the existing studies makes a subtle point. Not only is PTSD twice as prevalent in women in the general population, but women exposed to trauma are twice as likely to develop PTSD even when multiple traumatic events and sex differences in types of trauma are considered. The report also stated that men with PTSD were significantly more likely to exhibit a substance abuse disorder and/or antisocial personality disorder at the same time. These findings corroborate findings of an earlier national comorbidity survey that reported men with lifetime PTSD showed higher rates of substance abuse disorder and conduct disorder than women with lifetime PTSD.[10] This finding may be relevant to the question of violent behavior by males. That is, although women suffer from PTSD symptoms that affect their lives, they are not as likely to suffer from other disorders that cause them to engage in violent criminal behavior, ranging from vehicular homicide (usually involving substance abuse) to assault and murder (often involving substance abuse and conduct disorder). In addition women display a much greater PTSD response to assaultive violence than men do. This accounts for much of the differential between the rates of PTSD in women and men. Not only do women experience more symptoms than men, but they also have a longer course of illness—thirty-five months compared with only nine months for men. In the case of direct traumas, the duration increases to sixty months in women and twenty-four in men. Lifetime prevalence of PTSD in women is approximately twice as high as in men.[11]

PTSD IMPACT ON MILITARY SPOUSES

As I indicated previously, the impact of PTSD is felt during two phases of service—deployment and post-deployment. Both phases are receiving more study as a result of the Iraq and Afghanistan experience. Although I will focus mainly on the second phase, a few words are in order on the first. In January 2010, the *New England Journal of Medicine* reported the results of an extensive study based on examination of electronic medical-record data for all outpatient medical visits between January 1, 2003, and December 31, 2006, by wives of active-duty army personnel.[12] The study sample included 6,585,224 outpatient visits by 250,626 wives, of whom more than one-third had at least one mental health diagnosis during the four-year period. The wives were grouped into two categories: those whose husbands were deployed at the time of the visit and those whose husbands were not. The most common diagnoses were depression, anxiety, sleep disorder, acute stress reaction, and adjustment disorder. Nearly 37 percent of the women whose husbands were deployed and 30.5 percent of those whose husbands were home were diagnosed with mental health disorders.

Not surprisingly, the study report confirmed mental health research involving past warfare that said frequent or extended deployment leads to increased stress, anxiety, and depression among families of soldiers as well as among the personnel themselves. The authors noted that studies indicate that a large proportion of U.S. soldiers returning from Iraq and Afghanistan show considerable mental health problems but that the "psychosocial burden on families of deployed military personnel is less well understood and perhaps not comparable to that of previous deployments, given current service conditions." They commented, "Besides fear for the safety of their loved ones, spouses of deployed personnel often face challenges of maintaining a household, coping as a single parent, and experiencing marital strain due to a deployment-induced separation of an uncertain duration. Studies examining the effects of deployment on spouses have shown increased rates of marital dissatisfaction, unemployment, divorce, and declining emotional health."[13]

The last point is a crucial one. Although PTSD does not appear to be a factor in the spouses' mental health problems during deployment, it is a factor when the returning husband exhibits the symptoms of PTSD. The mental health problems of spouses, in addition to the veterans' psychological problems, contribute to setting the stage for troubled relationships that often explode into marital discord, domestic violence, divorce, and sometimes lethal violence. In examining a problem as complex as the effect of combat PTSD on marriage and family, it is essential to consider the whole family situation and all stressors that impact it. When the seeds of marital unrest are combined with the diminished capacity of both spouses to readjust to the relationship and to solve all the problems that exist, the volatile situation may escalate to the point of combustion.

Matthew J. Friedman, a psychiatrist specializing in PTSD, commented in the *New England Journal of Medicine*, "Since the family is the major source of social support, improvement in the mental health of spouses and children should also pay dividends in improving the mental health of troops throughout the deployment cycle." Friedman emphasized that the mental health problems of deployed soldiers and their families represented public health problems and that programs developed to prevent mental health problems among family members may well prevent psychiatric morbidity among the troops themselves.[14]

I turn next to the problems of return and readjustment, which are more directly identified with combat PTSD. It has been well known for a long time that veterans' development of PTSD following exposure to combat affects their marriages and family relationships and the mental health of their family members. A comprehensive report published in 2003 provides an extensive review of literature on the subject. The authors of the report called the impact of veterans' PTSD on spouses "secondary traumatization."[15] Wives of veterans with PTSD are subjected to a significant chronic stressor merely by living in close proximity with a person who suffers a pathological response to trauma. Beyond that, wives sometimes identify so strongly with their veteran husbands that they are secondarily exposed to the trauma. Most studies discuss problems of female military spouses. As the number of female veterans increases, new studies of male military spouses will be needed; information on this subject is currently inadequate.

Research shows that the experience of living with someone who has PTSD makes a person more susceptible to developing PTSD from unrelated trauma. Couples often find it impossible to reestablish their prewartime relationship. During the veteran's absence, wives often become more independent and more assertive as heads of household. The readjustment process can be difficult or impossible if the veteran is unable to adapt to the change. PTSD hampers the veteran's capacity to adapt to the original relationship, much less the changed one. Also, the veteran may have difficulty, physically or psychologically, resuming some aspects of the relationship responsibilities, as expected by his partner.[16]

The authors of the 2003 report note important observations gleaned from their examination of the literature. For example, when combat violence leads to PTSD in the veteran, it affects the veteran's intimate relationships in many ways. Emotional numbing and withdrawal are particularly damaging to relationships.

Emotional withdrawal, more than any other symptom, has led wives to seek separation or divorce. Angry outbursts are damaging as well. Some studies show that veterans are more likely to have only a few extremely violent and frightening abusive episodes than to exhibit the chronic, ongoing abusive tendencies typical in the domestic violence literature. Other studies, however, suggest a chronic atmosphere of violence within veterans' homes.[17]

As a reference point, a fairly standard definition of domestic or family violence is as "an incident resulting in physical harm, bodily injury or assault, or an act of threatened violence that constitutes fear of imminent physical harm, bodily injury, or assault between family or household members."[18] Although the definition of the crime of domestic violence varies somewhat from jurisdiction to jurisdiction, it typically is more general than definitions of many other crimes.[19] The crime of family violence, however, was created broadly to give police some latitude in taking appropriate protective steps in volatile and potentially dangerous situations. The parameters of the law enable police to take protective action and, in fact, generally require police not to ignore the situation even if the complainant has changed her or his mind.

In this context, it becomes easier to understand the pattern of domestic violence that is unfolding as veterans of Iraq and Afghanistan return home. The individual examples of violence—even the most extreme violence—begin to fit together into a recognizable configuration even though most media reports do not give sufficient detail for observers to understand all the factors in each case. Experts agree that the increasing number of veterans with PTSD raises the risk of domestic violence in families across the United States.[20] Research at the VA has established that male veterans with PTSD are two or three times more likely than veterans without the disorder to engage in intimate partner violence. Domestic violence frequently involves behavior that results in other criminal charges, such as assault, kidnapping, or murder. Behavior that fits within the general definition of domestic violence constitutes a crime in itself in all states, despite some variations among the laws.[21]

Many of the illustrative cases discussed previously in which veterans with PTSD symptoms or fully diagnosed PTSD committed murders of intimate family members, including wives, partners, or children, are relevant here. Most of the cases arose from combinations of combat exposure, PTSD, marriage instability, marriage disintegration, domestic violence, and/or substance abuse.

WOMEN WARRIORS: THE STRESS OF COMBAT

Vivienne Pacquette, a fifty-two-year-old noncommissioned officer who served two tours in Iraq and more than twenty years in the army, retired from the military in 2006. She continues to suffer from PTSD, and to cope with her disorder she avoids conversations with her sons, going out with her husband, and therapy sessions in which she has to "talk about seeing the reds and whites of her friends' insides after a mortar attack." After she enlisted in the 1980s, men often told Pacquette that women did not belong in the military. "Women were seen as weak and whiny," she said. She anticipated and later learned, however, that war was an equalizer. In early October 2004, her convoy of thirty vehicles was traveling from Kuwait to Mosul, Iraq, a violent city at the time. They were hit three times with roadside bombs, one exploding two hundred feet from Pacquette's unarmored Humvee. Two months later, a suicide bomber walked into a mess tent at a base across the street from hers and blew himself up, killing twenty-five people. Following that attack, in 2004 three of her friends were killed in a mortar attack on her motor pool.[22]

A military physician diagnosed Pacquette with PTSD in March 2005, but she refused treatment so that no one would know. She kept the disorder symptoms hidden during her time in Iraq. She still struggles with the symptoms. Back home, she distanced herself from family and friends, although her husband is steadfast in his support. Her therapist comments that rage, paranoia, and aggression are more accepted in men; women are expected to resume their domestic routines immediately upon arrival home. Women often feel ashamed and guilty because "they're not supposed to punch a wall, they're not supposed to get aggressive with their spouse."[23]

Female veterans of the Iraq War struggle with their own need for isolation. Nancy Schiliro, a twenty-nine-year-old who lost an eye as a result of a mortar attack in 2005, rarely left a darkened garage for nearly two years after returning home. Aimee Sherrod, also twenty-nine years old, had to limit the number of trips that she took outside her house. She avoided taking her son to places such as Chuck E. Cheese, where the arcade's bells made her jumpy. She couldn't take him to a park either because she felt uncomfortable in open spaces.[24] Many women struggle with the day-to-day activities of coming home from war just as their male counterparts do.

Another female veteran, Kristine Wise, experienced flashbacks when she saw road signs on her drive from San Diego to Bakersfield the first day after she returned from an eight-month deployment in Iraq. Her depression and panic attacks started before her discharge, but she had a difficult time convincing the VA to take her symptoms seriously. "They had a hard time comprehending I was a combat vet and didn't treat me with the same respect" they showed when dealing with men. She is now rated 10 percent disabled for PTSD.[25]

Although women are still technically prohibited from serving in combat, they are serving in forward positions and are many times exposed to the same traumas as men are.[26] As of late 2009, 11,713 women soldiers have been diagnosed with PTSD. Although women soldiers have been exposed to the same combat trauma as the men have, the VA is only in the early stages of fully acknowledging their gender-specific needs.[27] Since the number of women enlisting in the U.S. military has doubled in the past thirty years—and is expected to double again in the next ten years—the need for the VA health-care system to educate its staff and prepare for the problems of women is urgent.

Women's combat experiences are emerging in the literature about the Iraq and Afghanistan Wars as the deployment of U.S. troops continues. In addition to the media news stories featuring women veterans and soldiers, several books have appeared. Some, including Kirsten Holmstedt's *Band of Sisters: American Women at War in Iraq*, report mostly positive stories about women's experiences in wartime. Holmstedt's 2007 chronicle of the combat experiences of eleven women soldiers in Iraq presents a positive view of women's role in combat, with little mention of MST.[28] Another illuminating book about women's experiences in Iraq, however, emphasizes the prevalence of sexual trauma. In *The Lonely Soldier: The Private War of Women Serving in Iraq*, Helen Benedict portrays military sexual trauma as endemic and devastating to a large percentage of women soldiers.[29]

Women veterans have only recently started to turn to VA hospitals for diagnosis and treatment of their mental health problems. Expertise in counseling is developing as the number of women veterans with PTSD increases. In-depth reports about the unique experiences of women with combat PTSD are not yet available. A time lag commonly exists in this field because the symptoms of PTSD are not generally recognized quickly. Even when they are, veterans often delay getting help. Women typically face more obstacles than men in getting help because, as mentioned before, they are discouraged from even reporting harassment or assault. It is encouraging that the American Medical Association

(AMA) published the results of PTSD screening in a general sample of female patients in 2004.[30]

The AMA report reached some tentative conclusions about women's PTSD based on combat in Iraq and Afghanistan. None of them are surprising. Symptoms of PTSD are common in women treated at VA facilities. PTSD is associated with self-reported mental and physical health problems and poor health in these patients. Female veterans are a growing and understudied group that has been exposed to significant trauma. A national survey reported that 23 percent of female veterans were sexually assaulted during their military duty. Another survey reported that 48 percent of female veterans were assaulted during their military service. More than half of those reporting rape had been raped more than once. Women reported significant duty-related combat trauma, and many of them suffered trauma prior to their military experience that may have predisposed them to developing PTSD. As I noted earlier, the fact that women suffer PTSD at a rate of double that of males indicates that as women are increasingly exposed to combat trauma, the rate of resulting PTSD will be extremely high. Since women veterans tend to underuse VA facilities, at least at this point, and tend to delay seeking help even more than males do, it is reasonable to expect a significant increase in PTSD cases being reported by women in future years.

CRIMINAL CONNECTION

The extent to which women veterans with PTSD engage in criminal behavior remains an open question. Interviews with counselors who work with women indicate that alcohol and drug use among those with the disorder is prevalent. Alcohol and drug abuse brings inevitable contact with the criminal justice system. Soldiers and veterans have turned to alcohol in particular for what is euphemistically called self-medication for their symptoms, and certainly, women are no exception to this self-defeating behavior.[31] Active-duty military are struggling with substance abuse of all forms at disturbing rates. A 2010 report showed, for example, that misuse of prescription drugs among active-duty military personnel nearly tripled from 2005 to 2008 and that misuse of prescription drugs is two to four times greater in the military than in the general population.[32] Although drug and alcohol problems often manifest themselves after reentry into society, it is clear that substance abuse occurs during active duty. Alcohol and substance abuse are particularly noted in connection with both military sexual trauma and combat trauma.[33]

Although arrests for driving while intoxicated and drug possession do not make headlines and, therefore, are likely to escape attention, the combination of PTSD, substance abuse, and homelessness is certain to increase the number of veterans who appear in criminal court. Because women's PTSD symptoms appear to be different from men's, women with the disorder may commit far fewer violent crimes than men who have it. It is noteworthy that only one of the homicides compiled in the January 13, 2008, *Times* article discussed in chapter 8 involved a female veteran, Rebecca Braswell, a member of the Navy Seabees who served in Iraq. Braswell was convicted of the first-degree murder of her ex-husband. Her motive apparently stemmed from a bitter court custody fight concerning their daughter. No reference to PTSD or her military service experiences were made in news reports.[34] The PTSD differential between men and women plus general underreporting of minor criminal activity, as opposed to high publicity murders and other violent crimes, may account for a general lack of information about women veterans' post-deployment criminal activity.

FINAL OBSERVATIONS

In addition to the total number of female soldiers in the military, the proportion of female soldiers in individual units is important because women's isolation within their units is an important factor in the occurrence of MST. As the proportion of women in units increases, the risk of all forms of abuse should decrease. Not only will women find female colleagues with whom to share close living quarters, but their sheer numbers in relation to the numbers of men likely also will bring about gradual change in the male-dominated culture. Although this change may not happen until the proportion of women grows considerably, even small gains may discourage MST. Increasing the number of female officers will also accelerate change.

As the total number and unit-by-unit proportion of women in the military increase, other positive changes are likely to occur. These changes should lead to more reporting of harassment and assault, more follow-up on complaints, more positive outcomes of investigations and hearings concerning alleged abuses, and more satisfactory treatment for victims. Offenders who are charged with abuse should be held accountable rather than being summarily exculpated. The increased proportion of women at all levels of service will discourage the practice of transferring women who report sexual assault and will result in displacement of the male assailants instead. Although studies show that male soldiers are sometimes harassed and assaulted as well, as in the general society, women are the principal targets. A gradual feminization of military culture should benefit male victims as well.

10

Running the Gauntlet

MST and Sexual Violence Against Women Warriors

Despite the vast underreporting of MST, statistics that have come to light during the Iraq and Afghanistan Wars have consistently been alarming.[1] A comprehensive report issued in 2003 indicated that, whereas one in six women in civilian life experience sexual assault, the ratio climbs to one in three in military life.[2] A Department of Defense report issued in 2008 indicated that nearly three thousand military sexual assaults were reported in that year, and 163 were reported among forces in Iraq and Afghanistan.[3] Seventy-nine percent of women serving in the military since Vietnam reported experiences of sexual harassment.[4] Seventy-one percent of women and 4 percent of men in a sample of veterans seeking VA disability benefits for PTSD reported an in-service sexual assault.[5] Sexual assaults in the military are frequently not isolated incidents and often involve more than one perpetrator—37 percent of women veterans acknowledging rape during military service report multiple rapes and 14 percent of those raped report gang rape experiences.[6] Judged even by conservative standards, MST is a military and societal problem of epidemic proportions. Although both men and women are victims, servicewomen are at far greater risk. MST is a systemic problem exacerbated by higher numbers of women recruits entering an institution that continues to stereotype them while failing to protect them from either harm or retribution if they choose to report abuse.[7]

A recent Pentagon report issued in January 2012 not only confirmed the previous grave estimates of the military's sexual assault problem but raised the assessment of the problem to new heights. On January 19 of this year, Defense Secretary Leon Panetta reported that, consistent with the statistics since 2006, 3,191 reports of sexual assault throughout the military were made during 2011. Secretary Panetta, however, followed that announcement, which was confirmed in the Pentagon report released the next day, with a startling assertion that "realistically, the estimate for assaults 'actually is closer to 19,000.'" He emphasized that "'we assume this is a very underreported crime,' and that incidents of sexual assault are roughly six times as high as reports of the crime." According to the report, "[w]hile women comprise 14 percent of the Army ranks, they account for 95 percent of all sex crime victims."[8]

According to the U.S. Army report, the rate of violent sexual crimes has gone up 64 percent since 2006. Since many victims of sexual assault say they do not report the crimes because they doubt that perpetrators will be prosecuted, the secretary announced an initiative to combat the problem, including providing better training to military prosecutors. Congressional reaction was mixed, with some lawmakers pointing out that some of the proposed initiatives would not improve the situation and that Congress had already mandated many of the newly-announced initiatives. An example was leaving complete discretion in the hands of investigating complaints. Another problem appears to be continuing a policy of transferring soldiers who have been assaulted, rather than the perpetrators, to new units.[9]

With these alarming new statistics and assessments in mind, along with the promise of increased action on the part of the military, it is useful to examine some background information. The Department of Defense defines MST as rape, sexual assault, and sexual harassment. Under this classification, sexual assault is any unwanted sexual contact, and rape is assault that proceeds to penetration. Sexual harassment involves sexual activity not including contact.[10] Although some studies, as well as civilian criminal law, use different terms and definitions, I will generally use the terms as defined by the military. When the distinction between rape and sexual assault is not material, however, I will use the term sexual assault as referring to both.

The subject of sexual violence in the U.S. military has been exhaustively studied during the past two decades. Since 1988 more than twenty task forces, commissions, panels, and other research groups have studied and issued reports on the subject.[11] The prevalence of sexual trauma experienced by women in the

military is conclusively established, and yet the problem persists. Further studies are too often substituted for action to alleviate and prevent the problem. An
examination of some of the many studies and reports reveals the extent of MST,
the risk factors, and the consequences, including several clearly defined barriers.

The results of a study of sexual harassment and assault as predictors of PTSD
among female veterans of the Persian Gulf War were published in 1998. A
Department of Veterans Affairs Medical Research Service award supported the
study.[12] Women in the U.S. Army were interviewed upon returning from the
war and again eighteen to twenty-four months later. The conclusions were clear.
Stated succinctly, the rates of sexual assault (7.3 percent), physical sexual harassment (33.1 percent), and verbal sexual harassment (66.2 percent) were higher
than those found in civilian and peacetime military samples. Sexual assault was
more likely to lead to PTSD symptoms than was combat exposure. The frequency of physical sexual harassment was significant in predicting PTSD.

The report noted that, until recently, studies of the relationship between
combat exposure and PTSD symptoms had focused primarily on men. The
NVVRS, completed in 1988 and discussed in chapter 6, made women another
important focus group. The findings of the NVVRS confirmed that women
with high levels of combat exposure had more PTSD symptoms after wartime
service than men did. The authors noted, however, that no study at that point
had addressed the comparative effects of concurrent combat exposure and sexual assault. The preliminary data showed that the impact of wartime sexual
assault may be more harmful than combat exposure in producing PTSD.[13]

Other findings from the NVVRS were significant, especially when viewed
in light of the far more extensive combat experience of women in Iraq and
Afghanistan. The way in which physical sexual harassment and combat exposure combine to produce psychological outcomes may differ among women in
the current conflicts. In the NVVRS, the frequency of physical sexual harassment was linked with several specific factors that served as predictors, such as
lack of leadership support, lack of social support, and intervening events, but
combat exposure was not so linked. Controlling for predictive factors lessened
the impact of harassment on the soldier's or veteran's psychological functioning but did not have any significant effect on combat stress.[14]

Sexual harassment may have more obvious predictors because it takes place
in an interpersonal context and often involves a perpetrator who is known to

the victim. The setting for the behavior is usually social or work-related, which produces social and economic implications. Because of these and other factors, harassment causes humiliation, social alienation, and vulnerability to secondary consequences, such as loss of social status or job opportunities. Social and economic factors have less significance in the experience of combat stress. Sexual harassment or assault may also have a greater bearing on post-discharge events such as the capacity to have meaningful personal relationships.[15]

Later studies have corroborated the well-known findings as to the prevalence of sexual violence in the military. For example, in 2003 the Department of Defense financed a report revealing that almost a third of a nationwide sample of female veterans who sought health care through the VA had suffered sexual assault or attempted sexual assault while they were in the service. Another study of sexual trauma occurring in the military was reported in 2003 in the *American Journal of Industrial Medicine*.[16] The Department of Defense publishes annual reports about the number of sexual trauma complaints.

These studies provide a foundation for examining current information about female soldiers' experiences in Iraq and Afghanistan. Many more reports of individual experiences are becoming available now given the increased number of women serving in the military. In light of the extensive studies to date, preliminary assessments suggest that the new information will corroborate what is already known about MST and its impact on the military. It is useful to examine what is known from the studies about the prevalence and consequences of military sexual violence both in service and after the return to civilian life.

WHAT IS KNOWN ABOUT MST
Disparity in Statistics
In addition to the underreporting of sexual assault, the definitions and methods of compiling statistics used by the Department of Defense, the military services, the VA, and independent study groups make assessment difficult. For example, the Department of Defense reported that the prevalence of sexual assault among female active-duty service members declined from 6 percent to 3 percent between 1996 and 2002. An article published in 2003 and based on a survey conducted by the VA assessed the rate of female veterans who had experienced sexual assault at 30 percent, the rate of multiple rapes at 20 percent, and the rate of gang rapes at 30 percent.[17] The disparity in assessment has

been attributed to the Defense Department's failure to adopt current research protocols concerning the protection of human subjects and the anonymity of those responding.[18]

Military Attitudes toward Women

Several studies have found that negative attitudes toward women in the military significantly predict tolerance of sexual harassment. A correlation exists between disrespect for women when off duty (such as visiting adult clubs) and intimate partner violence. Moreover, male cultural practices outside the workplace influence attitudes and behavior in the workplace. Risk factors abound in the military environment. They include young women entering male-dominated working groups at low levels of authority and in numbers that make them a small minority in individual units, sexual harassment by officers, and unwanted advances in sleeping quarters and on duty.[19] The male-dominated environment may produce competitive and even hostile feelings toward women, who may be seen as an unwelcome challenge to traditional male activity or leadership. The attitudes may also reflect pre-combat attitudes toward women held in some quarters of the general society.

Many aspects of life in combat zones amplify the level of hostile behavior toward women. These aspects include a lack of privacy during daily routines, insufficient lighting, isolation, and a sexually charged atmosphere resulting in part from the heightened emotions relating to the risk and danger of combat. In addition, platoon leaders hand out condoms even though sex between soldiers is banned, thus giving out mixed messages to the potential offenders, who often include officers. Sexually oriented materials that denigrate women reportedly are readily available in Iraq. In combat conditions, there is often a general lack of adequate medical care and testing services for sexually transmitted infections, HIV, and pregnancy. Shortages of emergency contraception and medication, mental health counselors and rape trauma specialists, chaplains, victim advocates, attorneys, and rape evidence kits are common, and the capability to conduct a thorough criminal investigation is often lacking.[20]

Reporting Deficiencies

A VA survey of female veterans indicated that only one-quarter reported a sexual assault incident to a ranking officer. One-third said they did not know how to report abuse, and one-fifth believed that rape was to be expected in the military service. Military victims fear that the assailant, who is often higher in rank and command, will be more likely to be believed. Many also accept rape myths and blame and thus experience the self-doubt common among rape victims. Intoxication of the offender, the victim, or both often plays a role in sexual assaults. Finally, victims often fail to report sexual assault because they cannot escape continued contact with the assailant in the course of military duties.[21]

The Role of Military Inaction

A 2004 Department of Defense task force report on care of victims acknowledged the shortage of medical care, services, and trauma treatment for sexual assault, especially in combat zones, but made no action plan to remedy the problem. The report neglected to include the sexual offender's behavior among the causes of sexual violence. That is, despite situational factors, such as those mentioned previously, perpetrators make conscious choices to commit the crimes. The Pentagon report contained neutral language and positions and raised questions about victims' responsibility and credibility. This suggests there is a cultural barrier to implementing measures to prevent sexual violence in the military context. A hopeful sign is that, for the first time, a 2005 Defense Department report characterized sexual assault as a "crime," rather as simply "inappropriate behavior."[22] The policy of characterizing sexual violence in criminal terms apparently continues to be carried out.

PTSD and Other Consequences

Many studies conducted during the past twenty-five years have convincingly established that sexual assault causes severe mental health problems and long-term physical health problems. Two-thirds of victims display symptoms of PTSD, which is often referred to as rape trauma in this context. Ninety percent of victims experience PTSD within a month of the assault, and one-third continue to display symptoms six months later.[23]

Women veterans who experience MST suffer many adverse effects, including high rates of PTSD, health problems, depression, and substance abuse. Many also report suffering from both childhood violence and post-military violence. Studies show that those who are assaulted on duty are more likely to report chronic health problems, use prescription medication for emotional problems, fail to complete higher education, and have low annual incomes. Whether those results are caused by or merely correlate with MST is uncertain. In any event, the victims' quality of life is adversely affected over the long term with limitations on their physical and emotional health, education and financial achievement, and social activities.[24] In short, violence against women who serve in the military is a serious public health concern.

A PERSONAL STORY: JULIA

Julia endured sexual harassment during her three years in the Army Reserve before deployment to Iraq. From the outset, the noncommissioned officer in charge had her in his sights. She soon heard that

> he had to bed every female he saw. As soon as I was in the unit, another officer pulled me aside and said to be careful. He has to have sex with every female. He got one pregnant, and they kicked her out but let him stay. So I stayed away from him. Then the other officer started asking me to stay at his house. He kept escalating the situation and said he was becoming a photographer and wanted to photograph me in civilian clothes off the base. He asked me to give him a massage. When I refused, he made life hard for me and tried to 'write me up.' That's military justice. They can write you up and take away your school . . . your promotion. Eventually, I told someone higher up. He said he'd take care of it but he didn't do anything. He was a buddy of the officer.

Since reserve drills were only one weekend a month, Julia was able to ignore the harassment. But when her unit was activated, it became much worse. "They have control of you 24/7," she said. "There's nowhere to run . . . no escape. When you go to bed, they're there. When you get up, they're there. When you go to eat, they're there. . . . When you go to shower, they're there."

The same officer continued to harass her. No help came from either the men or women in her unit.

> Most of the women seemed jealous, and they were tough on me. A lot of the men acted like high schoolers. They were just perpetual high schoolers. Then the battalion commander took advantage of it. He promised to

protect me if I'd be with him. I felt trapped. . . . I just gave in at this point. Everyone suspected what was going on. They hated the commander, and because they couldn't get to him, they took it out on me. They made my life hell. I couldn't talk to anyone. I couldn't trust anyone, and every time I said anything, I made it worse for myself.

I finally had a complete meltdown. I tried to kill myself. . . . I was alone one day in an office on another base. I loaded my weapon and pointed the muzzle at my heart. I really wanted to kill myself. I was reaching for the trigger when somebody walked in. They took me to the clinic. For a while I went to the clinic every week. . . . One of my supervisors complained that I was spending too much time there, so I had to stop going. After my breakdown, they investigated the officer, but it was just a cover-up. They got him for spreading rumors about me, not for harassment. He got a reprimand. I denied any relationship with the commander, though, because I was afraid. . . . I was afraid he'd get me killed or that it would just make things worse for me. He used to threaten that if I didn't do what he asked, he'd send me on convoys . . . and that was the way to get killed.

He thought I was lying about the suicide. He kept saying that he was the only one on my side . . . that everyone else hated me. I believed him. I realize now that it was really sexual assault.

During the rest of the deployment, Julia managed to hold herself together, but she was severely depressed. She would do her job and return to her room and sit in the dark. She could not escape the anxiety, depression, and panic attacks.

THE PRINCIPAL RISK FACTORS

The typical risk factors that encourage sexual assault fall roughly into four categories. First is the culture of military violence that tolerates or does not discourage sexual harassment. Officers and peers may tolerate behavior that denigrates women, both on and off duty, and unwanted low-level sexual contact, such as brushing or touching. Second is the physical military work environment, in which the units that female soldiers are assigned to may be otherwise all male. Resentment can result from women performing traditionally male jobs. Third is the off-duty base environment, where sleeping quarters may be shared by men and women. Women may have few places to go safely for personal routines or leisure activities without fear of harassment or assault. Fourth is unsupportive or offensive behavior of ranking officers. At the low end of the spectrum, officers may not provide support for women under their command, and in addition, they may require women to perform both sex-role stereotypical jobs and assigned jobs. At the high end of the scale, ranking officers may themselves engage in sexual harassment, sexual assault, or coerced sexual relationships, or they may allow others to do so. They may threaten women with formal military discipline if they do not perform sexual acts or offer exchanges of sex for privileges or promotion—or protection. Even nonoffending officers may fail to give adequate information about reporting abuse, provide protection, or prosecute offenders.

CASE HISTORIES

At this point the main sources of information about military sexual trauma taking place in Iraq and Afghanistan are individual case histories presented in books, news media reports, blogs, and websites. Some of these sources emphasize the widespread sexual abuse of women soldiers, whereas other reports by women mention sexual harassment only in passing or, in some instances, avoid the subject entirely. Based on the experience of professionals and the authenticity of individual case reports, it seems fair to state that the military environment is inhospitable and risky for women soldiers, especially when they are in combat and isolated in small numbers within predominantly male units.

The first major news media report about violence against women soldiers in Iraq and Afghanistan appeared in a feature story in the *New York Times* titled "The Women's War." The article reported on the experiences of ten women deployed in Iraq and gave background statistics on the prevalence of sexual assault.

The lead case history in that article was the story of Suzanne Swift, a twenty-one-year-old army specialist. Swift went absent without leave (AWOL) on January 9, 2006, two days before her unit, the Fifty-Fourth Military Police Company, based in Fort Lewis, Washington, was redeployed to Iraq. After hiding out for six months, she was arrested on June 11 and taken back to Fort Lewis for disciplinary procedures.[25]

Swift told investigators that she did not report for deployment because she had been sexually harassed repeatedly by three of her supervisors—in Kuwait, in Iraq, and after her return to Fort Lewis. She said she was suffering from PTSD as a result of her experience in the war together with sexual harassment. The event that was most distressing was her squad leader's conduct in Iraq. She claimed that he had propositioned her for sex on the first day in Iraq and that she was coerced into having a sexual relationship with him for four months. She claimed she was manipulated into having sex. When she finally ended the relationship, he retaliated by humiliating her in front of her fellow soldiers. Swift said that she had grown accustomed to "sexually loaded remarks from fellow enlisted soldiers," which happened "all the time." But harassment by superior officers was more oppressive because of her duty to obey them and the consequences of refusal.[26]

The army's investigation determined that Swift's charges against two of her superiors, including the one who demanded sex from her, could not be substantiated for lack of evidence. The squad leader had already been discharged by the time the investigation began and subsequently was outside the army's jurisdiction. The sergeant whom she said harassed her received a stridently worded reprimand and was transferred. Swift, in the meantime, was diagnosed with PTSD by a civilian psychiatrist within days of her failure to report and later by the army's mental health division at Fort Lewis. She said that she had nightmares and fits of hysterical crying. In interviews, she seemed detached and unwilling or unable to express anger or pain.[27]

Swift had a summary court-martial and pled guilty to "missing movement" and being absent without leave. Her rank was reduced to private, and she served a twenty-one-day sentence in military prison. To receive an honorable discharge, she decided to complete her five-year enlistment. Although she checked into the inpatient psychiatric ward on the base, she was quickly released to duty. She said she was trying to forget the PTSD but was drinking heavily in order to get by. As the article went to press, she was uncertain about her future.[28]

Based on Swift's personal account of what happened, it is possible to identify the first and fourth factors of the sexual abuse scenarios. Coercive behavior by superior officers was a major cause of her problems. Since the information available comes almost entirely from Swift herself, conclusions about the relationship between her combat service and harassment, on the one hand, and her PTSD and going AWOL, on the other, are tentative, although her story rings true. It is not uncommon in such cases to see denials by accused offenders followed by their exculpation by the military authorities. Many women veterans report that they experience little female bonding in the war zone, in part because there are so few women in most units and in part because having close women friends exposes women soldiers to further ridicule.

According to Abbie Pickett, a twenty-four-year-old combat specialist with the Wisconsin National Guard at the time she was interviewed, "You're one of three things in the military—a bitch, a whore or a dyke." Although Sara Corbett, the author of the *New York Times* article, reported that some women said they felt at ease with the men in their platoon and were treated respectfully, this tended to be most common among reserve and medical units in which sex ratios were more even. Several women gave credit to their commanders for creating and enforcing a "more egalitarian climate" in which sexual harassment was not permitted.[29]

Pickett did not experience that hospitable climate. In 2001, two years before she was deployed to Iraq, she had been sexually assaulted during a humanitarian assignment in Nicaragua. She was nineteen at the time of the incident and had been afraid to report it, especially since the offender was a superior officer. During her eleven months in Iraq, in a company of 140 men and nineteen women, she found that sexual harassment was common. It was more intense in a combat zone because there was no opportunity to escape from it. Whether she was waiting in food lines or carrying out her assignment—trying to fix the army's broken-down trucks—she was usually the only woman in sight and the object of constant persecution.

Pickett appears in one of the featured personal histories in Helen Benedict's *The Lonely Soldier*. Benedict expands on the details of Pickett's personal story to reveal a clear picture of the factors that contribute to sexual assault and resulting PTSD. Although there were nineteen women in Pickett's company, the women were usually divided among different convoys, leaving them mostly on their own. Although the male troops had the opportunity to develop collegial or bonding experiences, the women's isolation from one another made relationships far more difficult. In the book, Pickett is quoted as saying, "Female bonds are really important because sometimes you need to let your guard down and be yourself, instead of having to put on a mask for everyone. Soldiers are always fronting." For women, the lack of opportunity to cease "fronting" meant that "someday it's all going to crash."[30]

Pickett was aware that several officers, including her commanding officer, had engaged in illegal activity. When she was recommended for a Bronze Star with Valor, her commanding officer reportedly said that she would not receive the award under his command. She never received the award. After she reported the corruption she had witnessed, she became aware that the leaders were watching her closely. She was repeatedly accused of wrongdoing by her leadership, and she even started thinking about suicide.

Pickett was charged with an Article 15, a serious matter punishable by demotion by two ranks and up to two months in prison. The charge was based on a trivial matter, failure to check the oil and gas in her truck before starting it up, and she was given a choice of accepting the punishment or having a court-martial. She initially chose the latter. Eventually, her commander offered her a reprimand if she would give up her right to a trial. If she chose a trial, she would risk her career and have to stay longer in Iraq, and any soldiers she subpoenaed as witnesses would have to stay behind while the rest of the unit went home. She relented and was allowed to leave Iraq for Kuwait. Back home, she persisted in reporting the corruption. She later heard that some of the offending officers suffered repercussions.[31]

Pickett also experienced combat stress in her role as combat lifesaver, particularly during one devastating mortar attack on her unit. A VA clinician formally diagnosed her with PTSD a year after deployment. She believes the cause was a combination of combat, harassment, and the earlier sexual assault. It is easy to identify the first and fourth factors—military culture and the conduct of officers—as the main causes of the sexual harassment and resulting stress reaction.

Many other female soldiers are profiled in "The Women's War," including Keri Christensen, a veteran who is married and has two children. The experience of combat and sexual stress led her to let her military enlistment expire, despite being six years away from retirement benefits. She was exposed not only to the shame of repeated sexual harassment but also to being demoted and marginalized after reporting the incidents.[32]

Another classic case involved an anonymous female veteran who had served in Kuwait. After being sexually assaulted while deployed, she began exhibiting PTSD symptoms, including jumpiness, intrusive thoughts, and nightmares. She went to the local VA hospital for help. She was put into group therapy, but the group turned out to consist entirely of male Vietnam veterans. Many of them were trying to work through sex crimes they had committed in Vietnam. Others had been domestic violence offenders. The female reservist "freaked out," in her words, and went into "a complete tailspin." She began to drink heavily, lost her job, moved away from her family, and contemplated committing suicide. After a stay at a residential program for women with PTSD, she began to recover. When the media coverage of the Iraq War began, however, she began to feel the stirrings of her PTSD again as she felt deep concerns about the eventual fate of women soldiers being deployed to Iraq. Would the VA know what to do with the large numbers of traumatized female veterans and how to protect them from being retraumatized in the male-oriented system?[33]

The MST factors involved in these case histories are unmistakable. Not only do combat conditions raise the level of military violence, but the male-dominated culture plus unsupportive or abusive treatment by superior officers combine to push the combat stress of many women soldiers beyond their endurance. Identifying these factors in individual cases is an essential step in reducing and eventually preventing MST.

HOW WOMEN WILL CHANGE THE PTSD PICTURE

As I have noted, an increase in the number of women in the military is bound to bring about changes in military culture and, in the process, reduce the incidence of psychiatric casualties stemming from MST. When the proportion of women recruits, especially women officers, increases, positive changes in military customs seem likely. The culture of war may even change for the better. When women are in a distinct minority—as enlistees and officers—logic suggests that they are likely to conform to male-dominated institutional features and MST continues at present unacceptable levels. When women gain a substantial foothold in both capacities, they are more likely to initiate equitable changes. The culture of the military as an extension of manhood, with all its ramifications, will eventually undergo a positive transformation.

With this transformation, issues and decisions may be approached less aggressively. There may be less resistance in the military to adopting strategies that defer aggressive responses in favor of nuanced responses to provocations. This may be especially important in situations involving peacekeeping and winning over civilian populations, according to some commentators.[34] This is a subject of great controversy, and there is no consensus on whether feminizing the military will weaken or strengthen it. The result of growing feminization remains to be seen. One scholar, Jean Bethke Elshtain, discussed the clash of two feminist positions, those advocating civic equality, the "right to fight," and those supporting "no more war." Elshtain points to many problems facing the military, including the specter of deploying mothers with young children or even infants and the long-term effects of this practice. She also notes the problems arising from the interaction of males and females in the service, all of which I have discussed in detail. Elshtain questions the importance of the civic equality argument on behalf of women, since studies show that only a minority of women actually want to take part in combat.[35]

Other scholars, such as Pulitzer Prize–winning historian Walter A. McDougall, a Vietnam veteran, question the wisdom and value of the civic equality position, claiming that the military is a difficult organization to change. McDougall argues that changes attributable to greater recruitment of women will not be sensible or beneficial.[36] He stated his position in 2000, before the Iraq and Afghanistan campaigns. Some of his predictions have not proved true since, generally speaking, women have served with distinction. Others, such as his concern about the interaction of men and women, have been accurate, however.

On the subject of psychiatric casualties, researchers have determined that women experience more PTSD, take longer to recover, experience different symptoms, have fewer symptoms that lead to violent behavior, and also comprise most of the victims of MST. Moreover, women have special problems and concerns about their role in their family and society. Studies exploring the effect of combat stress on women are under way. For example, the VA has funded a major study at Yale University to determine whether there are gender differences in the way female and male combat veterans readjust to civilian life.[37]

As the number of women exposed to combat increases, PTSD in women veterans is becoming an increasingly important problem. The study of the impact of active service on women soldiers has produced very little definitive information so far, aside from the findings previously mentioned. In general, women who suffer from PTSD report having a lower quality of life than men who suffer from PTSD do.[38] In addition to the sex differences in acquiring

PTSD from military combat, women on active duty and women veterans face unique problems because of their particular roles in the family and society.[39]

It seems reasonable to predict that, considering the critical roles that women play in the family, community, and society, increasing numbers of women veterans with PTSD caused by war, MST, or both, will have a far-reaching impact. This phenomenon will further affect the social services needed for the veterans and their families. However, because women suffering from PTSD tend to exhibit less violent behavior than men, the increase of female PTSD sufferers is not likely to result in an influx of serious criminal cases into the court system. Women veterans suffering from PTSD may commit alcohol and drug-related offenses, but they will likely not commit violent crimes. The effect of PTSD on women veterans will be serious and long term. PTSD typically erupts first—in men and women—in the home. Sometimes these cases involve family violence, and often they are associated with the breakup of marriages. It may be that long-term changes in the stability and durability of the family as a social institution contributes to the problems by weakening the internal bonds and structure of the relationship.[40] All in all, PTSD in women veterans threatens to cause even more of a disruption to the social fabric of home, community, and society than PTSD in male veterans.

PART IV

BATTLES ON THE HOME FRONT

11

Trials of Homecoming

The coming-home stories of the veterans interviewed for this book suggest what political and military leaders, the psychiatric community, and the courts should do to prevent or greatly reduce the problems of PTSD. Although all these veterans suffer from PTSD and some of them have had legal problems, none of them have been charged with major crimes. Their experiences in combat, reintegrating into civilian society, and suffering from PTSD illustrate vividly the issues that I have discussed in the previous chapter. Their difficulties in picking up the pieces of their former lives upon returning demonstrate the need for creative change in the institutional approach to PTSD. Their stories graphically reveal the broad spectrum of war experiences that can lead to PTSD and the many ways in which PTSD presents itself.

Although several of the veterans began to have symptoms of PTSD while in combat, others had no symptoms until they returned home from deployment. These veterans—even those who had reported symptoms or been treated while in service—were not adequately screened or counseled for mental health problems upon discharge. None received adequate psychiatric treatment while deployed. Their stories demonstrate that many factors contribute to the timing of the first appearance of PTSD symptoms. Among these factors are combat assignment, trauma, available support, and personal qualities and experiences prior to entering the service. In the case of the interviewees, all these factors were markedly diverse.

By the same token, all the veterans came home to different situations. All of them had difficulty transitioning, some more than others. None of them felt that the military provided adequate preparation for making the transition from deployment to civilian life. All believed that they reentered society unequipped for the problems they would face.

Each of the veterans faced a different set of challenges. Linda found employment to support herself, but her alcohol abuse led to a series of drunk-driving convictions. Julia returned home to a job plus a plan for continuing her education, but she was derailed by depression and anxiety that led to her psychiatric hospitalization. Dax returned home to resume civilian life burdened by both physical combat injuries and PTSD. But when he got off the bus, his girlfriend was there waiting for him. Six months later, they were married. Ray returned to a stable marriage and had set up a plan for continuing his education. He was the only one of the seven who succeeded in maintaining his equilibrium while navigating the transition process. His wife's support plus his own determination were crucial.

RON, ART, JAY, AND ALAN

Ron, Art, Jay, and Alan all had severe problems, including homelessness, alcohol and drug abuse, criminal behavior, divorce, and unemployment, before being able to get the resources needed to find the path to recovery. Each of them hit bottom before beginning to recover. All of them found their own paths to treatment at the VA. Nearly all of them made poor decisions along the way in part because they were not aware of how their military experiences would affect their civilian lives.

When Ron was discharged, he returned to his hometown and resumed working at his pre-deployment job collecting garbage. He was addicted to drugs, a habit he acquired in what he called the "insanity in Southeast Asia." He had trouble sleeping and kept one of his twenty guns within reach at all times. Emotionally he was still in combat and saw everyone as either friend or enemy. "I couldn't seem to think any other way than how they taught me. If you're not with me, you're against me. Everything was white or black. . . . No gray." He admits that he did "a lot of insane thinking. In the '80s, I started getting active in a Vietnam Vet association, and it always turned into party time."

Ron's drug habit dominated his life. "I was selling drugs because my habit was out of whack. I was done with the garbage in four hours and had the whole day to hustle. . . . I sold cocaine from my house. . . . After I started speed-balling, I couldn't keep up. It was the only way I knew of making myself feel good. . . . It was a serious problem," he said. "I still run into people who say they thought I was dead."

Art had a similar problem.

In the service, I started to have flashbacks and was hypervigilant. I was treated for PTSD. . . . We got out of Kuwait in April of 1991. No one talked to me about getting back to civilian life. When I got out two months after leaving Kuwait, I had my duffel bag and my uniforms on hangers. I . . . stayed in North Carolina. I got married shortly after. . . . We had been dating before I left. For six months we stayed married and then got it annulled. . . . It was all my fault . . . drinking, mostly. Before I went in . . . I wasn't an alcoholic. When I got out, I drank a lot of Bacardi. I couldn't get a job. I had no experience in anything. There's no equivalent job to being in the artillery. We were not technicians. We were hit men. We just shot weapons.

Art returned to his home town and started to use drugs.

We had no drugs in Kuwait. I got to drugs after my divorce. I was hanging around in the streets. . . . I was using crack cocaine and beer. That was my breakfast, lunch, and dinner . . . and I stole from everybody. If they left it lying around, it was mine. My mother kicked me out, and then my sister did too. I was sleeping in abandoned buildings, shelters, and finally got to a VA treatment center. I was there four months and left before they found out I was drinking. I was homeless, tired, and hungry. I ran on the streets for three years. . . . I was the only one who didn't think I needed help. . . . I finally got to the VA for help and was diagnosed with PTSD but not enough to get a disability. I was shot down three times. I've still got anger in me. I thought I'd be taken care of for life when I joined the service, but when they let you go, they let you go.

Jay's experience was similar to Art's. When he returned home, he couldn't identify what was wrong. He recalls,

Even my family knew I wasn't the same person as when I went in. I was very edgy and couldn't stand noise. I isolated myself. . . . My coworkers couldn't joke with me; I would flare up really easily. . . . I'm not using drinking and drugs as an excuse but I started medicating myself. It was the only thing I knew to numb myself from reality.

I did that for a long time. . . . I finally knew it was getting out of control so I went to rehab . . . for nineteen days. . . . I had no clue what PTSD was until the late '80s when I saw something about it on TV. I had no contact with the VA until I was down and out in 2004. I told a social worker at the VA then that I had bad nightmares so real I thought I was in Vietnam, and she explained PTSD to me. I thought it meant I was crazy. I was not a drug user when I was growing up. But after I was back, I started using heroin and marijuana and, later, cocaine. I got so paranoid I thought the world would crash.

My first arrest was not until 1995, when I was forty-four years old. . . . It was for drug possession. I didn't do jail time but got five years probation for possession of cocaine. No one asked about combat service or substance abuse. . . . I was homeless in New York City for ten months in 2003 and 2004. When I was using, I came close to throwing myself under a bus. I hit bottom and had no place to turn. I'd used up all my options. . . . One day in the Bronx, my niece saw me, and she was in tears. . . . She told my brother, and he came to get me. I got to the VA after that.

After his deployment in Iraq, Alan also began a long downward descent fueled by alcohol abuse and poor decision making. He got married as soon as he returned. As he put it,

It was partly to avoid boredom because I'd be living off base. . . . I didn't really know what to do. I couldn't reenlist because of my alcohol problem. I was drunk at my wedding. . . . During the four days we had before I left for Iraq, we both were drinking hard. . . . But, she didn't drink as much when I got back. . . . She told me she was scared of me. . . . I talked and wrote to her when I was over there, but seeing her in person after being away for so long and being through so much, it was weird to the point where I was not comfortable. . . . The night I got off that bus, I got hammered with Jack Daniels and beer.

If you're not around the same people you went through that stuff with, normal people aren't going to understand. Like my wife. . . . She didn't understand, and she begged me to help her understand. I wouldn't open up to her; I didn't know how. Half the shit I wouldn't want her to hear.

If I was in her shoes, I'd probably been scared of me too . . . waking up in the middle of the night and having cold sweats and night terrors. For the first few weeks, I had to sleep on the floor with my back to the wall because that's how I slept over there. I was always looking out the window and making sure nobody was around, jumping at the slightest loud noise, and driving the car and scanning the roadside for IEDs. I still catch myself doing stuff like that.

I kept drinking while I was in the service until my command basically said that's it. I got out of the Marines four months early and got a discharge under honorable conditions. I get all my full disability benefits and all the VA benefits. . . . I felt like I needed to be in Iraq to feel normal. . . . So, it's a catch-22. . . . I didn't really know what I wanted. I guess I just drank to feel normal.

There was a lot of domestic violence. While I was a marine, the military police came to our apartment a bunch of times. . . . It would always get swept under the rug. When I got out and we got our own place, I got arrested. . . . I lucked out when I had to go in front of a judge. . . . Because I was a combat vet, I was treated pretty decent. I did get busted for DUI [driving under the influence]. A week or two later, I hit a tree. The judge was pretty lenient with me. . . . It helped me not having to pay a $500.00 fine to say that I was an unemployed, disabled vet.

LINDA AND JULIA

Linda had no problems in Iraq but had a difficult time when she returned to civilian life. Her anxiety and alcohol abuse seemed to stem from being unable to start fresh. When she enlisted, her life was unsettled, and when she returned home, she had no more sense of direction and did not receive any guidance or support in making the transition. She had fallen behind her friends in everything—education, career, and relationships. She had not received any employment training or experience in making decisions. Now she felt hopeless, discouraged, and depressed.

She recalled,

When I got back, I went to see a counselor who explained what my problems were. I didn't know what it was. . . . I didn't really have time to figure it out. We were busy taking supplies to the infantry and waiting to get shot at. After I got back, my grandfather died. That's what started my drinking like real bad. I would stay in my room for months. I would have a bottle of wine and pass out. I'm not sure if I didn't want to feel anything or if I was trying to feel something. . . . I felt numb, but I also cried a lot. . . . I had two DUIs, two major car crashes. I should be dead right now. The cop that was at the scene told me I had alcohol on my breath, but it was from the night before. . . . He caught the history of my being in Iraq and everything. He said . . . I could take you to jail but I'm not going to. I did go back to college for a little while, but I just couldn't decide my major. I kept switching.

Julia was not exposed to any combat trauma while in Iraq, but she suffered sexual harassment and assault at the hands of superior officers and was unable to find support either from the women in her unit or from other officers. Despite her psychiatric problems during deployment, she was discharged without transition assistance and so her psychiatric problems were left untreated. The situation she faced at home was highly stressful. The officer who had coerced her was charged with sexually assaulting a civilian, and prosecutors wanted her testimony for the court-martial.

"When I got the phone call telling me that I had to testify," she related,

I said I'd rather kill myself than testify. I did not want anything to do with this. They sent someone to my house to make sure I didn't harm myself and took me the next day to the VA hospital. A judge found that I needed to be kept there for . . . fifteen days. I gave testimony to a military grand jury from my hospital room. . . . After that, I went into treatment with a psychiatrist at the VA.

Although less than a year has passed since Julia was released from the hospital, she has gained strength from her treatment. She no longer feels suicidal but remains vulnerable.

DAX

Dax had met his wife just three months before leaving for Iraq on his third tour. "We were girlfriend and boyfriend, and we knew we loved each other," he said, but

> she was afraid of . . . the war changing me. I said, "I've already been twice, it's not like it's gonna change me now," and I told her I had volunteered for this third tour. She didn't like that. I told her, "If . . . you still want me when I get back I'll be here for you," and so when I got back she was there waiting on me, getting off the bus; six months after getting off the bus we were married.

Dax and his unit received minimal screening or treatment for PTSD during deployment.

> Before getting on a plane for home, we were sent to Kuwait. . . . They put you in what they call . . . a detox center . . . for two weeks where you can get recivilianized, where you're around people again. . . . They're detoxing you from war, and during that time, they put you in large groups of everybody you've been in combat with, and ask you "Does anybody feel suicidal?" You gonna answer that? Or, "Does anybody feel that they're gonna have a problem?" That means I'm gonna stay here longer, or you can send me home now to my wife or girlfriend. So you say, "I'm fine," and then you can get on the plane. . . . One thing that I would love to see changed is, before people are able to go back to the states and again before they're discharged from any military service, they need to be seen by a doctor and a psychologist. Nobody in their chain of command needs to be in that room because that's more stress. They don't want to look weak in front of their peers and especially the person that they're trying to please above all things. They need to be in that room, and they need to be asked a series of questions. If you do that . . . I guarantee you the

number of people who are committing suicide, and the number of people who are going through life in a deranged state will be lowered extremely.

After returning to the States, Dax was put through a physical test. "I collapsed during the test, and they found the injuries to my spine. After that, they discovered that I had PTSD." Most people don't get symptoms of PTSD until six months after being out of combat. Dax was formally diagnosed with PTSD in 2005. While he was in the service, there was little opportunity to talk to anyone about PTSD symptoms. During combat,

> I didn't have time to think about myself, nor should I have. . . . I should've been thinking about the person to my left and right who was depending on me to make sure they got home, and that's what I did. After I got home, I realized that I had problems . . . and I missed being in combat and being with my boys.
>
> I didn't even think I had PTSD. I had spent a long time over there. . . . Stress just became part of my daily life, and then I came back to the civilian world. It's hard to readjust from being in a combat situation all the time where you don't ask whether somebody is going to shoot; it's shoot first and ask questions later. . . . The only reason I knew something was wrong was because I couldn't sleep. I was trying not to sleep because I was used to a situation where if you sleep, somebody's going to die.

RAY

Ray's experience was more positive. Although he was diagnosed with PTSD after returning home, it did not derail him. As a sniper, he had been given some control over using his skills. He avoided alcohol and drug abuse. He developed insights into the nature of his PTSD. He reflected,

> I don't think I had a PTSD issue when I was in Iraq. I was too caught up in life . . . in things going on. . . . I didn't feel any symptoms until I returned home. It wasn't until I was home that I started feeling problems. . . . I had a horrible time trying to readjust. . . . I felt bulletproof when I was in. . . . We were always doing silly things . . . firefights or

being overly brave to the point of stupidity. It was easy to get caught up in the flow of that. It was really hard when I just stopped. One day you're in and you feel really important. You feel like you make a difference, and the next day you are getting attitude from the guy at McDonald's. You would never be given that attitude in the military as a ranger or as a sniper. Everyone is getting out of your way and saying, "Yes, sir."

PTSD for me has nothing to do with what it looks like on TV or [what I] see in pamphlets at the VA. . . . I don't think it has to do with [seeing combat death] because . . . I don't think it's any more traumatic than the death of a close family member. . . . It could be a crippling sadness for five or ten years, but it wouldn't be PTSD. . . . The things I see on TV describing it seem more like grief. To me, PTSD is unexplained anxiety, unexplained nervousness, unexplained depression, like clinical depression . . . not just "Oh, I'm sad." I just couldn't get out of it. It felt like it was in my joints and the whole well-being of my body; it was mostly anxiety.

There are stressful situations. I'll be at a place even now that will be an open outdoor market. . . . You go to this place that has restaurants and there is a band playing, water fountain, and all the billboards with lights all around, and that will just send me into a panic. My heart rate is racing. Now, I can recognize what is happening. . . . But before, it just made me agitated. . . . I wasn't scared that someone was going to come get me. I wasn't having a flashback. I just could no longer handle stressors like that in my life. And, it took me a while to realize that might be connected to the military. . . . I couldn't adjust; I couldn't cope.

I didn't hear cars backfire thinking it was a gun. I just was very irritable and anxious, and I had a hard time with that. . . . One day I was in the military, and the next day I was out and never really had a chance to figure it out. . . . Part of the survival mechanism of a soldier is to make racial jokes about your enemy—to dehumanize your enemy because that's what you need to do to handle it. . . . When you're in, that's your enemy; that's the one who wants to kill you, and you want to kill them. . . . I had more in common with [the person I was trying to kill] than the [people] back home. . . . It's easy to talk about killing someone. . . . But you never think about what it's like to live with that after. You live the rest of your life having killed somebody. They don't show you that in the movies.

I needed to get out of the military. I was mentally ready to go home. . . . People get it wrong that snipers don't have a hard time. A lot of people make the connection between the distance between you and the enemy and the experience that you had. So, many people say someone who was in a hand-to-hand fight has more trauma than someone who was in a pistol fight. And that person has more trauma than someone who was in a rifle fight, and that person has more trauma than someone who was a sniper, and that person has more trauma than someone sitting in America pushing a red button and killing somebody. . . . My feeling is that the sniper is the worst off because the sniper has to decide when the person is going to die . . . and it's not necessarily a combatant. A sniper in a situation could be watching a person drink a cup of coffee, and the sniper has to say, "Well, should I give him another sip or should he be shot now?" That's a harder decision to make than fighting for your life.

CONCLUSION

Taking into account these veterans' wide variety of combat experiences and PTSD symptoms, some tentative conclusions become evident. Mental health problems arising during active duty were generally treated inadequately. Those who had problems faced either indifference or the stigma attached to making complaints. Transition counseling for mental health problems was inadequate, and the veterans were abruptly released into the civilian world. Veterans who had been directionless at the time of enlistment were no better off at discharge. Some were worse off because significant time had passed during which there was little opportunity for decision making or emotional growth. Poor decision making after reentry was common: the veterans married impulsively, struggled with relationships, and abused alcohol and drugs.

The timing of the initial symptoms was a function of multiple factors, and the constellation of PTSD symptoms in each individual case was complex and unique. Each veteran's awareness and understanding of his or her psychiatric illness came through self-discovery, usually after crisis intervention by family members or strangers. All the veterans had difficulties in readjusting to civilian life regardless of how difficult the combat experience had been. Substance abuse was common and sometimes explained as a coping mechanism. The combination of adjustment difficulties, economic problems, and relationship problems led to dysfunction in civilian life and antisocial behavior. Some behavioral difficulties led to criminal activity and arrest, but in the courts, the veterans were generally treated well. Their criminal troubles reflected more their substance abuse and poor coping skills than it did a carryover of violence.

With these personal stories and previous discussions in mind, I will recommend measures for the courts, psychiatric professionals, and civilian and military leadership to take in order to deal more effectively with PTSD.

12

Finding Solutions

Courts, Psychiatry, and the Politics of PTSD

Hundreds of thousands of veterans have already returned home from the Iraq and Afghanistan Wars. Many thousands more will return as U.S. involvement draws to a close. Current predictions, based on the present experience of recent veterans and the past experience of Vietnam veterans, are that large numbers will appear in courts as criminal defendants. They will face psychological, social, and economic problems in addition to serious legal problems. In many cases, the veterans will offer PTSD as a formal defense in legal proceedings; in others, symptoms of the disorder will be taken into account without appearing in the official record.

Many states have responded to veterans' needs by establishing special courts for veterans. These generally consist of special criminal courts for veterans accused of committing nonviolent crimes. The focus of these courts is on treatment and rehabilitation rather than adjudication and punishment. Is this appropriate? How should courts handle veterans' criminal cases? What must judges and lawyers know about combat PTSD? What steps can political and military leaders take to minimize or prevent PTSD and thereby avoid legal entanglements? Given the certainty that military force will continue to be used from time to time in the future, what can be done to reduce the prevalence of PTSD among soldiers and war veterans? What can psychiatric professionals do to deal more effectively with combat PTSD so that society as a whole—and courts in particular—will not have to bear the heavy burden of dealing with the fallout from psychiatric casualties of war and their consequences? A fresh perspective, together with a thoughtful and

194

effective approach to prevent or reduce PTSD and its destructive impact not only on individual sufferers but on courts and society, is needed.

PERSPECTIVES

The full impact of PTSD on society and the courts, as well as on the military, is now inescapably upon us. It is clear that combat PTSD is not merely a military or political problem. It is a personal, social, economic, and public health problem with enormous ramifications. Although PTSD inevitably will accompany combat stress, civilian and military leaders have the means to reduce, if not prevent, its impact.

Since PTSD is a problem for the whole of American society, it is essential to distinguish the roles and responsibilities of those who deal with PTSD. Because war begins with political leaders' decisions to engage in combat, civilian decisions must be considered the point of origin of combat PTSD. Political leaders, particularly the president and Congress, are primarily responsible for policy decisions and for framing the military's objectives as well as determining what resources will be allocated to the military budget. Civilian leaders, therefore, not military leaders, initiate the conflicts that eventually lead to PTSD for soldiers and veterans. The process goes full circle, and eventually, civilian society bears the impact of psychiatric (as well as physical) casualties. Civilian political leaders have the initial—and the overriding—duty to minimize the number of mental health and physical casualties of war. They initiate, authorize, and oversee military actions, as well as allocate funds for the military.

The role of the military is complicated. The military is charged, first and foremost, with accomplishing the policy objectives provided by political leaders, all the while attempting to preserve and protect from harm the soldiers who carry out the operations. Military leaders carry out civilian directives, decide on priorities, set standards, and generally manage the machinery of war. Once a military operation is under way, military leaders must cope with the problem of PTSD among their soldiers. Although the ultimate responsibility for positive change falls on civilian political leaders, military leaders have a coordinate responsibility to carry out their objectives while preserving and protecting the troops within their command, including the troops' psychological health.

Within the psychiatric profession, civilian psychiatrists have a single ethical duty to their patients. In comparison, military psychiatrists may experience dual and conflicting responsibilities to both their patients and the military's goals. It is undeniable that an important military goal is to restore soldiers' health in order to return them to service and maximize fighting strength. In addition to their ethical responsibilities to patients as individuals, therefore, military psychiatrists cannot help but be aware of institutional pressures to return patients to combat as quickly as possible, even before those patients have reached optimum improvement. Moreover, military psychologists' role is complicated by their knowledge that patients will likely be sent back to the stressful situation that caused or contributed to the psychiatric disorder in the first place.

Courts enter the picture late in the combat PTSD story. Their basic function is to decide in a fair, even-handed, and effective manner legal disputes initiated by litigants. Their doors must be open to all litigants and all properly filed cases. Courts make decisions on the basis of legal standards and authority regardless of the subject matter of cases. Although they consider standards and doctrines from other disciplines, such as psychiatry, they are bound only to reach decisions based on legal standards and authority. The discretion necessarily given to judges creates the potential for inconsistency in this arena.

I will shortly identify some measures that all three institutions—the civilian and military leaders, the psychiatric profession, and the courts—can take to deal effectively with combat PTSD, with particular attention to how those measures impact the operation of courts when veterans are litigants. Whatever improvements civilian and military leaders undertake with regard to PTSD may reduce the ultimate impact on the psychiatric profession and the courts. The psychiatric profession plays an integral role. Ideally, it should provide a realistic definition of the disorder in the *DSM* and should, when possible, anticipate and treat psychiatric problems before veterans reenter civilian society. Courts come into the picture only after all other efforts to prevent, minimize, or resolve PTSD problems have failed. Courts are not only the front lines for society's unresolved conflicts but also the last resort for many people—victims and perpetrators alike.

RECOMMENDATIONS

I recommend in general terms measures that the civilian and military leaders, the psychiatric profession, and the courts should consider in order to deal more effectively with combat PTSD. These recommendations, some of which may be self-evident and some less so, follow from an independent assessment of the past and present configuration of combat PTSD. The underlying premises of the recommendations, which are meant to stimulate further discussion, are that combat PTSD is (1) a long-standing condition; (2) a subject the public has become more aware and accepting of; (3) a subject still burdened and governed by misunderstanding, stigma, and expediency; (4) a worsening condition because of multiple psychological and cultural factors; (5) a prevalent and destructive disease that has reached an unacceptable level; and (6) a responsibility of civilian and military leaders, who have the ultimate authority to identify, eliminate, and alleviate the disorder.

WHAT CAN POLITICAL AND MILITARY LEADERS DO?

When making decisions to use military force, leaders should take into account human costs, including potential psychiatric and physical casualties, as well as economic costs. When use of force is contemplated, civilian leaders must establish clear policy objectives to guide military planning. Objectives should include measures necessary to protect and preserve service members, including their mental health. The military must formulate its objectives with a view to minimizing mental health injury. Candor and transparency within the political and military institutions are essential. The predicted human costs to society as a result of war may weigh against military action. Cost-benefit analysis of both economic and noneconomic factors is essential. Potential loss of confidence in government, injury and loss to members of society as a result of criminal behavior and other consequences of PTSD, and overall cost to society as a result of impaired decision making, even apart from physical and emotional injuries, must be fully accounted for in the analysis. They must also be accounted for during the military planning phase of war.

The military must maintain enlistment screening to identify potential recruits who are urgently at risk of suffering psychiatric disorders. Although the historical record shows that screening benefits have limitations, screening may eliminate the greatest risks. As psychiatrists and military leaders recognize, it is important to study resilience and vulnerability in order to understand how to minimize PTSD as well as how to treat it. In the mental health field, resilience has been defined as "the ability to maintain a state of normal equilibrium in the face of extremely unfavourable circumstances." Vulnerability may be defined for this purpose as "the potential for casualty when exposed to a hazard or threat."[1] The military's interest in finding the key to the resilience/vulnerability dichotomy is mainly to determine how to identify individuals who are less susceptible to combat PTSD so that the number of soldier breakdowns and psychiatric casualties can be kept to a minimum.

National Guard and Army reservists should be similarly screened before being called into active duty. These soldiers are in a different position from typical volunteers. Many of them enlisted without any realistic expectation of activation and deployment in a war zone. Some may not be suitable for active duty in today's counterinsurgency military actions. In addition to augmenting the regular troops, however, the participation of National Guard and Reserve troops probably engage more members of the public in the wars' progress. The consequences they may confront after entering combat have devastating potential. Many of them leave behind spouses or partners, children, jobs, mortgages, and other responsibilities that may languish during their absence, which immediately heightens their stress levels.

Since PTSD can emerge at many different phases of military service based on many factors, all phases of service and all factors must be examined carefully to ascertain what has contributed to PTSD in a given individual. The phases of service include basic training, advanced training, conditioning of recruits, deployment to noncombat assignments, combat exposure, combat engagement, intervals between deployments, redeployments, immediate post-discharge readjustment, and long-term post-discharge. An additional detriment is the cascade of consequences, in the form of poor life decision making, that is attributable in whole or in part from PTSD. Combat trauma is not the only source of danger, fear, conflict, and stress in a war zone, nor is it the sole cause of PTSD. One commentator pointed out, "In examining the term risks for veterans of the Afghanistan and Iraq wars, we must acknowledge the socio-economic-cultural context and the personal variables that dynamically shape soldiers' adaptation across the life span."[2] PTSD can result from a combination of pre-deployment factors, deployment variables, and post-deployment factors.

Military leaders must recognize the full significance of the moral compunction against killing that is innate in most people. Mental conditioning that takes place in training distances individuals from their violent actions and may exacerbate PTSD later.[3] Future research may show that similar results occur with respect to the distancing involved in increasing use of remote weaponry, such as the drones that are now so widely used. The remote machinery of war, such as drones, are not likely to be a panacea for long-term psychic and moral damage of war. A serious moral and practical question remains whether the natural resistance to killing can or should be overcome to fight wars more effectively. In any event, it is well established that dealing with mixed messages—for example, kill noncombatants to protect U.S. troops but protect and persuade noncombatants when at all possible—troubles soldiers. Fully recognizing moral conflict as a cause of PTSD will enhance the opportunities to prevent the disorder and moral injury.

Political and military leaders must also take steps to prevent and eliminate MST. The recent public acknowledgement of the immense scope of the problem is a welcome first step. There is much to do, however, to remedy the situation. Women should be integrated into units in sufficient numbers to provide safety and reasonable comfort. This will protect them and make assistance and treatment more available. The military must promote a greater proportion of women to leadership positions to discourage and control MST and promote treatment.[4] Discretion as to investigations and prosecutions must not reside in the hands of individual unit commanders. Most importantly, the military must promote nonviolence in relationships among its troops, especially with respect to female soldiers. Creating an environment of equal treatment and mutual respect is fundamental.

Reducing the prevalence of alcohol and drug abuse in the military is another basic step. Drug programs for active-duty and reserve personnel involving screening, monitoring, supervising, and educating are essential and should be offered on an ongoing basis. Substance abuse within the military undermines effectiveness, contributes to MST and other violence, and increases the likelihood of mental health problems when veterans reenter civilian society. Political and military leaders must acknowledge and handle misconduct on the part of soldiers and veterans openly and forthrightly with a view to understanding the intricacies of the contributing factors—even in the face of unwanted political fallout.

Both political and military leaders must pursue with open minds a thorough examination of the surge in military-related suicides. They must acknowledge that the surge signals serious structural problems within the entire military system. Although investigations to explore the causes of the suicide epidemic apparently are under way, no clear answers have yet emerged. Relationship breakdowns, prescription drug abuse, and operational tempo (the pace of deployments and redeployments) have been identified as critical factors in military suicides.[5] Other likely contributing factors are depression (caused by the inability to readjust, failed marriage, and unemployment, for example), burnout (fatigue and exhaustion from a year's deployment under trying circumstances and multiple deployments), perceived mistakes in action (such as killing or failing to save civilians), killing of combatants, guilt because of failure to save colleagues, anger or impulsiveness after discharge, difficulty making decisions once out of the military, alienation from civilian society, unpreparedness to resume education or establish careers, and PTSD and other mental disorders. Severe physical injuries and disabilities may present seemingly unconquerable obstacles for individuals who are coping with other readjustment problems.

Suicide-prevention strategies must encompass the policy goals that have been promulgated, such as avoiding recruitment of people who are potential suicide risks, providing treatment to soldiers who appear to be at risk, expanding treatment opportunities after discharge, and counseling survivors. At the same time, it is essential to recognize that those are only general policy statements and to avoid conflating the diverse strategies. Most importantly, military and civilian leaders must recognize that a successful approach requires their penetrating and candid acknowledgment of the human costs of engaging in military action. These costs include psychiatric casualties related to PTSD and suicide. All efforts will be doomed to failure in the absence of introspection, forthright acknowledgment, and determination to make the necessary changes.

The military should aim to provide thorough post-deployment screening for mental health problems before discharge and thereafter at a suitable interval to identify psychiatric problems. It must provide all necessary treatment, support services, family counseling, and employment assistance before soldiers return to civilian society. The goal must be to prevent problems of readjustment rather than expect civilian society to deal with them after they occur. Although some progress may be under way, present measures are inadequate since veterans should be exceptionally disciplined, trained, educated, and prepared to be productive members of civilian society, rather than casualties, as happens too often.

According to the Stanford study discussed in chapter 7, the first step is for the Department of Defense to provide an adequate transition process, including screening, treatment, and support services before soldiers reenter civilian life. PTSD must be addressed early to lessen its severity, avoid the strong stigma attached, and avoid development of comorbid conditions, such as substance abuse and depression. Barriers to mental health care must be eliminated so that veterans can get the treatment they need.

It is essential for veterans, their families, and the public that lifetime monitoring for PTSD and treatment, when necessary, be an integral part of the care available to veterans.

WHAT CAN MENTAL HEALTH PROFESSIONALS DO?

Critics argue that the present PTSD formulation in the *DSM-IV-TR* is confusing and question the (1) trauma concept; (2) assumption of a specific trauma factor; (3) lack of specificity of the criteria, namely, that they overlap with too many other disorders; (4) criterion creep or spread into too many diverse situations; and (5) excessive malingering encouraged by the formulation, which corrupts legitimate use of the diagnosis.

Others challenge the formulation for different reasons. Some respected mental health professionals argue that PTSD is overdiagnosed and that it represents a medicalizing (turning a human condition into a medical problem) of the process of recontextualization, a psychiatric term meaning integration of a trauma into normal experience so that the sufferer can move on with life.[6] This argument fails to recognize the full import of PTSD's disabling symptoms. Although the present formulation of PTSD may need improvement, the legitimacy of the condition cannot seriously be in doubt.

Because the *DSM* serves as a diagnostic resource and standard for purposes of treatment and health-care reimbursement, the APA constructs criteria for each disorder for those purposes. Although the *DSM* drafters attempt to classify as accurately as possible the disorders' symptoms as they exist, it is inevitable that professionals will disagree about how to define the boundaries between closely-related disorders. Regardless of how traumatic stress is defined at any moment, the condition is and will continue to be a serious problem for soldiers and veterans. The symptoms of the disorder lead to social, economic, and legal problems as the veterans attempt to readjust to civilian life. The veterans, their families, their friends, and those they come into contact with suffer the consequences.

To acquire disability benefits or defend themselves against charges of criminal activity, including those involving substance abuse, veterans need a diagnosis, a formula in a sense, that embodies the PTSD concept. A vague or ambiguous narrative of problems will not suffice in medicine, psychiatry, law, health care, or any other field veterans must navigate to survive—and thrive—in society. Veterans need a shorthand way of efficiently explaining both their suffering and their situation. The PTSD diagnosis was created for that purpose—to acknowledge, identify, and develop guidelines for the body of symptoms. That the disorder is a social construct does not detract from its basic validity. PTSD encompasses a cluster of variable conditions, symptoms, causes, and effects. Understanding of it may still be at a primitive stage, and future research probably will change the formulation of its causes and components in order to enable improved treatment. The present DSM disorder represents an imperfect attempt to identify the elements of an age-old mental health disease or injury. In considering how PTSD affects veterans, one must remember that, in addition to those who are actually diagnosed with the disorder, many others suffer but are never diagnosed because they do not seek treatment. The 2008 Rand report discussed in chapter 7 concluded that many veterans do not seek help, and of those who do, only half receive "minimally adequate" treatment. For example, in the last year of the Rand study, only slightly more than half of the veterans who had depression or PTSD sought help, and of those, half received minimal care.[7] In addition, countless others have some symptoms of PTSD but lack the full range of symptoms necessary to qualify for a diagnosis. There are no reliable statistics on this category of people with partial PTSD.

As mentioned in chapter 2, an APA committee is currently working on the *DSM-5*, which is due to be published in 2013. Since publication is approximately a year away and many changes are possible, I will not attempt to speculate about proposed revisions. Although the committee has announced a number of proposed changes, several of which may particularly affect combat PTSD, none would directly address the changes that I believe are worthy of consideration, as outlined in the following paragraphs.[8]

The psychiatric profession must promote consideration of PTSD as a public health issue rather than simply as an individual mental health problem. The broad reach of combat PTSD within American society, in terms of the number of veterans who develop the disorder and the number of people whose lives are directly affected thereby, qualifies it as a public health issue, meaning one that involves the health of communities or populations. Combat PTSD belongs in the category of current public health issues, which includes chronic conditions such as obesity, repetitive head trauma from sports, and diseases such as heart disease and diabetes.

Viewing PTSD as a disorder that targets specific populations is valuable for identifying causes and fashioning remedies. Classifying the disorder in this manner also helps focus attention on the need for public action to address the disorder's widespread effects. Individual veterans should not be left alone to deal with a condition caused by their public service. Given the large number of veterans reintegrating into civilian life now and over the next few years, combat PTSD will continue to be a public health problem of huge proportions for the foreseeable future.

The psychiatric profession should closely study resilience and vulnerability with regard to PTSD, as well as the effects of drugs such as propranolol, which may block the reconsolidation (restabilizing) of traumatic memories, on the manifestation of PTSD symptoms. The relationship of PTSD to substance abuse and to criminal behavior also needs urgent attention.

The profession should work to eliminate military mental health professionals' conflicts of interest. This recommendation focuses on a problem that has existed throughout all wars. Military psychiatrists need clear guidelines to fulfill their professional responsibilities to individual patients, while simultaneously meeting the needs of their military employer. Soldiers who are suffering from psychiatric injury during service would benefit from having psychiatrists who are committed to follow ethical standards and who are free of military pressure governing the patient relationship.

Addressing the phases and factors of PTSD, as noted previously, is important. PTSD models or paradigms reflect multiple causes and contributing factors. As my individual interviews demonstrate, the kinds of traumatic events that can produce a PTSD reaction are extremely varied. Recognizing that varied fact patterns result in PTSD is crucial. This would relieve the burden on veterans to fit their symptoms into a framework that does not accommodate their situation. In view of the uniform set of *DSM* criteria for PTSD, professional recognition of the variations in PTSD causes, symptoms, and patterns of emergence is essential. The DSM criteria for PTSD should be re-examined in DSM-5 or a future revision to reflect such variations in order to facilitate diagnosis and treatment of veterans, as well as for other practical uses such as criminal defenses.

Psychiatrists must consider how factors unique to combat PTSD, such as the training and mental conditioning that precede combat service, moral injury, and displacement from home, contribute to acquiring the disorder. Psychiatry must take into account the moral conflict that humans experience when under pressure to kill or injure other humans, including civilians. Psychiatry must recognize not just the fear of danger but also moral repulsion from being required to act in ways that run counter to human instincts.

Care is needed to avoid making changes in PTSD criteria that might be useful for civilian applications but that, in the process, might water down the criteria and thereby undermine the legitimacy or credibility of PTSD for use by veterans and soldiers. For example, changes that would expand civilian claims of PTSD by bystander observers of traumatic injury might be useful for purposes of civil lawsuits. At the same time, changes that make it too easy to assert might promote skepticism and doubt about the legitimacy of the disorder when claimed by veterans in traumatic situations arising in the course of combat.

Changes that are made to the *DSM* category for PTSD should clarify the disorder based on research, eliminate confusion and uncertainty caused by the normal-abnormal paradox, and avoid overlap with other disorders. Criteria change should not take place as a reaction to popular cultural trends. Any changes in PTSD criteria, especially definitional changes or increased specificity, should be made with careful consideration of the potential impact on practical applications of PTSD by soldiers and veterans who assert the diagnosis as a defense in criminal cases.

Mental health professionals must research and investigate the relationship between PTSD and criminal behavior. Studies are needed to establish the mechanisms that lead to criminal behavior. Specifically how do symptoms arising from military service cause or contribute to specific criminal behavior? Better understanding of the connection between PTSD and violence would greatly benefit soldiers, veterans, their families, and society in general. Resilience and vulnerability merit research and study by the psychiatric profession as well as the military.

Given the prevalence of MST within the military, the psychiatric profession must understand and adapt the PTSD criteria to this pervasive problem and include symptoms stemming from MST. PTSD resulting from MST is closely related in causation and symptoms to PTSD following a sexual assault in civilian society. The occurrence of sexual trauma within a military context—especially combat—is intensified, however, because of the unique stressors that are present in the military setting.

The relationship of substance abuse to mental health problems requires special attention. The combination of the two in a military context creates a unique recipe for disaster. In addition, the prevalence of military suicides warrants a close study of the relationship of PTSD and substance abuse to suicide risk.

Finally, psychiatrists must recognize the interactive relationship of law and psychiatry when *DSM* disorders are presented in court. When judges and juries apply psychiatric criteria to specific factual scenarios, the interpretations and results give new fact-specific meaning to the *DSM* criteria. That process affects the way psychiatric terms will be applied to other legal situations. In other words, giving factual substance to *DSM* criteria, which are rules or guides to defining disorders, creates meaningful terms for effective use by courts. Psychiatrists also need to remember that in legal applications, PTSD is the cause of specific crimes, not general criminal behavior. Fact patterns of particular crimes are complicated and involve many elements other than PTSD.

To further aid judges in determining the relevance of PTSD in specific cases, psychiatrists must examine partial PTSD with respect to criminal behavior. Provision should be made for interpretation of partial symptoms, in the absence of full diagnosis, as an explanation for criminal behavior, when appropriate. Also, better diagnostic consistency and mental health support should be given to those suffering from partial PTSD.

COURTS, CULTURE, AND THE PTSD DEFENSE

Some states have enacted laws or started programs to facilitate alternative sentences for veterans, especially for those suffering from substance abuse or mental health problems. California and Minnesota were the first to enact sentencing statutes with the goal of providing treatment for veterans with PTSD. In the early 1980s California passed its first statute allowing the Department of Corrections to enter into agreements with other agencies to provide counseling and treatment for defendants. It amended the statute in 1984 to allow veterans suffering from substance or psychological abuse to receive treatment in federal facilities. The statute turned out to be ineffective, however, at providing veterans with federal treatment instead of incarceration. Courts ruled against federal treatment because suitable federal programs did not exist.[9]

A new version of the statute became effective in 2007. Under this statute, a defendant must make an initial showing of combat service in the U.S. armed forces. The defendant must then show that his or her substance abuse or other psychological disorder resulted from military service. Once those showings are made, the trial court has discretion to consider placing the defendant in a treatment program. The 2007 version, while resolving some of the problems that existed under the prior law, retracted some benefits for veterans convicted of serious crimes. Under the 1984 law, veterans could receive treatment regardless of the length of their imprisonment. The new law applies only when the veteran is eligible for and actually receives probation.[10] The statute is worth noting as a step forward, but many problems remain unresolved.

A Minnesota statute also provides treatment options for veterans. It requires the sentencing court to ask affirmatively whether the defendant is currently serving or has served in the military. The Minnesota law also provides more flexibility in considering treatment options. Both of these state laws provide for consideration of military service in connection with sentencing, following conviction, but not during the trial itself.[11] Subsequent to California's and Minnesota's statutes, other states, including Illinois, New Hampshire, Oklahoma, New York, and Ohio have enacted legislation to address veterans' issues, including veterans' substance abuse and mental health problems, civil service employment, and a wide variety of benefits.[12]

In addition to legislation, many U.S. state courts, the first of which was in Buffalo, New York, are establishing special courts for criminal trials of veterans. The move is unusual, even within the realm of problem-solving courts, such as mental health courts or drug courts, because the basis for admission to the court commonly hinges on the defendant's personal status rather than the nature of the offense involved. Basing admission on veteran status provides for special treatment for a class of defendants regardless of whether that status is relevant to the crime charged. Although the way veterans courts operate varies from state to state, the foundational premise appears to be that veterans deserve special consideration from criminal courts because of their military service. Although few would dispute that veterans deserve special consideration from the government, many believe courts are not the appropriate vehicle to deliver the special treatment.

Three highly visible signs of the inadequate handling of psychiatric casualties of war are the growing suicide rates of military personnel, the frequency of MST, and the mounting numbers of homicides charged against soldiers and veterans of Iraq and Afghanistan. Although less dramatic and harder to measure, the growing numbers of PTSD cases accompanied by dysfunctional behavior, such as homelessness, disrupted relationships, domestic violence, substance abuse, and nonfelony criminal arrests on the part of soldiers and veterans point to a chronic medical and social problem. All of these signs and symptoms indicate dysfunction in the handling of mental illness problems of veterans by civilian and military leadership. The criminal cases and personal stories involving combat PTSD recounted in earlier chapters are evidence of inadequate programs to assist veterans in reentering civilian life. States and communities have responded by creating veterans courts to remedy the less serious problems arising during military service.

Some veterans courts were established within existing court systems by virtue of the administrative authority of judges. Others were established through legislation by state or local governments. As of March 2011, about fifty jurisdictions around the United States have established veterans courts.[13] More courts of this type can be expected to join the ranks in ensuing months. Although individual variations exist, most courts are available only to veterans charged with misdemeanors or nonviolent felonies. The emphasis of many courts is on finding mentoring programs and outside treatment for nonviolent offenders. Veterans courts are generally available to all veterans charged with nonviolent crimes, that is, all veterans except those charged with sex, violent, or weapons-related offenses.[14] A difference of philosophy exists among proponents as to whether all veterans should be admitted to these courts or whether they should be open only to veterans who have been deployed to combat zones. Some people believe that only veterans with mental health problems stemming from wartime experiences should be eligible.[15] A few are open to nonveteran offenders who otherwise meet the guidelines as to types of crimes eligible and other factors that apply to veterans. Successful completion of the prescribed program results in reduction or dismissal of the charges, sometimes called graduations. Not surprisingly, given the selection process, most courts report successful results.

Other special courts organized around a category of offenses, such as drug charges, or contributing factors, such as mental health problems, screen cases so that some defendants can be diverted to treatment or counseling in addition to or instead of prosecution. When successful, diversion can be appropriate and worthwhile for the offenders and the state. Wisconsin, for example, has a veterans court program that works closely with an outreach agency of the VA.[16] The goal of the program is to provide VA services to veterans in an effort to help avoid "unnecessary criminalization and incarceration of Veteran offenders with mental illness."[17]

Still, veterans courts are used to provide special privileges for a class of defendants based on who they are rather than what they are accused of doing or what problems they have. The program can be described as inconsistent with and undermining the prevailing standard of fair treatment for all people that is mandated by the equal protection clause of the 14th Amendment to the U.S. Constitution. When states create a special procedure only for veterans, however well-intentioned they may be, they are using judicial authority and resources beyond their proper limits to remedy problems created by the failure of the federal government—both civilian and military leadership—to provide services to veterans before they reenter civilian society and become involved in the criminal justice system as defendants.[18]

Indeed, veterans do deserve special assistance from the government to help them successfully reintegrate into civilian society. Veterans and their families should not be left on their own to cope with homelessness, unemployment, mental illness, substance abuse, relationship breakdown, and other problems that can lead to criminal activity. They need appropriate support before transitioning to civilian life. The failure of current support systems has left it to states and cities to fill in the gaps, sometimes with resourceful measures that may be subject to constitutional challenge.

Although the establishment of veterans courts has been enthusiastically praised for the most part, critics have pointed out shortcomings. Some critics have noted that most veterans courts take only the types of cases that are easiest to deal with, leaving the difficult ones for the criminal justice system to adjudicate. Other commentators have charged favoritism in setting different standards for veterans' criminal conduct. One critic, for example, observed, "Excusing criminal conduct to an entire class of potential defendants is unconscionable and leaves an entire class of innocent victims without proper closure to violent crimes."[19] Another argued that veterans courts create a "class of privileged offenders," a "dangerous precedent."[20]

Although I agree that many such measures are not consistent with U.S. standards of equal justice, they are not "unconscionable." It is evident that efforts by judges and others to establish courts for special handling of veterans' criminal problems stems from compassion, conscience, and concern for veterans. It is unconscionable when civilian and military leaders fail to take measures that prevent veterans with PTSD from lapsing into criminal behavior in the first place. Special courts created to provide screening to determine whether cases are appropriate for diversion to social service agencies serve a legitimate purpose. Screening and diversion programs have become accepted procedures within criminal courts to connect defendants with resources outside the court system, such as drug counseling, mental health treatment, or mediation of minor controversies. But screening and diversion should be available to all defendants, whether veterans or not, who are in similar situations.

If the purpose of veterans courts is to provide a forum so that a group of defendants, even though they may be deserving in some respect, can receive special treatment in the guilt or sentencing phase of criminal cases, the practice would run counter to the U.S. system of justice. Many other categories of defendants could legitimately argue that they should have similar opportunities. Their drug addiction or mental health problems may have arisen because of circumstances beyond their control, and they may be deserving of special treatment for that reason. Although American society owes a great debt to its veterans, it is not the function of courts to develop policy and procedures that seek to remedy the problems that may have resulted from their military service.

It is the duty of the executive and legislative branches of government to intervene in veterans' lives and to solve their problems. With due respect to the argument that courts should assume that role, I suggest that it misapprehends the courts' purpose in American government. The basic function of courts is to see that all defendants are given due process and that the law is fairly and impartially applied. Intervening in veterans' lives to make them whole again is the duty of the institutions and leaders who sent these men and women to war in the first place. Courts are not agencies created or equipped to solve the social problems of society through policymaking and delivery of social services.

Moreover, any suggestion that it is acceptable to wait until veterans have been charged with crimes before the executive and legislative branches intervene to assist in making them whole is far off the mark. The time for intervention is before criminal behavior takes place. Although there are not yet adequate statistics on how victims overall respond to the proceedings in veterans courts, some victims have objected to special treatment of defendants in individual cases. In some jurisdictions victim consent is required, but in others courts have discretion to accept cases without such consent.[21]

The real harm is not only that one class of defendants is singled out for special treatment, which may cause others to lose trust in the fairness of the court system, but also that similar opportunities are not made available to others who could also benefit from them. An even greater harm is that, by focusing on resolving veterans' problems in court after crimes have been committed, attention is diverted from holding accountable those who bear the initial responsibility for preventing and avoiding the criminal behavior in the first place—civilian and military leaders. Any assumption, express or implied, that federal government leadership is doing all it should and that it is up to families, communities, states, and courts to do the rest is grievously mistaken.

On an encouraging note, several studies from 1993 and 2000 have supported the idea that veterans who are convicted of crimes have lower recidivism rates than other criminals. Beyond that, more recent studies show that veterans who have completed specialized treatment programs have an even lower rate of recidivism. This suggests that veterans may be ideal candidates for handling by problem-solving courts and rehabilitation programs.[22]

Although veterans deserve appreciation and consideration from the government, special treatment from courts is problematic when it undermines the principle of equal protection of the law. The courts' proactive approach to addressing veterans' criminal problems reflects genuine concern and insightful recognition that mental health problems resulting from service in combat bear on criminal and other antisocial behavior, but courts are bound to proceed with great care to meet their constitutional obligation of providing equal justice to all.

An unspoken assumption regarding veterans courts is that criminal involvement of veterans stems largely from their military service. That assumption has roots in past observations about a correlation between combat and crime. Historical literature contains many references to combat veterans' propensity for criminal behavior, and many studies have reported on the number of veterans who have been incarcerated after returning home. Unfortunately, these studies rarely provide meaningful comparative figures about nonveterans' conviction or incarceration rates. Moreover, they do not distinguish between psychological and behavioral aspects of war. That is, they do not distinguish between criminal behavior resulting from psychological damage caused by war and that resulting from learned behavior that is acceptable in wartime but criminalized in civilian society.[23]

A move to expand the criminalization of behavior, especially behavior related to possession and sale of illegal drugs, the target of the war on drugs, began in the 1970s and has continued to the present. The category of domestic violence crimes has also been expanded over the past few decades to include conduct that previously evaded criminal handling. The potential for criminal activity among veterans, therefore, has increased over time.

One area in which veterans courts have established a useful model for handling criminal cases is in consolidating multiple factors that contribute to criminal behavior—specifically, substance abuse and mental health problems—within the ambit of problem-solving courts. Alcohol and drug abuse, as well as the misuse of prescription medications, have been long-standing problems within the military as indicated by studies and experiential evidence. The most commonly abused drug among both active-duty soldiers and veterans is alcohol. A recent study reported that more than 43 percent of active-duty military reported binge drinking and almost 20 percent reported frequent, heavy drinking. Binge drinkers within the military also admitted to other alcohol-related problems, such as high-risk behavior and alcohol-related violations of the law.[24]

These findings corroborate an earlier study of recent Iraq and Afghanistan War veterans in which 40 percent tested positive for hazardous drinking and 22 percent for alcohol abuse. Less than one-third of the hazardous drinkers had received any VA counseling for their problems. Among National Guard members and reservists, the likelihood of alcohol-related problems increased with the existence of mental illness or use of medication. In addition, veterans face a serious risk of overdose on prescription medicines, especially opioid analgesics for pain relief from combat injuries and antidepressants for mental health treatment. A study found that Vietnam veterans with combat PTSD face a heightened risk of dying from a drug overdose.[25] The lethal combination of prescription medications and alcohol is a pervasive problem for all soldiers and veterans.

In addition to the *Porter v. McCollum* ruling, in which the Supreme Court concluded that combat PTSD must be taken into account when sentencing a veteran, another federal case, *United States v. John Brownfield Jr.*, gave special weight to military service as a sentencing factor. Judge John L. Kane Jr. of the U.S. District Court for Colorado wrote a lengthy memorandum of decision to explain his decision to sentence an Iraq veteran who plead guilty to bribery of a public official to probation rather than prison. With this decision, the judge deviated from the federal sentencing guidelines, which is permitted when satisfactorily explained. In his memorandum, Judge Kane detailed the defendant's personal and military history and combat experiences. Although the defendant had not been diagnosed with PTSD, he was awaiting a mental health assessment. His traumatic experiences and symptoms, as detailed, were consistent with PTSD. Judge Kane explained that the sentencing guidelines do not account for Brownfield's three tours in war zones. He added, "It would be a grave injustice to turn a blind eye to the potential effects of multiple deployments to war zones on Brownfield's subsequent behavior."[26] The case received considerable media attention.

An unusual development took place in 2010 in another federal case involving the criminal prosecution of Britten Walker, a veteran of three combat tours in Iraq and Afghanistan. Walker had been arrested in January 2010 after assaulting a federal police officer and a doctor at the VA medical facility in Buffalo, New York. Walker allegedly committed the assaults after making a series of threats to kill a VA worker, bomb several television stations, and bomb cars on the New York State Thruway. Walker complained to reporters that the VA was not equipped to handle all the soldiers coming back with problems. The judge assigned to the case appointed a psychiatrist to evaluate Walker for combat-related trauma. When the report came back, the judge released Walker from jail to attend a thirty-day treatment program for veterans suffering from PTSD. After Walker completed the program successfully, the judge released him on condition that he must attend an outpatient mental health program. Five months later, the judge transferred the case to the Buffalo Veterans Treatment Court for adjudication, dismissing the federal case without prejudice.[27]

This was the first criminal case to be transferred from federal court to a state or local veterans treatment court. The transfer raised the unsettled controversy over whether such action unfairly shifts the focus of courts from "serving the retributive interests of victims to the rehabilitative interests of perpetrators."[28] As of early 2011, Walker was several months into his rehabilitative program.[29]

On a less controversial level, state court judges and juries have frequently applied PTSD as a defense or a mitigating factor in sentencing. Judges' rulings at the trial level have no precedential value but may be persuasive to other trial courts dealing with the same issue. Decisions of judges on federal and state appellate courts, however, do have value as precedent within their jurisdictions. What juries decide as matters of fact, once instructed by judges to consider criminal defenses, have no value as precedent and no persuasive value to other courts. Only when trial judges decide whether jury verdicts should be set aside or upheld do the trial court decisions acquire persuasive value, and then, it is the judge's decision, not the jury's, that carries persuasive weight.

Iraq and Afghanistan veterans face a very different atmosphere in the court system from that faced by Vietnam veterans. PTSD is out in the open, accepted, and understood far better than it was in the past. Courts are likely to be more receptive to the defense. Because PTSD has gained recognition and acceptance in criminal courts today, the current focus should be on determining the role to assign to PTSD in veterans' cases.

One proposal made in an academic journal is to create an affirmative defense (one that the defendant has to plead and prove) that specifically names PTSD. This defense would be used if, at the time of the crime, the defendant, as a result of a specific "extreme trauma" that caused PTSD, acted in response to what he or she perceived as a threat of unlawful force. Aside from practical problems with this proposal, it would not be wise to base a special defense on a particular psychiatric disorder, much less to base a legal defense on it. It is one thing to have a special diagnostic category for PTSD. It is quite another to single out a class of defendants—those who claim to have had PTSD when the offense occurred—for special treatment. This proposal flies in the face of fundamental guarantees of equal protection of the law and fair trial.[30]

WHAT CAN THE COURTS DO?

Having surveyed the unprecedented ways in which courts are currently dealing with veterans who are charged with crimes, I focus on steps that courts can take to deal more effectively and fairly with criminal charges against soldiers and veterans with PTSD. As I noted previously in chapter 1, the PTSD syndrome can be very complex. Although interpretation and explanation must be as clear as possible, the difficulties must be recognized and taken into account. My assumption is that changes in the *DSM-5* that affect soldiers and veterans will be of minimal use in court. I further assume that, at best, change in the way the military handles the PTSD problem will be gradual.

Courts must address and resolve the equal protection problems inherent in the existing model of veterans courts by converting them to problem-solving courts open to nonveteran defendants who meet the standards for acceptance, for example, being charged with a nonviolent crime. Creating veterans courts to deal with their unique problems has done a significant service by officially recognizing the interrelationship of human behavior, stress, mental health problems, and substance abuse and addiction problems. The veterans courts, although varied in nature and jurisdiction, are essentially hybrid problem-solving courts that bring together the functions of several specialty courts. Examining the key components in some veterans courts reveals the wisdom of a multilayered approach for comprehensive treatment of complicated problems. Opening these courts to nonveterans with similar problems would maintain the hybrid approach and resolve equal protection and fairness problems. Such courts, like most existing veterans courts, should be designed to deal with nonviolent offenses. Victims could be given an opportunity to request that cases be adjudicated in regular criminal courts rather than the problem-solving courts.

Courts must have personnel, including judges as well as interested lawyers, who have had instruction in mental health matters regarding the epidemiology, symptoms, *DSM* criteria, causes, and consequences of PTSD. These personnel must be aware of the spectrum of PTSD manifestations and the full range of causes and contributing factors. Educational programs must address and correct past myths and misunderstandings. For PTSD to be properly evaluated and applied in court, both lawyers and judges must have a clear understanding of possible applications in criminal matters. Otherwise, they may not recognize and understand relevant evidence, and judges may rule improperly on evidence that is presented. Moreover, legal instructions to juries may be off the mark unless lawyers and judges understand precisely the purposes for which PTSD evidence may be offered. Understanding the relationship between PTSD and other mental health problems related to military service and criminal conduct is essential, given the long history of the relationship between combat PTSD and criminal behavior.

Since, as noted previously, PTSD can emerge at many different phases of military service as a result of many different factors, court personnel must be aware of all phases of military service and all relevant factors in order to identify the causes of PTSD in a defendant. Combat trauma is not the only source of danger, fear, conflict, and stress in a combat zone, nor is it the sole cause of PTSD. As one commentator pointed out, "The examination of the long-term risks for veterans of any war also requires an evaluation of the unique socio-economic-cultural contexts that dynamically shape soldiers' recovery and adaptation across the life span."[31] PTSD can result from a combination of pre-deployment factors, deployment variables, and post-deployment factors.

Given the present inadequate screening for PTSD, lawyers and judges working in criminal arraignment courts may actually be the first responders to veterans' problems with PTSD. They need to know how to identify veterans whose situations are suitable for referral to problem-solving courts. They must provide screening and diversion in coordination with VA assistance for veterans, along with other types of diversion during the arraignment process in criminal courts. To do this effectively, they must surmount barriers to mental health care and must realize how PTSD affects veterans' abilities to assist in making legal decisions.[32]

Three different stages of court proceedings are involved. Arraignment courts are the front lines for screening and identifying appropriate cases. Problem-solving courts for veterans (and others who are allowed access), in which resolution without adjudication is appropriate, constitute the second stage. Cases that are not appropriate for referral to problem-solving courts and cases in which resolution fails constitute the third stage. In arraignment courts, procedures must be in place to identify cases that may be appropriate for diversion, that is, interim referral to social support agencies, including substance abuse programs and mental health counseling. Cases in which defendants comply with court orders and treatment programs may properly be disposed of without the full adjudication process. Military personnel, like all defendants, need lawyers to help them negotiate the criminal process.

Court and legal personnel must receive education about substance abuse and addiction and their relationship to mental health issues, especially PTSD. Although the burden for alleviating and reducing the serious substance abuse and addiction problem remains with the military, courts will have to deal with the consequences of these problems as well. Judges must understand the benefits and detriments of short-term incarceration for offenders who relapse during the treatment process as well as the importance of avoiding burdening defendants in appropriate cases with the collateral consequences of convictions, including loss of civil rights. In some cases, deferring prosecutions may be a wiser course than requiring guilty pleas.[33]

Judges, like psychiatrists, must appreciate the interactive role of law and psychiatry. They must understand that court applications of PTSD, as testified to by psychiatrists, bring about changes in the meanings of the *DSM* criteria. The fact-specific nature of criminal cases brings to life the language of psychiatry as mental health experts present it in court. Cases in which defendants have psychiatric disorders may well turn on factual determinations rather than on the expert testimony about the disorders. In cases that go to trial, judges and other court personnel need to identify the specific purposes for which PTSD is presented and the relevant standards. As shown in chapter 6, the PTSD symptoms and diagnosis may be presented for a variety of purposes, including the insanity defense, self-defense, mental state, and mitigation. Each purpose has different standards and potential outcomes for veterans and nonveterans. Courts should provide specialized training for judges and others on PTSD that includes overviews of the nature of trauma, the symptoms of PTSD, how to deal with mental health professionals and the *DSM*, the concept of delayed onset and the one-month recovery period, the special problems involved in MST, and the range of criminal behavior that can be affected by PTSD. These subjects apply to PTSD in nonveterans as well as veterans.

Judges, lawyers, and court personnel must be educated on how PTSD relates to criminal behavior. When laws that protect privacy and confidentiality allow, the courts should cooperate with researchers concerning the relationship of combat PTSD to criminal behavior. Previously, research has been limited to appellate case reports, media accounts of high-profile cases, and occasional government studies that looked at the correlation of military combat, PTSD, and criminal behavior. Information available with respect to trial court proceedings has been difficult to obtain because of the lack of accessible records.

Judges must be educated concerning the proper role of problem-solving courts within the judicial process. The responsibilities of judges, lawyers, and others in these courts should be reconsidered. Problem-solving courts can play an important role in helping veterans and others to recover. Studies show that the process of readjustment is facilitated by ensuring that mental health services are available in order to shorten recovery time. Mediation will assist more than adversarial proceedings in cases that involve continuing relationships, such as marriages.

CONCLUSION

Psychiatric casualties of war have been misunderstood and mismanaged throughout the history of warfare. Although mistakes in interpretation and understanding may have been excusable before the psychiatric profession fully understood mental health problems, excuses no longer exist. Initiating or conducting military operations in ways that increase the likelihood of psychiatric casualties and failing to provide an adequate, effective transition to civilian life, with ongoing support services, is no longer justifiable. Although Congress and the military have implemented programs that address mental health issues, present measures are not yet as effective as they should be.[34]

Courts should be reactive participants in the combat PTSD story line, despite advocacy of proactive intervention by some proponents of veterans courts. Courts do not initiate or select their cases, and they should not overreach in an effort, however well meaning, to remedy the shortcomings of the other branches of government. They must remain steadfast in their role of providing equal justice to all. Despite their constitutional limitations, courts can improve the way they adjudicate criminal cases involving veterans, however, by providing fair, impartial, effective, and enlightened resolution of cases involving PTSD.

EPILOGUE:
THE FUTURE OF PTSD

War may be the least comprehensible human enterprise—too often initiated without clear goals or a meaningful assessment of consequences. Once war is underway, propelled by a life of its own and stubbornly defended with escalating rhetoric, the *fog of war* sweeps in to obscure plain truth. Regardless of the cause at stake, unintended consequences throw expectations into disarray; events spin out of control. Fueled by uncertainty, doubt, and a growing burden of mistakes, omissions, and half-truths, war is prolonged even in the face of mounting human and economic costs. Afterward, the meaning of a war remains obscure until the ebb and flow of events reveal unmistakable truths, subject to ongoing revision and reinterpretation.

The wars in Iraq and Afghanistan are hardly an exception. Although the decade-long conflicts have been widely reported by professional—and non-professional—journalists, bloggers, and filmmakers to an unprecedented extent, the meanings of the wars are only remotely understood. The public has heard countless personal stories from U.S. soldiers, and many more will emerge in the coming years.

FUTURE PERSPECTIVE: PERSONAL STORIES
The future outlook for soldiers and veterans of these wars is disheartening in some respects but encouraging in others. Many veterans, including those whose stories appear in these pages, continue to experience the adverse consequences of PTSD. Most of the veterans interviewed have, nonetheless, shown courage

219

and determination in restoring balance to their lives, accepting the consequences, and expressing optimism for the future. Although nearly all of them
have partially recovered from PTSD, it is sobering to realize that many other
veterans are not so fortunate.

Jay is grateful for his position as a peer counselor in a veterans center. He
says,

> I got a felony conviction for possession of narcotics. I'm grateful that I
> ended up here. Honestly, if I were not working here, I probably wouldn't
> be able to hold a job because of my mental illness. Even now I have bad
> days. I'm on meds all the time. . . . I still get depressed. . . . I don't know
> if it's PTSD or depression, but I see others with mental illness worse than
> mine and I don't feel so bad. I don't hold anyone else accountable for my
> life. I'm just grateful for every day that I can come here. People here show
> appreciation and support.

Although his life is not what he expected it to be, Jay feels grateful every
day that he escaped the despair that he once felt and that he has a place to go
where he can help other veterans.

Art works at a home for veterans. "It is nearly two years since I've been in
this job," he says.

> I love this job. I get to help people like myself. It's helping me too. No
> matter how bad a day gets for me, the people I visit are worse off. I still
> have trouble sleeping. I'm not cured, but I try not to think about it. I can't
> stand fireworks, though. I'm not scared of the fireworks but scared of
> what I will do because of the feeling I get . . . you know, go to a bar, have
> drinks, smoke crack. So I stay inside the house and turn the TV up. I
> wonder what would have happened if I'd stayed in twenty years. Would
> I be like this? Would I have grown out of it? My mother says in twenty
> years I probably would have died. I go to a Narcotics Anon meeting every
> night. . . . It keeps the focus off me. It's not about me anymore. It's about
> helping others, and as long as I do that, I help myself too. In that sense,
> PTSD is a positive force in my life. The other veterans—mostly from
> Korea or Vietnam—talk to us because we know.

Art's life so far has not met his expectations, but he focuses on gratitude for the help he received and the opportunities he has.

Ron volunteers at a social center for veterans. "I got clean ten years ago," he says.

I went to a religious program, although I wasn't looking for religion at that time. I made it through and learned more about PTSD with a clear mind and with God's help. . . . I'd had drug overdoses and nearly died because my liver barely functioned. I can look at myself today. I know I should be dead. . . . I should have died in Vietnam. I live with the symptoms of PTSD and nightmares . . . but I feel that God has truly blessed me.

The other veterans live with uncertainty, but they are not discouraged. Linda continues to have PTSD symptoms and gets counseling for her PTSD and her alcohol abuse. "I'd like to continue my art career," she says.

I think I had a lot of potential, and I'm trying to find out where I could get a job in art. . . . I came back from Iraq and felt I had missed out on everything. . . . I missed out on my social years. I just feel like I wasted them. Sometimes I feel like I want to be back in college because I miss walking outside my dorm and seeing someone I know all the time. . . . I have three or four jobs right now, but I can't stay like this my whole life. I'm going to miss out on life, and I don't want to. I just don't know what decision to make. That freaks me out.

Alan has taken positive steps in his recovery. "I'm a full-time student," he reports. "I just started at community college and declared my forestry major. I'll finish my credits at the community college and transfer to a state university. I went through a twenty-one-day program at the hospital. Now I'm out at a recovery house. . . . Doing a hell of a lot better. Sober a month and a half now." He has not found a new relationship but maintains a friendship with his former wife. He's optimistic about education and a career but is still working at absorbing the past experiences. Although he continues to have symptoms, he feels that he's come far in his recovery.

Julia returned from deployment with severe psychiatric problems. After being compelled to testify against the officer who had coerced her into a sexual relationship with him, she went into treatment with a psychiatrist at the VA. Although less than a year has passed since Julia was released from the hospital, she has gained emotional stability from her treatment. She no longer feels suicidal but remains vulnerable. She feels confident about her career goals.

Ray recovered from his worst days of PTSD without breaking stride. He completed his education and kept his marriage stable. If anything, he understates the progress he has made as well as the depth of his insights into PTSD. He still has bad times.

> Since I've been in school, I had a panic attack. I didn't lose consciousness but ended up falling. . . . I just don't know what caused it. People would never know I was in the military if I didn't tell them. What happened to me was a loss of control. It's made me a control freak. But I feel like I'm more adjusted now . . . and calmer. I feel like all these things are much better, but I don't know whether it's because time has gone by or because I've been able to self-diagnose and to cope better.

Dax has a full medical retirement for his combat injuries. As he put it,

> To this day I wake up and my pain level's an 8 out of 10. . . . I can be walking and suddenly my legs will go, ooh, not now, and drop out from underneath me, and once that happens I'm at 10 out of 10 pain. . . . I know what I've gotta live with on a day-to-day basis, and I'm okay with that. . . . As far as PTSD goes, it's an enemy that very few people understand or . . . know where it comes from or who's gonna get it. . . . They say that post-traumatic stress disorder is your body changing to where a chemical imbalance [exists and] you live in hypervigilant state.
>
> Nothing in particular happened to give me PTSD—even the kill-box situation that turned my hair gray in twenty-four hours. When I was over there, everything was fine. . . . I took care of my boys and did my job. . . . I'd have to say it was prolonged exposure, multiple tours, when you start changing your life and adapting to your situation, your surroundings, when it's not just a couple of weeks or months, but years. Stress becomes your normal. It's almost like your heart has a valve, and when there's stress, it starts pumping. It's either fight or flight. When

you're exposed to that for years, the valve never quite shuts off. Because of that and because you're trained not to sleep, somebody comes up and scares you—not meaning to—you do what you're trained to do. When I got back, when my wife walked into the room, she made sure she said something before coming in. That's PTSD. . . .

I went through all the classes for PTSD, and I'm not on medication for it now. It took me to the end of 2008 to get better. But you never get over PTSD. The effects are still there, but I've got a buffer . . . now that I never had before. . . . I can teach about it, and we have classes for new vets so they can learn how to deal with it. . . . We want the young ones to hear the live stories [from older veterans]—to learn from something other than a textbook and a doctor, to make the young vets open up by talking with people who've been in combat like them.

I'm medically retired. I'm not able to work. So what I do is I try to help veterans with their paperwork as far as getting the benefits they deserve, and they deserve a hell of a lot that they're not getting, and a lot less of the headaches that they're getting because of it. There's a lot of things that need to be changed in this system, and it needs people in it that are mature enough to put the politics aside.

I'll be thirty next September. I can't go back in the military. If I could, I'd do it in a heartbeat. I miss most the camaraderie—the brotherly love. One of the ways I can contribute is by helping those who come back—to make sure they don't have to deal with what I did when I got back . . . and to be respected for putting their lives on the line.

FORESEEING COMBAT TRAUMA

Psychiatric casualties have occurred in all wars, long before PTSD was identified. Conditions in recent wars have been more conducive to PTSD because of many factors, including increased firepower, widespread use of lethal weapons against American soldiers, and the absence of clear lines of demarcation between combatants and civilians. These factors may well have precipitated violence toward civilians and increased incidence of psychiatric problems attributable to moral injury. Redeployments and the absence of clear and consistent military objectives have contributed to the stress. Favorable survival rates, made possible by improvements in medical care, have also led to greater incidence of psychiatric injuries as soldiers who historically would not have survived injuries do survive.[1]

The economic approach generally used in evaluating the costs of war is far too limited. Human costs, including psychiatric disorders, divorces, emotional distress in veterans' spouses and children, impaired decision making, and loss of employment skills, as well as injuries and deaths, have adverse impact on the quality of life in American society, which, after all, is what the government seeks to preserve by going to war. Before undertaking any military intervention, it is crucial to make short-range and long-range assessments of human costs. Short-range assessments should take into account the potential risks to mental and physical welfare during deployment and during the first five to ten years after deployment. Short-range consequences include marriage and family readjustment problems, domestic violence, unemployment, criminal law violations, drug and alcohol abuse, suicide, and homelessness. Long-range effects of war include the impact of the lifelong mental and emotional impairment of individuals. The effects of PTSD can have a cumulative effect on veterans and their family members. Because PTSD can adversely affect the capacity to make wise life decisions, it is not enough to consider only the immediate results of combat trauma. The effects may last a lifetime.

THE FUTURE OF WAR

The mental health injuries of veterans that have surfaced in the wake of deployments to Iraq and Afghanistan are the first warning signs of a tidal wave of social, economic, and legal problems for American society. Although the mental injuries of combat may at times seem invisible during wartime, they emerge unmistakably in the form of social, domestic, medical, economic, and criminal dysfunction once soldiers reenter civilian society.

Even as American troops remain in Iraq and Afghanistan, turmoil in other places threatens to draw political leaders into new military interventions. At the same time, every day brings new stories of human events involving the psychiatric injuries of war along with their devastating consequences. The public must be wary of a rush to judgment about the nature and causes of these events as well as the necessity of these potential interventions. Perspectives on the meaning and consequences of the recent wars and of future interventions will be subject to ongoing reinterpretation and change.

Global events and policies are far too unstable to permit reliable predictions about future wars and future psychiatric casualties. Present warnings indicate, however, that the pattern may be shifting from a series of infrequent major wars to a state of persistent tension, punctuated by sporadic outbreaks of hostilities with terrorist groups and small-scale insurgencies, along with the potential of larger conflicts with world powers. Military leaders and Defense Department officials have said that the United States may be locked in a hostile relationship with a network of terrorist groups for a generation.[2] This novel state of affairs has all the elements needed to produce explosive outbreaks of PTSD and other psychiatric casualties. Based on recent experience, few people would dispute that the demands of a decade of American warfare have already traumatized the present generation of soldiers and their families to an unprecedented extent.

Theories circulate about the differences among the various types, or generations, of warfare—third, fourth, fifth, and more. Whatever future changes in warfare may turn out to be, however, it is likely that technological changes will increase, not decrease, the level of operational stress on individual combatants. Future wars may well involve multiple deployments, increased firepower, and protracted wars unmarked by signs of what victory might be. Wars without clear and achievable objectives, well-defined durations, and articulated goals will be as disastrous in the future as they have been in the past. When accompanied by lowered standards for enlistment borne of necessity, multiple deployments, and public indifference or opposition, these military actions seem bound to result in high levels of psychiatric casualties. Such wars, lacking clear objectives, are likely to generate high levels of unintended consequences leading to ambivalence and doubt—the *perfect storm* for PTSD.

This state of affairs translates into constant challenge, not only to the military, but to the medical, mental health, social service, legal, and economic resources of American society. Many soldiers will be killed in combat, and many more will return to repair their fractured lives while facing months, years, decades, or even lifetimes of overcoming mental and physical disability. It is essential to minimize—or avoid—this outcome that threatens to drain American family, social, political, and economic life of the vitality of hundreds of thousands of promising young women and men.

Although we cannot control the provocations of those who would seek to draw us into conflict contrary to our best interests, we can control the way we respond. In each instance, the potential damage to the people put in harm's way in the name of preserving a democratic way of life deserves to be weighed along with any potential benefit. When civilian leaders decide, after due deliberation and exploration of alternatives, that use of military force is unavoidably and urgently needed, it is essential that clear, realistic, and strict guidelines be given to the military as to what the objectives are, how to achieve them, and how to prevent or minimize mental and physical casualties.

Recent comments by former secretary of defense Robert Gates reflect his new appreciation of the human costs of war. Secretary Gates reportedly commented in an interview that he is "wary of wars of choice." According to the report, "The human costs of the wars in Iraq and Afghanistan had made [Gates] far more wary about unleashing the might of the American armed forces."[3] Awareness of this sort could lead to wiser decisions concerning the deployment of military force.

The picture of the nation besieged by endless war is bleak. Political courage will be needed to stem the drain of conflict on human and economic resources. Creative use of diplomatic negotiation to resolve disputes and respond to threats will be essential. Independent and effective media coverage of war will be important to ensure unfiltered news about the status of conflict. Courts, in dealing with veterans' cases, should adjudicate and manage veterans' criminal cases with sensitivity and wisdom while maintaining the guarantee of equal protection of the law. Commitment on the part of civilian and military leaders to take into account war's human costs is a vital step toward wise policy decision making.

Since the post-Vietnam years, when the relationship between individuals and the government underwent radical change, the evolution of American social culture has continued to accelerate. It would appear that people see themselves as autonomous and not morally bound to their government's actions. At the same time, with consumerism and self-interest appearing to gain a strong grip on the attention of the public, there is legitimate concern about the will of the people to hold the government accountable for its foreign policy decisions, including foreign interventions. A citizenry that becomes disengaged and disinterested in what its government does and fails to do places its own independence, autonomy, and political power at grave risk of being usurped by those, at home and abroad, who would exploit it for their own interests, contrary to the best interests of the American public. Citizens as well as political leaders must meet their responsibilities wisely, courageously, and steadfastly in the national interest in order to fulfill America's historic promise of moral, as well as political and economic, leadership in the world. The determination, dedication, and courage of the veterans who have sacrificed in America's name will help to seal that promise.

NOTES

1. THE BATTLE THAT NEVER ENDS

1   U.S. Department of Veterans Affairs Fifth Annual Report, 2007, quoted in William B. Brown, "Another Emerging 'Storm': Iraq and Afghanistan Veterans with PTSD in the Criminal Justice System," *Justice Policy Journal* 5 (Fall 2008): 13; and Larry Minear, *Through Veterans' Eyes: The Iraq and Afghanistan Experience* (Washington, DC: Potomac Books, Inc., 2010), 9. See also "PTSD in Service Members and New Veterans of the Iraq and Afghanistan Wars," *PTSD Research Quarterly* 20, no. 1 (Winter 2009): 1, 2; Michelle Tan, "2 Million Troops Have Deployed since 9/11," *Marine Corps Times*, December 18, 2009; Michelle Tan, "A Million Soldiers Deployed since 9/11," *Army Times*, December 20, 2009.

2   Brown, "Another Emerging 'Storm,'"13.

3   John O'Connor, "TV: Vietnam Veterans, U.S. Crime and Prison," *New York Times*, July 15, 1982.

4   Ibid.

5   Erin M. Gover, "Iraq as a Psychological Quagmire: The Implications of Using Post-Traumatic Stress Disorder as a Defense for Iraq War Veterans," *Pace Law Review* 28 (2007–2008): 561n5.

6   Margaret E. Noonan and Christopher J. Mumola, *Veterans in State and Federal Prison, 2004*, Bureau of Justice Statistics Special Report (Washington, DC: U.S. Department of Justice, 2007), http://bjs.ojp.usdoj.gov/content/pub/pdf/vsfp04.pdf.

7   Chris Rohlfs, "Does Military Service Make You a More Violent Person? Evidence from the Vietnam Draft," *Journal of Human Resources* 45 (November 2010): 17.

8   Greg A. Greenberg et al., "Risk of Incarceration among Male Veterans and Nonveterans: Are Veterans of the All Volunteer Force at Greater Risk?" *Armed Forces & Society* 33 (April 2007): 337.

9 Jonathan Shay, *Odysseus in America: Combat Trauma and the Trials of Homecoming* (New York: Scribner, 2002).

10 Charles W. Hoge, *Once a Warrior, Always a Warrior: Navigating the Transition from Combat to Home—Including Combat Stress, PTSD, and mTBI* (Guilford, CT: Globe Pequot Press, 2010), 17.

11 Robert D. Haycock, *Arming Commanders to Combat PTSD: A Time for Change—Attacking the Stressors vice the Symptoms* (Fort Leavenworth, KS: School of Advanced Military Studies, U.S. Army Command and General Staff College, 2009), 33.

12 For more on post-traumatic growth, see Richard Tedeschi and Lawrence Calhoun, "Posttraumatic Growth: A New Perspective on Psychotraumatology," *Psychiatric Times* 21, no. 4 (April 1, 2004), http://www.psychiatrictimes.com/print/article /10168/54661?printable=true; Daisuke Nishi et al., "Posttraumatic Growth, Posttraumatic Stress Disorder and Resilience of Motor Vehicle Accident Survivors," *Biopsychosocial Medicine* 4, no.7 (2010), http://www.bpsmedicine.com /content/4/1/7; and Jim Rendon, "Post-Traumatic Stress's Surprisingly Positive Flip Side," *New York Times*, March 22, 2012, http://www.nytimes.com /2012/03/25/magazine/post-traumatic-stresss-surprisingly-positive-flip-side.html ?pagewanted=print.

13 Ben Shephard, *A War of Nerves: Soldiers and Psychiatrists in the Twentieth Century* (Cambridge, MA: Harvard University Press, 2001), 385.

14 David Dobbs, "Soldiers' Stress: What Doctors Get Wrong About PTSD" (quoting Richard McNally), Scientific American Magazine, April 13, 2009, 98 https://www .scientificamerican.com/article.cfm?id=post-traumatic-stress-trap.

15 Hoge, *Once a Warrior, Always a Warrior*, 5.

16 Ann Scott Tyson, "Youths in Rural U.S. Are Drawn to Military," *Washington Post*, November 4, 2005.

17 Shephard, *War of Nerves*, 344.

18 Richard A. Gabriel, *The Painful Field: The Psychiatric Dimension of Modern War* (New York: Greenwood Press, 1988), 9.

19 Daryl S. Paulson and Stanley Krippner, *Haunted by Combat: Understanding PTSD in War Veterans Including Women, Reservists, and Those Coming Back from Iraq* (Westport, CT: Praeger, 2007), 8; Gabriel, *Painful Field*, 7.

20 Bessel A. van der Kolk, "The History of Trauma in Psychiatry," in *Handbook of PTSD Science and Practice*, ed. Matthew J. Friedman, Terence Martin Keane, and Patricia A. Resick (New York: Guilford Press, 2007), 19.

21 Timothy P. Hayes, "Post-Traumatic Stress Disorder on Trial," *Military Law Review* 190/191 (2006–2007): 69.

22 Ruwan M. Jayatunge, "History of PTSD: The History of Post-Traumatic Stress Disorder," *GI Rights News* (blog), January 4, 2010, http://girightsnews.blogspot.com /2010/01/history-of-ptsd.html.

23 Gabriel, *Painful Field*, 8.

24 van der Kolk, "History of Trauma in Psychiatry," 19; Shay, *Odysseus in America*, 1.

25 Jonathan Shay, *Achilles in Vietnam: Combat Trauma and the Undoing of Character* (New York: Atheneum, 1994), 52.

26 Adam Phillips, "'Theater of War' Seeks to Heal Soldiers: Ancient Greek Warrior Plays Promote Frank Discussion of Post-Traumatic Stress," *Voice of America*, August 23, 2010, http://www.voanews.com/english/news/usa/arts/Theater-of-War-Seeks-to -Heal-Soldiers-101313629.html.

27 Gabriel, *Painful Field*, 10–11.

28 Gabriel, *Painful Field*, 14, 16–17.

29 Franklin D. Jones et al., eds., *War Psychiatry*, Textbooks of Military Medicine (Falls Church, VA: Office of the Surgeon General, U.S. Army, 1995), 6.

30 "Nostalgia: A Vanished Disease," *British Medical Journal* 10 (April 1976): 857.

31 Jones, *War Psychiatry*, 6.

32 Roger J. Spiller, "Shellshock," *American Heritage Magazine* 41 (May/June 1990): 3.

33 Ibid.

34 Ibid., 4.

35 Terri Tanielian and Lisa H. Jaycox, *Invisible Wounds of War: Psychological and Cognitive Injuries, Their Consequences, and Services to Assist Recovery* (Santa Monica, CA: Rand, 2008), xi, 3–6.

36 Ibid.

37 Ibid., xxi.

38 Thomas L. Hafemeister and Nicole A. Stockey, "Last Stand? The Criminal Responsibility of War Veterans Returning from Iraq and Afghanistan with Post-Traumatic Stress Disorder," *Indiana Law Journal* 85, no. 1 (2010): 90n12.; Michael P. Atkinson et al., "A Dynamic Model for Post-Traumatic Stress Disorder among U.S. Troops in Operation Iraqi Freedom," *Management Science* 55 (September 2009): 1454, 1461.

39 Hafemeister and Stockley, "Last Stand?," 91n14.

40 Michael J. Davidson, "Post-Traumatic Stress Disorder: A Controversial Defense for Veterans of a Controversial War," *William and Mary Law Review* 29 (Winter 1988): 415.

41 Hafemeister and Stockley, "Last Stand?," 91–92.

42 Ann R. Auberry, "PTSD: Effective Representation of a Vietnam Veteran in the Criminal Justice System," *Marquette Law Review* 68 (Winter 1985): 647.

43 Haycock, *Arming Commanders*, 1–2.

44 Barry R. Schaller, *Understanding Bioethics and the Law: The Promises and Perils of the Brave New World of Biotechnology* (Westport, CT: Praeger, 2008).

45 Barry R. Schaller, *A Vision of American Law: Judging Law, Literature, and the Stories We Tell* (Westport, CT: Praeger, 2001), 1, 78.

2. COMBAT PTSD: A MOVING TARGET

1 Tanielian and Jaycox, *Invisible Wounds of War.*

2 Jasmine Morales, "Soldiers Learn How to Get out of the 'Battle Mind' and Back into the 'Peacetime Mind,'" The United States Army, March 23, 2009, http://www.army.mil /article/18608/; "PTSD Treatment Programs in the U.S. Department of Veterans Affairs," U.S. Department of Veterans Affairs, January 1, 2007, http://www.ptsd.va.gov /public/pages/va-ptsd-treatment-programs.asp.

3 Charles W. Hoge et al., "Combat Duty in Iraq and Afghanistan, Mental Health Problems, and Barriers to Care," *New England Journal of Medicine* 351, no. 1 (July 2004): 20; Minear, *Through Veterans' Eyes*, 157–58.

4 "Many Vets Struggle with PTSD," *South Source*, n.d., http://source.southuniversity.edu/many-vets-struggle-with-ptsd-20290.aspx.

5 Hoge, *Once a Warrior, Always a Warrior*, 1.

6 Ibid., xx.

7 Psych Central News Editor, "PTSD Nearly Doubles Risk of Dementia," *Psych Central*, June 2010, http://psychcentral.com/news/2010/06/08/ptsd-nearly-doubles-risk-of-dementia/14401.html; Crystal Phend, "Smaller Brain Linked to Soldiers' PTSD Risk," *MedPage Today*, December 8, 2009, http://www.medpagetoday.com /PublicHealthPolicy/MilitaryMedicine/17380.

8 Hoge, *Once a Warrior, Always a Warrior*, 6.

9 Ibid., 38–39.

10 Matthew J. Friedman et al., eds., *Handbook of PTSD Science and Practice* (New York: Guilford Press, 2007), 3.

11 Ibid., 4.

12 American Psychiatric Association, *Diagnostic and Statistical Manual of Mental Disorders, DSM-III-R*, 3rd ed. rev. (Washington, DC: American Psychiatric Association, 1987), 247–51.

13 American Psychiatric Association, *Diagnostic and Statistical Manual of Mental Disorders, DSM-IV-TR*, 4th ed. (Washington, DC: American Psychiatric Association,

2000), 463–69. All additional definitions and criteria not otherwise cited are from the *DSM*, including the *DSM-III*, *DSM-III-R*, *DSM-IV*, and *DSM-IV-TR*.

14 Hoge, *Once a Warrior, Always a Warrior*, 10–11.

15 Hafemeister and Stockey, "Last Stand?," 95.

16 Friedman, *Handbook of PTSD Science and Practice*, 1.

17 Ibid., 81–82; Lisa DeLuca, "Combat PTSD and Iraq War Soldiers: Why Afghanistan and Iraq Combat Veterans Often Don't Seek PTSD Therapy," *Suite 101.com*, May 15, 2009, http://post-traumatic-stress-disorder.suite101.com/article.cfm/combat _ptsd_iraq_war_veterans.

18 Hans Pols and Stephanie Oak, "War and Military Mental Health: The U.S. Psychiatric Response in the 20th Century," *American Journal of Public Health* 97 (December 2007): 2136.

19 Edgar Jones, "Flashbacks and Post-Traumatic Stress Disorder: The Genesis of a 20th-Century Diagnosis," *British Journal of Psychiatry* 182 (2003): 158.

20 Gabriel, *Painful Field*, 25.

21 Bruce Ackerman, "Don't Panic," *London Review of Books* 24, no.3 (February 2002), 15.

22 Gabriel, *Painful Field*, 25.

23 Rachel Yehuda and Alexander C. McFarlane, "PTSD Is a Valid Diagnosis: Who Benefits from Challenging Its Existence?" *Psychiatric Times*, July 2009.

24 Jones, "Flashbacks and Post-Traumatic Stress Disorder," 158–63.

25 Pols and Oak, "War and Military Mental Health," 2132.

26 Hoge, *Once a Warrior, Always a Warrior*, 26.

27 Wilbur J. Scott, "PTSD in DSM-III: A Case in the Politics of Diagnosis and Disease," *Social Problems* 37 (1990): 295.

28 Bernice Andrews et al., "Delayed-Onset Posttraumatic Stress Disorder: A Systematic Review of the Evidence," *American Journal Psychiatry* 164 (September 2007), http://ajp.psychiatryonline.org/cgi/content/full/164/9/1319.

29 N. Hunt and I. Robbins, "The Long-Term Consequences of War: The Experience of World War II," *Aging & Mental Health* 5, no. 2 (2001): 183–90.

30 Hays, "Post-Traumatic Stress Disorder on Trial," 73.

31 Hoge, *Once a Warrior, Always a Warrior*, 37–39.

32 Hays, "Post-Traumatic Stress Disorder on Trial," 73–74.

33 Hoge, *Once a Warrior, Always a Warrior*, 6.

34 Ibid., 6–7.

35 Ibid., 3.

36 Hafemeister and Stockley, "Last Stand?," 96–97.

37 David Dobbs, "The Post-Traumatic Stress Trap," *Scientific American* 300 (2009): 64–69.

38 "Should More Veterans Get PTSD Benefits?" *New York Times*, July 8, 2010; Dobbs, "Post-Traumatic Stress Trap," 65–66.

39 "Belmont Report: Ethical Principles and Guidelines for the Protection of Human Subjects of Research," 44 Fed. Reg. 76 (April 18, 1979).

40 Brett T. Litz et al., "Moral Injury and Moral Repair in War Veterans: A Preliminary Model and Intervention Strategy," *Clinical Psychology Review* 28 (December 2009): 695–706.

41 Matthew J. Friedman, "Post-Vietnam Syndrome: Recognition and Management," *Psychosomatics* 22 (1981): 931–43.

42 Litz, "Moral Injury and Moral Repair in War Veterans," 695–706.

43 Amy Blumenshine, "Addressing Moral Injury among Military Veterans, *InterActs* (February 2010): 12.

44 Casey T. Taft, Dawne S. Vogt, and Amy D. Marshall, "Aggression among Combat Veterans: Relationship with Combat Exposure and Symptoms of Posttraumatic Stress Disorder, Dysphoria, and Anxiety," *Journal of Traumatic Stress* 20 (April 2007): 135–45.

45 "Crime Linked to Combat Stress," PTSD Support Services, December 20, 2010, http://www.ptsdsupport.net/crime_linked_to_combat_stress.html.

3. ACROSS THE AGES: PTSD FROM THE CIVIL WAR TO KOREA

1 Eric T. Dean Jr., *Shook over Hell: Post-Traumatic Stress, Vietnam, and the Civil War* (Cambridge, MA: Harvard University Press, 1997), 26.

2 Scott, "PTSD in DSM-III," 295.

3 John Huston, *Let There Be Light*, directed by John Huston, filmed at Edgewood State hospital, commack, Long Island, NY (1946; Nobility Studios, 1980), DVD.

4 Jones et al., *War Psychiatry*, 8.

5 Hays, "Post-Traumatic Stress Disorder on Trial," 70.

6 Hannah Fisher, "American War and Military Operations Casualties: Lists and Statistics," Navy Department Library, Department of the Navy, July 13, 2005, http://www.history.navy.mil/library/online/american%20war%20casualty.htm; "Civil War: Casualties and Costs of the Civil War," Digital History, http://www.digitalhistory.uh.edu/historyonline/us20.cfm; "Civil War Statistics," http://www.phil.muni.cz/~vndrzl/amstudies/civilwar_stats.htm.

7 Dean, *Shook over Hell*, 51.

8 Ibid., 55–57, 59, 68–69.

9 Ibid., 70, 72, 74.

10 Ibid., 75–77.

11 Ibid., 90.

12 Ibid., 91–98.

13 Ibid., 98–99

14 Betty B. Rosenbaum, "The Relationship between War and Crime in the United States," *Journal of Criminal Law and Criminology* 30 (January/February 1940): 725–40.

15 Dean, *Shook over Hell*, 111, 114.

16 Ibid., 116–17.

17 Ibid., 120–23, 126, 134.

18 Ibid., 134, 159–60.

19 Gabriel, *Painful Field*, 26-27.

20 Spiller, "Shellshock," 5, 6.

21 Ibid., 6–7.

22 Jones, *War Psychiatry*, 9; Hays, "Post-Traumatic Stress Disorder on Trial," 71.

23 Jones, *War Psychiatry*, 10; Hays, "Post-Traumatic Stress Disorder on Trial," 71.

24 Jones, *War Psychiatry*, 10.

25 Ibid., 10–12.

26 Spiller, "Shellshock," 8.

27 Hans Pols, "Waking Up to Shell Shock: Psychiatry in the U.S. Military during World War II," *Endeavour* 30 (December 2006): 144.

28 Ibid., 145.

29 Spiller, "Shellshock," 8.

30 Fisher, "American War and Military Operations Casualties."

31 Pols and Oak, "War and Military Mental Health," 2136.

32 Gabriel, *Painful Field*, 27–28.

33 Hays, "Post-Traumatic Stress Disorder on Trial," 71.

34 Scott, "PTSD in DSM-III," 296.

35 Pols, "Waking Up to Shell Shock," 145.

36 Ibid., 146.

37 According to Pols, "It has since become known that Marshall fabricated most of his statistics. This, however, does not detract from his enormous influence on US Army training practices." Pols, "Waking Up to Shell Shock," 147n23.

38 S. L. A. Marshall, *Men against Fire: The Problem of Battle Command in Future War* (New York: University of Oklahoma Press, 1947), 78; Pols, "Waking Up to Shell Shock," 148.

39 Pols, "Waking Up to Shell Shock," 148.

40 Ibid.; Marshall, *Men against Fire, 79.*

41 Jones, *War Psychiatry*, 12.

42 Ibid., 14.

43 Spiller, "Shellshock," 9.

44 Hans Pols, "War Neurosis, Adjustment Problems in Veterans, and an Ill Nation: The Disciplinary Project of American Psychiatry during and after World War II," *History of Science Society* 22 (2007): 81.

45 Richard Polenberg, "The Good War? A Reappraisal of How World War II Affected American Society," *Virginia Magazine of History and Biography* 100 (July 1992): 295, 298.

46 Pols, "War Neurosis, Adjustment Problems in Vietnam, and an Ill Nation," 82.

47 Bob Hebert, "An Overdue 'Welcome Home,'" *New York Times*, May 15, 2010.

48 Pols, "War Neurosis, Adjustment Problems in Vietnam, and an Ill Nation," 83–84.

49 Ibid.

50 Hays, "Post-Traumatic Stress Disorder on Trial," 296.

51 Shephard, *War of Nerves*, 341.

52 Gabriel, *Painful Field*, 28–29.

53 Shephard, *War of Nerves*, 342; Haycock, *Arming Commanders to Combat PTSD*, 11, 12.

54 Dave Grossman and Bruce K. Siddle, "Psychological Effects of Combat," in *Encyclopedia of Violence, Peace and Conflict*, ed. Lester Kurtz (San Diego: Academic Press, 1999), found online at http://www.killology.com/print/print_psychological.htm; "Weather Report—Korean War," *Korean War Educator*, http://www.koreanwar-educator.org/topics/weather/weather.htm; Delaware Commission of Veterans Affairs, "Korean War Veterans' '50s Frostbite Injuries Return to Haunt Them,'" *Centurion* 5 (October–December 1996).

55 Jones, *War Psychiatry*, 16.

56 Hays, "Post-Traumatic Stress Disorder on Trial," 75.

57 Jones, *War Psychiatry*, 16.

58 Gabriel, *Painful Field*, 8.

4. THE POLITICS OF PTSD: VIETNAM

1 Spiller, "Shellshock," 3.

2 Ibid.

3 Pols and Oak, "War and Military Mental Health," 2137.

4 Ibid.; Simon Wessely, "Twentieth-Century Theories on Combat Motivation and Breakdown," *Journal of Contemporary History* 41 (April 2006): 281–82.

5 Gabriel, *Painful Field*, 29.

6 Ibid.

7 Pols, "War and Military Mental Health," 2138.

8 Gabriel, *Painful Field*, 30.

9 Ethan Watters, "The Way We Live Now: Idea Lab; Suffering Differently," *New York Times*, August 12, 2007.

10 Richard A. Kulka, *Trauma and the Vietnam War Generation: Report of Findings from the National Vietnam Veterans Readjustment Study* (New York: Brunner/Mazel, 1990), 23.

11 Jones, *War Psychiatry*, 17; Pols and Oak, "War and Military Mental Health," 2138; History Place, "The Vietnam War: The Bitter End 1969–1975," 1999, http://www.historyplace.com/unitedstates/vietnam/index-1969.html; William Gardner Bell and Karl E. Cocke, eds., "Introduction," in *Department of the Army Historical Summary: Fiscal Year 1973* (Washington, DC: Center of Military History, U.S. Army, 1977), http://www.history.army.mil/books/dahsum/1973/chI.htm.

12 Shephard, *War of Nerves*, 341.

13 Ibid., 340.

14 Ibid., 344.

15 Ibid., 348.

16 Ibid., 351, 352.

17 See the personal stories of Rich and Lee in Shephard, *War of Nerves*, 352.

18 Ibid., 348.

19 Ibid., 349.

20 Jones, *War Psychiatry*, 17.

21 Shephard, *War of Nerves*, 350.

22 Jones, *War Psychiatry*, 17, 19.

23 Ibid., 6, 20.

24 Shephard, *War of Nerves*, 349.

25 Ibid., 353.

5. THE CAMPAIGN FOR PTSD

1 Dean, *Shook over Hell*, 8, 9.

2 Ibid.

3 Jerry Lembcke, "The 'Right Stuff' Gone Wrong: Vietnam Veterans and the Social Construction of Post-Traumatic Stress Disorder," *Critical Sociology* 24 (January 1998): 37.

4 Ibid., 40, 41, 46.

5 Ibid., 48, 49, 56, 57.

6 Dean, *Shook over Hell*, 9.

7 Ibid., 12, 13.

8 Ibid., 14–15.

9 Ibid.

10 Ibid., 23.

11 Shephard, *War of Nerves*, 355.

12 Scott, "PTSD in DSM-III," 298; PBS, "The Mai Lai Massacre," *Vietnam Online*, March 29, 2005, http://www.pbs.org/wgbh/amex/vietnam/trenches/my_lai.html; West's Encyclopedia of American Law, "My Lai Massacre," *Encyclopedia.com*, 2005, http://www.encyclopedia.com/topic/My_Lai_incident.aspx#2.

13 Scott, "PTSD in DSM-III," 298.

14 Ibid., 299.

15 Ibid., 300, 301.

16 Shephard, *War of Nerves*, 357.

17 Ibid., 360–61.

18 Scott, "PTSD in DSM-III," 305.

19 Shephard, *War of Nerves*, 367.

20 Scott, "PTSD in DSM-III," 307–8.

21 Ibid., 308.

22 Ibid.

23 Shephard, *War of Nerves*, 368.

24 Dave Grossman, *On Killing: The Psychological Cost of Learning to Kill in War and Society*, rev. ed. (New York: Little, Brown, 2009), 4.

25 Ibid., 266–67.

26 Ibid., 268–70, 276–77.

27 Ibid., 251–63.

6. VIETNAM VETERANS IN THE DOCK

1 Wellborn Jack Jr., "The Vietnam Connection: Charles Heads' Verdict," *National College for Criminal Defense* 9 (January–February 1982): 7.

2 "War Echoes in the Courts," *Newsweek*, November 23 1981, 103. See *State v. Heads*, 385 So.2d 230, 231–32 (La. 1980), for a complete statement of the facts; and Samuel P. Menefee, "The 'Vietnam Syndrome' Defense: A 'G.I. Bill of Criminal Rights'?" *Army Lawyer*, February 1985, 14–15.

3 Jack, "Vietnam Connection," 7–8.

4 See, for example, criminal cases involving John R. Coughlin and Stephen W. Gregory, discussed in Menefee, "'Vietnam Syndrome' Defense," 1, 6.

5 C. Peter Erlinder, "Paying the Price for Vietnam: Post-Traumatic Stress Disorder and Criminal Behavior," *Boston College Law Review* 25 (1983–84): 314.

6 *State v. Heads*, 370 So.2d 564 (La. 1979).

7 Jack, "Vietnam Connection," 7–8.

8 Menefee, "'Vietnam Syndrome' Defense," 6.

9 Jack, "Vietnam Connection," 8, 9.

10 Ibid., 9, 10.

11 Ibid., 15–18, 320–21.

12 Menefee, "'Vietnam Syndrome' Defense," 14.

13 Jack, "Vietnam Connection," 12–17; Erlinder, "Paying the Price for Vietnam," 321.

14 Hafemeister and Stockey, "Last Stand?," 122; Michael J. Davidson, "Post-Traumatic Stress Disorder: A Controversial Defense for Veterans of a Controversial War," *William and Mary Law Review* 29 (Winter 1988): 423

15 Davidson, "Post-Traumatic Stress Disorder," 422n55.

16 Hafemeister and Stockey, "Last Stand?," 100.

17 Ibid., 101.

18 John P. Wilson and Sheldon D. Zigelbaum, "The Vietnam Veteran on Trial: The Relation of Post-Traumatic Stress Disorder to Criminal Behavior," *Behavioral Science and Law* 1, no. 3: (1983): 69, 83.

19 Ibid., 83.

20 Hafemeister and Stockey, "Last Stand?," 101, 102.

21 William E. Copeland, Gordon Keeler, Adrian Angold, and E. Jane Costello, "Posttraumatic Stress without Trauma in Children," *American Journal of Psychiatry* 167, no. 9 (September 2010): 1059–65, http://www.ncbi.nlm.nih.gov/pmc/articles/PMC2936664/.

22 Kulka, *Trama and the Vietnam War Generation*, xxiv, 3.

23 Ibid., xxviii.

24 Ibid., xxviii, 7, 186.

25 Ibid., 187–88.

26 Ibid., 279–80

27 Ibid., xxviii, xxix.

28 Daniel J. DeNoon, "Fewer Vietnam Vets Suffer from PTSD," *CBSNEWS*, August 17, 2006, http://www.cbsnews.com/stories/2006/08/17/health/webmd /main1908799.shtml; Bruce P. Dohrenwend, J. Blake Turner, Nicholas A. Turse, Ben G. Adams, Karestan C. Koenen, and Randall Marshall, "The Psychological Risks of Vietnam for Veterans," *Science* 313, no. 5789 (August 18, 2006): 979–82.

29 *State v. Felde*, 422 So.2d 370 (La.1982), *cert. denied*, 461 U.S. 918 (1983); Case No. 82-CR-310 (Cir.Ct.Door County, Wis., 1982). See also Susan Milstein, "War Is Hell. It's Also a Good Defense," *The American Lawyer* (October 1983): 100.

30 "Pleading PTSD: Novel Defense for Vietnam Vets," *Time*, May 26, 1980.

31 No. 19205 (Cir.Ct.Montgomery County Md. 1979); No. 80-00135-01-S (D.Mass. 1980); Erlinder, "Paying the Price for Vietnam," 325, 326.

32 541 F.Supp. 142 (D.Mass. 1982).

33 Menefee, "'Vietnam Syndrome' Defense," 20, 21.

34 Auberry, "PTSD," 647.

35 Auberry, "PTSD," 647–48; Milstein, *War is Hell, The American Lawyer*, 100.

36 No. 1484-79 (N.J. Super.Ct. 1981).

37 Ford, "In Defense of the Defenders: The Vietnam Vet Syndrome," *Criminal Law Bulletin* 19 (1983): 434, 440, quoted in Menefee, "'Vietnam Syndrome' Defense," 15.

38 Ibid.

39 Felde, supra n34.

40 Menefee, "'Vietnam Syndrome' Defense."

41 Ibid., 10.

42 Ibid., 10–12.

43 Ibid., 13.

44 Elizabeth J. Delgado, "Vietnam Stress Syndrome and the Criminal Defendant," *Loyola Law Review* 19 (1985): 473, 489.

45 Menefee, "'Vietnam Syndrome' Defense," 14.

46 Doug Magee, "The Long War of Wayne Felde," *The Nation*, February 5, 2008.

47 Erlinder, "Paying the Price for Vietnam," 334–36.

48 No. 19205 (Cir.Ct.Montgomery County, Md. 1979); Auberry, "PTSD," 659.

49 Auberry, "PTSD," 659; Erlinder, "Paying the Price for Vietnam," 340.

50 David Beneman, "Understanding Affirmative Defenses," *www.fd.org*, http://www.fd.org /pdf_lib/Beneman_Affirmative_Defenses_materials.pdf; "Affirmative Defense," *Free Dictionary*, http://legal-dictionary.thefreedictionary.com/Affirmative+Defense.

51 Delgado, "Vietnam Stress Syndrome," 474.

52 Erin M. Gover, "Iraq as a Psychological Quagmire: The Implications of Using Post-Traumatic Stress Disorder as a Defense for Iraq War Veterans," *Pace Law Review* 28 (2008): 561, 576–77.

53 653 S.W.2d 404–6 (Tenn. 1983); Delgado, "Vietnam Stress Syndrome," 473.

54 Sup. Ct. Order No. 2908-2-PC (Sup.Ct.Ariz. 1983); No. CR-75687 (Supreme Court Maricopa County, AZ, 1984).

55 Erlinder, "Paying the Price for Vietnam," 342–43.

56 Lembcke, "'Right Stuff' Gone Wrong," 49–51.

57 Peter Karsten, "The US Citizen-Soldier's Past, Present, and Likely Future," *Parameters*, Summer 2001, 61–73.

7. BREEDING GROUND FOR PTSD: IRAQ AND AFGHANISTAN

1 Tanielian and Jaycox, *Invisible Wounds of War*.

2 White House, *Strengthening Our Military Families: Meeting America's Commitment* (Washington, DC, January 2011), http://www.defense.gov/home/features/2011 /0111_initiative/strengthening_our_military_january_2011.pdf; John Matson, "Legacy of Mental Health Problems from Iraq and Afghanistan Wars Will Be Long-Lived," *Scientific American*, June 27, 2011; Moni Basu, "Seven Months in Iraq, Six Years Back Home: A Soldier's War on Two Fronts," CNN, May 22, 2011, http://www.cnn.com/SPECIALS/2011/war.at.home/part1/index.html.

3 Tanielian and Jaycox, *Invisible Wounds of War*, 5.

4 Charles W. Hoge et al., "Combat Duty in Iraq and Afghanistan, Mental Health Problems, and Barriers to Care," *New England Journal of Medicine* 351, no. 1 (July 2004): 16, 19.

5 Ibid., 19; Hafemeister and Stockey, "Last Stand?," 89n11.

6 Matthew J. Friedman, "Acknowledging the Psychiatric Cost of War," *New England Journal of Medicine* 351 (July 2004): 75, 76.

7 Hafemeister and Stockey, "Last Stand?," 91.

8 Charles W. Hoge et al., "Mental Health Problems, Use of Mental Health Services, and Attrition from Military Service after Returning from Deployment to Iraq or Afghanistan," *Journal of the American Medical Association* 295, no. 9 (March 2006): 1023, 1027–28.

9 Karen H. Seal et al., "Trends and Risk Factors for Mental Health Diagnoses among Iraq and Afghanistan Veterans Using Department of Veterans Affair Health Care, 2002–2008," *American Journal of Public Health* 99 (2009): 1654.

10 Michael P. Atkinson et al., "A Dynamic Model for Post-Traumatic Stress Disorder among U.S. Troops in Operation Iraqi Freedom," *Management Science* 55 (September 2009): 1454; "Research: High PTSD Rates for Iraq War Veterans," Stanford Knowledgebase, September 19, 2009, http://www.stanford.edu/group/knowledgebase /cgi-bin/2009/09/19/high-ptsd-rates/.

11 Atkinson, "A Dynamic Model," 1454; "Research: High Rates," 1454, 1461.

12 Ibid., 1454, 1463–66.

13 Ibid., 1454, 1465–66.

14 "PTSD and Dementia: More Study Needed to Determine Why Veterans with PTSD Are More at Risk than Others," *Science Daily*, August 31, 2010, http://www.sciencedaily .com/releases/2010/08/100831073805.htm.

15 Atkinson et al., "Dynamic Model," 18, 21, 23.

16 Office of the Inspector General, *Observations and Critique of the DoD Task Force on Mental Health* (Washington, DC: U.S. Department of Defense, 2008), 2n70.

17 Alyson Sincavage, "The War Comes Home: How Congress' Failure to Address Veterans' Mental Health Has Led to Violence in America," *Nova Law Review* 33 (Spring 2009): 492.

18 Ibid., 494.

19 Ibid., 495.

20 For general information about the laws see Veteran's Mental Health Act, S.2162, Sec. 101-705 (2008); National Defense Authorization Act for Fiscal Year 2008, H.R. 1585, 110th Cong. (2007); H.R. Res. 1098, 110th Cong. (2008).

21 Sincavage, "War Comes Home," 496.

22 Inspector General, *Observations and Critique of the DoD Task Force.*

23 Hafemeister and Stockey, "Last Stand?," 91; Bethany H. Carland-Adams, "Primary Suicide Risk Factor for Veterans Is Post-Traumatic Stress Disorder," *Journal of Traumatic Stress* 22 (August 2009): 303.

24 Hafemeister and Stockey, "Last Stand?," 91.

25 "Army Suicides Reach Record," *UPI.com*, July 16, 2010, http://www.upi.com/Top _News/US/2010/07/16/Army-suicides-reach-record/UPI-79341279295982/.

26 Mark Thompson, "Is the U.S. Army Losing Its War on Suicide?," *Time*, April 13, 2010.

27 Ibid.

28 Elisabeth Bumiller, "Pentagon Report Places Blame for Suicides," *New York Times*, July 29, 2010.

29 Erica Goode, "After Combat, Victims of an Inner War," *New York Times*, August 2, 2009.

30 Lisa R. Rhodes, "Army Begins Phase Two of Five-Year Study on Suicide, Prevention," U.S. Army, October 7, 2010, http://www.army.mil/article/46242/.

31 "Mental Health Status of World Trade Center Rescue and Recovery Workers and Volunteers—New York City, July 2002–Aug. 2004," *Morbidity and Mortality Weekly Report*, September 10, 2004, 812–15.

32 Megan A. Perrin et al., "Differences in PTSD Prevalence and Associated Risk Factors among World Trade Center Disaster Rescue and Recovery Workers," *American Journal of Psychiatry* 164, 9 (September 2007): 1385

33 *Porter v. McCollum*, 130 S.Ct. 447; 175 L.Ed.2d 398 (2009).

34 For an overview of the problems involved in prevention and treatment see Tanielian and Jaycox, *Invisible Wounds of War*.

35 Jim Malone, "Polls Show Americans Weary of Afghan Conflict," *VOA News*, June 22, 2011.

8. THE WAR AT HOME: VETERANS IN CRIMINAL COURT

1 Julie Sullivan, "Trauma in Iraq Leads to Drama in Oregon," *The Oregonian*, October 31, 2009.

2 Ibid.

3 Melody Finnemore, "Firestorm on the Horizon—PTSD," *Oregon State Bar Bulletin*, April 2010, http://www.osbar.org/publications/bulletin/10apr/firestorm.html; Kim Murphy, "Did the War Make Him Do It?" *Los Angeles Times,* November 28, 2009, http://articles.latimes.com/2009/nov/28/nation/la-na-soldier28-2009nov28.

4 Sullivan, "Trauma in Iraq Leads to Drama in Oregon."

5 Julie Sullivan, "Did an Oregon Veteran Bring the War Home?" *The Oregonion*, October 31, 2009, http://www.juliesullivan.info/ptsd.murder.html; Sullivan, "Trauma in Iraq Leads to Drama in Oregon."

6 Sullivan, "Trauma in Iraq Leads to Drama in Oregon."

7 Ibid., 5.

8 Ibid.

9 Melody Finnemore, "Playing His Part: Markku Sario Finds a Stage in Law and Performing Arts," *Oregon State Bar Bulletin*, July 2010, http://www.osbar.org /publications/bulletin/10jul/profiles.html.

10 Deborah Sontag and Lizette Alvarez, "Across America, Deadly Echoes of Foreign Battles," *New York Times*, January 13, 2008.

11 Ibid.

12 Matthew Purdy, "Personal Tragedies Illuminate the Consequences of War," *Nieman Reports*, Summer 2008.

13 David Botti, "Article on Veterans Committing Murder Stirs Debate," *Newsweek*, January 14, 2008, http://www.thedailybeast.com/newsweek/blogs/soldiers -home/2008/01/14/article-on-veterans-committing-murder-stirs-debate.html.

14 Kyle Burchett, David Ferreira, and Glenn Sullivan, "Postdeployment Homicide," *Newsletter of Section VII of the American Psychological Association*, Spring/Summer 2008, 12.

15 Ibid.,13.

16 Ibid., 14.

17 Ibid.

18 Ibid.

19 Sontag and Alvarez, "Across America."

20 Lizette Alvarez, "After the Battle, Fighting the Bottle at Home," *New York Times*, July 8, 2008.

21 Ibid.

22 Ibid.

23 Sontag and Alvarez, "Across America."

24 Ibid.

25 Ibid.

26 "The Cases," *New York Times*, January 12, 2008.

27 *United States v. Gregg*, 451 F.3d 930 (8th Cir. 2006), http://caselaw.findlaw.com /us-8th-circuit/1464470.html.

28 Deborah Sontag and Lizette Alvarez, "In More Cases, Combat Trauma Is Taking the Stand," *New York Times*, January 27, 2008.

29 *United States v. Gregg*, 451 F.3d; Dale Wetzel, "Iraq Veteran's Arguments Stifled at Murder Trial, Lawyer Says," *Associated Press*, March 24, 2006.

30 *United States v. Gregg*, 451 F.3d at 930.

31 Sontag and Alvarez, "In More Cases."

32 Ibid.

33 Ibid.

34 Lizette Alvarez and Deborah Sontag, "When Strains on Military Families Turn Deadly," *New York Times*, February 15, 2008.

35 Ibid.

36 Ibid.

37 R. Jeffrey Smith, "Sharp Rise in Violent Crimes Cited among Returning Iraq Vets in Colo. Unit," *Washington Post*, July 28, 2009, http://www.washingtonpost.com /wp-dyn/content/article/2009/07/27/AR2009072702331.html.

38 Katherine van Wormer, "The Dynamics of Murder-Suicide in Domestic Situations," *Brief Treatment and Crisis Intervention*, May 2008, 274; Vernon J. Geberth, "Domestic Violence Homicides," *Law and Order Magazine* 46 (November 1998): 51–54.

9. WOMEN'S WAR: THE FACES OF PTSD

1 Patricia Kime, "Studies on Female Vets Influence VA Health Care," *Army News*, August 8, 2011, http://www.armytimes.com/news/2011/08/military-women-veterans -VA-policy-080811w/.

2 Sara Corbett, "The Women's War," *New York Times*, March 18, 2007.

3 Helen Benedict, "The Plight of Women Soldiers," *The Nation*, May 18, 2009.

4 Ibid.; Daniel Engber, "What Can Female Soldiers Do? A Primer on the Latest Wrangling over Women in the Military," *Slate*, May 19, 2005, http://www.slate.com /id/2119241/.

5 Author interviews with Helen Hart Gai (September–November 2010).

6 See Kirsten A. Holmstedt, *Band of Sisters: American Women at War in Iraq* (Mechanicsburg, PA: Stackpole Books, 2007); Kirsten Holmstedt, *The Girls Come Marching Home: Stories of Women Warriors Returning from the War in Iraq* (Mechanicsburg, PA: Stackpole Books, 2009).

7 Caron Zlotnick et al., "Gender Differences in Patients with Posttraumatic Stress Disorder in a General Psychiatric Practice," *American Journal of Psychiatry* 158 (November 2001): 1923.

8 David F. Tolin and Edna B. Foa, "Sex Differences in Trauma and Posttraumatic Stress Disorder: A Quantitative Review of 25 Years of Research," *Psychological Bulletin* 132 (2006): 961.

9 Ibid., 959, 964–77.

10 Zlotnick et al., "Gender Differences in Patients," 1925.

11 Glenn Craig Davis and Naomi Breslau, "Are Women at Greater Risk for PTSD than Men?" *Psychiatric Times* 15 (July 1998): 2.

12 Alyssa J. Mansfield et al., "Deployment and the Use of Mental Health Services among U.S. Army Wives," *New England Journal of Medicine* 362 (January 2010): 101.

13 Ibid.

14 Matthew J. Friedman, "Prevention of Psychiatric Problems among Military Personnel and Their Spouses," *New England Journal of Medicine* 362 (January 2010): 169.

15 Tara Galovski and Judith A. Lyons, "Psychological Sequelae of Combat Violence: A Review of the Impact of PTSD on the Veteran's Family and Possible Interventions," *Aggression and Violent Behavior* 286 (2003): 1.

16 Ibid., 8.

17 Ibid., 5–6.

18 Connecticut General Statutes § 46b-38a(1).

19 See National Center for Victims of Crime, "Domestic Violence," *Library/Document Viewer*, 2008, http://www.ncvc.org/ncvc/main.aspx?dbName=DocumentViewer &DocumentID=32347; Jessica Martin, "A Growing Problem for Veterans: Domestic Violence," *Washington University in St. Louis Newsroom*, November 6, 2008, http://news.wustl.edu/news/Pages/12902.aspx.

20 Martin, "Growing Problem for Veterans."

21 See National Center for Victims of Crime, "Domestic Violence"; Martin, "Growing Problem for Veterans."

22 Damien Cave, "A Combat Role, and Anguish, Too," *New York Times*, November 1, 2009.

23 Ibid.

24 Ibid.

25 Susan Donaldson James, "Traumatized Female Vets Face Uphill Battle," *ABC News*, March 2, 2010, http://abcnews.go.com/Health/female-veterans-traumatized-war -fight-battle-va-healthcare/story?id=9979866.

26 Society for Women's Health Research, *PTSD in Women Returning from Combat: Future Directions in Research and Service Delivery* (Washington, DC, 2008), 2.

27 James, "Traumatized Female Vets Face Uphill Battle."

28 Holmstedt, *Band of Sisters*.

29 Helen Benedict, *The Lonely Soldier: The Private War of Women Serving in Iraq* (Boston: Beach Press, 2009).

30 Dorcas J. Dobie et al., "Posttraumatic Stress Disorder in Female Veterans," *Archives of Internal Medicine* 164, no. 4 (February 2004): 394.

31 Jacqui Goddard, "Operation Home Front Helps Women Veterans Heal," *Christian Science Monitor*, April 27, 2010, http://www.csmonitor.com/USA/Society/2010/0427 /Operation-Home-Front-helps-women-veterans-heal.

32 Office of National Drug Control Policy, *Prescription Drug Abuse* (Washington, DC: White House, August 18, 2011), http://www.whitehouse.gov/ondcp/prescription -drug-abuse.

33 California Department of Alcohol and Drug Programs, "Women Veterans: Women on the Front Lines," http://www.adp.ca.gov/veteran/womenvet.shtml.

34 "The Cases," *New York Times*, January 12, 2008.

10. RUNNING THE GAUNTLET: MST AND SEXUAL VIOLENCE AGAINST WOMEN WARRIORS

1 Christine Hansen, *A Considerable Sacrifice: The Costs of Sexual Violence in the U.S. Armed Forces* (Buffalo, NY: Baldy Center for Law and Social Policy, 2005), http://www.law.buffalo.edu/baldycenter/pdfs/milcult05hansen.pdf; PBS, "Fact Check: Military Sexual Trauma," *Now*, September 7, 2007, http://www.pbs.org/now/shows/336/fact-check-military-sexual-trauma.html.

2 Anne G. Sadler et al., "Factors Associated with Women's Risk of Rape in the Military Environment," *American Journal of Industrial Medicine* 43(2003): 262–73.

3 Department of Defense, *Fiscal 2008 Report on Sexual Assault in the Military* (Washington, DC, 2009), 9; Janet Bagnall, "What the Military Won't Talk About," *Montreal Gazette*, October, 12, 2010; Sadler, "Factors Associated with Women's Risk of Rape," 266; Brittany L. Stalsburg, "Military Sexual Trauma: The Facts," fact sheet, Service Women's Action Network, 2008, http://www.servicewomen.org/wp-content/uploads/2011/01/SWAN-MST-fact-sheet1.pdf.

4 Sadler, "Factors Associated with Women's Risk of Rape," 266.

5 Sadler, "Factors Associated with Women's Risk of Rape," 266; Maureen Murdoch et al., "Prevalence of In-Service and Post-Service Sexual Assault among Combat and Noncombat Veterans Applying for Department of Veterans Affairs Posttraumatic Stress Disorder Disability Benefits," *Military Medicine* 169 (2004): 392–95.

6 Sadler, "Factors Associated with Women's Risk of Rape," 266.

7 Stalsburg, "Military Sexual Trauma."

8 Anna Mulrine, "Pentagon Report: Sexual Assault in the Military Up Dramatically," *Christian Science Monitor*, January 19, 2012, http://www.csmonitor.com/layout/set/print/content/view/print/452550.

9 Ibid.

10 "Military Sexual Trauma," U.S. Department of Veterans Affairs, January 1, 2007, http://www.ptsd.va.gov/public/pages/military-sexual-trauma-general.asp.

11 Hansen, *Considerable Sacrifice*; Stalsburg, "Military Sexual Trauma."

12 Wolfe et al., "Sexual Harassment and Assault as Predictors of PTSD Symptomology among U.S. Female Persian Gulf War Military Personnel," *Journal of Interpersonal Violence* 13 (February 1998): 40–57.

13 Ibid., 52–53.

14 Ibid., 53.

15 Ibid.

16 Sadler, "Factors Associated with Women's Risk of Rape," 266.

17 Ibid.

18 Hansen, *Considerable Sacrifice*.

19 Ibid.

20 Ibid.

21 Ibid.

22 Ibid.

23 Ibid.

24 Ibid.

25 Corbett, "Women's War."

26 Ibid.

27 Ibid.

28 Ibid.

29 Ibid.

30 Benedict, *Lonely Soldier*, 129, 141.

31 Ibid., 145–47.

32 Corbett, "Women's War."

33 Ibid.

34 Gerard J. DeGroot, "Is the United States Seriously Considering Military Women as . . . Peacekeepers?," 1996, http://userpages.aug.com/captbarb/degroot.html; Hadara Graubart, "Head 2 Head: Women at War," *Psychology Today*, November 1, 2007, http://www.psychologytoday.com/articles/200711/head-2-head-women-war.

35 Jean Bethke Elshtain, *Women and War* (New York: Basic Books, 1987); Jean Bethke Elshtain, "'Shooting' at the Wrong Target: A Response to Van Creveld," *Millennium* 29 (2000): 443–48.

36 Walter McDougall, "The Feminization of the American Military," *Foreign Policy Research Institute E-Notes*, February 4, 2000, http://www.fpri.org/enotes/military.20000204.mcdougall.feminizationofamericanmilitary.html.

37 "Effects of Combat on Returning Female Veterans Focus of Fippinger Grant," *Yale News*, November 6, 2009, http://opac.yale.edu/news/article.aspx?id=7064; "Yale-Led Study to Examine Post-Combat Trauma among Women Veterans," *Yale News*, November 10, 2010, http://dailybulletin.yale.edu/article.aspx?id=7992.

38 Society for Women's Health Research, *PTSD in Women Returning from Combat*.

39 Ibid.

40 "Does the American Family Have a History? Family Images and Reality," Digital History, n.d., http://www.digitalhistory.uh.edu/historyonline/familyhistory.cfm.

12. FINDING SOLUTIONS: COURTS, PSYCHIATRY, AND THE POLITICS OF PTSD

1 Ayesha S. Ahmed, "Post-Traumatic Stress Disorder, Resilience and Vulnerability," *Advances in Psychiatric Treatment* 13 (2007): 369–75.

2 Brett T. Litz, "The Unique Circumstances and Mental Health Impact of the Wars in Afghanistan and Iraq," fact sheet, National Center for Post-Traumatic Stress Disorder, January 5, 2007, http://www.nami.org/Content/Microsites191/NAMI _Oklahoma/Home178/Veterans3/Veterans_Articles/5uniquecircumstancesIraq -Afghanistanwar.pdf.

3 Grossman, *On Killing*, 252.

4 Michael Tsang, "Yale-Led Study to Examine Post-Combat Trauma among Women Veterans," *Veterans Today*, November 18, 2010.

5 Bob Brewin, "Army Reserve and Guard Suicide Rates More Than Doubled Last Year," *Nextgov*, Janurary 19, 2011, http://www.nextgov.com/nextgov/ng_20110119_4296.php.

6 David Dobbs, "Soldier's Stress: What Doctors Get Wrong about PTSD," *Scientific American*, April 13, 2009.

7 Tanielian and Jaycox, eds., *Invisible Wounds of War*, xxi, xxii.

8 "G 05 Posttraumatic Stress Disorder," American Psychiatric Association DSM 5 Development, August 20, 2010, http://www.dsm5.org/ProposedRevision/Pages /proposedrevision.aspx?rid=165.

9 Adam Caine, "Fallen from Grace: Why Treatment Should Be Considered for Convicted Combat Veterans Suffering from Post Traumatic Stress Disorder," *University of Missouri–Kansas City Law Review* 78 (Fall 2009): 225–26.

10 Ibid., 228–29.

11 Ibid., 232.

12 Alyson Sincavage, "The War Comes Home: How Congress' Failure to Address Veterans' Mental Health Has Led to Violence in America," *Nova Southeastern University Law Review* 33 (Spring 2009): 495; "Significant State Sentencing and Corrections Legislation in 2009," National Conference of State Legislatures, October 5, 2010, http://www.ncsl.org/?TabId=19122; Amanda DeBard, "War Veterans Benefit from New State Laws," Stateline, December 31, 2008http://www.stateline.org/live /details/story?contentId=365276 ; "State Veteran Programs and Benefits," http://www.oregon.gov/ODVA/BENEFITS/statebenefits.shtml.

13 Bill Murphy Jr., "More Cities and States Try Veterans Courts," *Stripes Central* (blog), March 31, 2011, http://www.stripes.com/blogs/stripes-central/stripes-central-1.8040 /more-cities-states-try-veterans-courts-1.139605.

14 Caine, "Fallen from Grace," 234–35.

15 William H. McMichael, "Special Courts Help Vets Regain Discipline Camaraderie, By Turning to Mentors Who've Served," *Military Times Newspaper*, February 14, 2011, http://www.nadcp.org/MilitaryTimes%20-Veterans-Treatment-Courts.

16 "Wisconsin State Approving Agency (SAA) Montgomery GI Bill Information," Wisconsin Department of Veterans Affairs, http://saa.dva.state.wi.us/.

17 Department of Veterans Affairs, "VA Services for Veterans Involved in the Justice System: The Veterans Justice Outreach (VJO) Initiative," fact sheet, November 2009, http://www.oregon.gov/ODVA/docs/PDFs/Criminal_Justice_Portal/VJOFactSheet .pdf?ga=t.

18 Sincavage, "War Comes Home," 505.

19 Ibid.

20 Ibid.; Justin G. Holbrook, *Veterans' Courts and Criminal Responsibility: A Problem Solving History and Approach to the Liminality of Combat Trauma* (Chester, PA: Widener University School of Law, 2010), 45–46.

21 "A Guide to Allegheny County Veterans Court," Allegheny County Veterans Court, http://www.drexelmed.edu/Portals/0/BHE/allegheny%20county%20veterans %20court.doc

22 Melissa Pratt, "New Courts on the Block: Specialized Criminal Courts for Veterans in the United States," *Appeal* 15 (2010): 41.

23 Holbrook, *Veterans' Courts and Criminal Responsibility*, 1–3, 19.

24 Drug Policy Alliance, *Healing a Broken System: Veterans Battling Addiction and Incarceration* (New York, 2009), 4.

25 Ibid., 3, 4.

26 United State v. Brownfield Jr., Criminal Case No. 08-cr-00452-JLK, http://graphics8 .nytimes.com/packages/pdf/us/20100303brownfield-opinion-order.pdf.

27 Holbrook, *Veterans' Courts and Criminal Responsibility*, 1, 3.

28 Ibid., 3.

29 McMichael, "Special Courts Help Vets Regain Discipline."

30 Erin M. Gover, "Iraq as a Psychological Quagmire: The Implications of Using Post-Traumatic Stress Disorder as a Defense for Iraq War Veterans," 28 Pace L.Rev. 561 (2007–08), 584.

31 Litz, "Unique Circumstances and Mental Health Impact."

32 Evan R. Seamone, "Attorneys as First-Responders: Recognizing the Destructive Nature of Posttraumatic Stress Disorder on the Combat Veteran's Legal Decision-Making Process," *Military Law Review* 202 (2009): 146–51.

33 Drug Policy Alliance, *Healing a Broken System*, 7–9.

34 Hafemeister and Stockey, "Last Stand?," 87.

EPILOGUE: THE FUTURE OF PTSD

1 C. J. Chivers, "In Wider War in Afghanistan, Survival Rate of Wounded Rises," *New York Times*, January 7, 2011.

2 Andrew J. Bacevich, "Endless War, A Recipe for Four-Star Arrogance," *Washington Post*, June 27, 2010; "General Foresees 'Generational War' against Terrorism," *Washington Post*, December 13, 2006.

3 Thom Shanker and Elisabeth Bumiller, "Looking Back, Gates Says He's Grown Wary of 'Wars of Choice,'" *New York Times*, June 18, 2011.

SELECTED BIBLIOGRAPHY

Following is a selection of books that I consulted, most of which are cited in the notes section. This bibliography is by no means a complete record of all sources consulted.

Benedict, Helen. *The Lonely Soldier: The Private War of Women Serving in Iraq*. Boston: Beacon Press, 2009.

Dean, Eric T., Jr. *Shook over Hell: Post-Traumatic Stress, Vietnam, and the Civil War*. Cambridge, MA: Harvard University Press, 1997.

Gabriel, Richard A. *The Painful Field: The Psychiatric Dimension of Modern War*. New York: Greenwood Press, 1988.

Grossman, Dave. *On Killing: The Psychological Cost of Learning to Kill in War and Society*. Rev. ed. New York: Little, Brown, 2009.

Hammes, Thomas X. *The Sling and the Stone: On War in the 21st Century*. Minneapolis, MN: MBI Publishing, 2006.

Hoge, Charles W. *Once a Warrior, Always a Warrior: Navigating the Transition from Combat to Home—Including Combat Stress, PTSD, and mTBI*. Guilford, CT: Globe Pequot Press, 2010.

Holmstedt, Kirsten A. *Band of Sisters: American Women at War in Iraq*. Mechanicsburg, PA: Stackpole Books, 2007.

Jones, Franklin D., et al. *War Psychiatry*. Textbooks of Military Medicine. Falls Church, VA: Office of the Surgeon General, U.S. Army, 1995.

Keegan, John. *The Face of Battle*. London: Penguin Books, 1976.

Kulka, Richard A. *Trauma and the Vietnam War Generation: Report of Findings from the National Vietnam Veterans Readjustment Study*. New York: Brunner/Mazel, 1990.

Minear, Larry. *Through Veterans' Eyes: The Iraq and Afghanistan Experience*. Washington, DC: Potomac Books, 2010.

Paulson, Daryl S., and Stanley Krippner. *Haunted by Combat: Understanding PTSD in War Veterans Including Women, Reservists, and Those Coming Back from Iraq*. Westport, CT: Praeger, 2007.

Shay, Jonathan. *Achilles in Vietnam: Combat Trauma and the Undoing of Character*. New York: Atheneum, 1994.

———. *Odysseus in America: Combat Trauma and the Trials of Homecoming*. New York: Scribner, 2002.

Shephard, Ben. *A War of Nerves: Soldiers and Psychiatrists in the Twentieth Century*. Cambridge, MA: Harvard University Press, 2001.

Stanford, David, ed. *Doonesbury.com's The Sandbox: Dispatches from Troops in Iraq and Afghanistan*. Kansas City, MO: Andrews McMeel, 2007.

Tanielian, Terri, and Lisa H. Jaycox. *Invisible Wounds of War: Psychological and Cognitive Injuries, Their Consequences, and Services to Assist Recovery*. Santa Monica, CA: Rand, 2008.

Tick, Edward. *War and the Soul: Healing Our Nation's Veterans from Post-Traumatic Stress Disorder*. Wheaton, IL: Quest Books, 2005.

Van der Kolk, Bessel A. "The History of Trauma in Psychiatry." In *Handbook of PTSD Science and Practice*, edited by Matthew J. Friedman, Terence Martin Keane, and Patricia A. Resick. New York: Guilford Press, 2007.

INDEX

ABOUT THE AUTHOR

Barry R. Schaller is a clinical visiting lecturer in law at Yale Law School and a visiting lecturer at Trinity College. Since retiring from the Connecticut Supreme Court, Justice Schaller has continued to serve on the Connecticut Appellate Court. He has served in all three branches of state government. His first book, *A Vision of American Law*, published in 1997, received the Quinnipiac Law School Book Award for excellence. His second book, *Understanding Bioethics and the Law*, was published in 2007. He serves as an expert on bioethics and the law at the Peter Jennings Project for Journalists and the Constitution. He earned his BA from Yale College, his JD from Yale Law School, and he holds an honorary Doctor of Laws degree from Quinnipiac Law School.